THE SCOTTISH CASTLE

by

STEWART CRUDEN

SPURBOOKS

1981

First published by Thomas Nelson & Sons Ltd.
This edition published by Spurbooks
(A division of Holmes McDougall Ltd.)
Allander House
137-141 Leith Walk
Edinburgh EH6 8NS

ISBN 0 7157 2088 0

Printed in Great Britain by
Holmes McDougall Ltd., Edinburgh

Preface

THIS book does not offer a series of descriptions of Scottish castles. It attempts to explain them, and ventures some criticisms.

Castles provide material for archaeological study as valid as megalithic burial chambers and Iron Age hill-forts. No less than prehistoric monuments they illustrate aspects of human behaviour and ideas at certain periods in the past, and, properly interpreted, help us to understand them. To the prescient observation of Lethaby "the wall, the pier, the arch, the vault, are elements which should be investigated like the lever and the screw"[1] we would add the curtain-wall, the gatehouse, the arrow-slit, the gun-port and other characteristic features of castellated architecture. We might also add that in architecture performance is not everything, that architecture is not a science to be studied but an art to be practised, and that it is not only by Commodity and Firmness that we should judge it, but by Delight also. And this derives from a purely aesthetic impulse, unselfconscious though it might be and often was, as the following pages should show.

Archaeology is an historical method. The materials of archaeology are of secondary importance. What matters is the inference to be drawn from them. The comparison of resemblances, the search for "parallels" and "influences", are not ends in themselves, although description is. Recording bodies may justly say with Wordsworth, "I've measured it from side to side, 'tis three feet long and two feet wide", but description, and the wearisome search for origins can only illustrate "how", not "why". An attempt is made in the following pages to explain the "why" as well as the "how" of Scottish castles. However successful this attempt might be it does demonstrate, I believe, a remarkable continuity in building tradi-

[1] W. R. Lethaby in 1911: (1955), 2.

tion, and from the end of the fourteenth century a stubborn adherence to a native partiality for vertical building.

It was not my original intention to work out a preconceived notion along these lines. Indeed, an architectural development which could be demonstrated as a truly continuous process was not suspected when the work began as a study of early stone castles. About them it seemed that a reappraisal was long overdue to refute the heresy of time-lag which has bedevilled the study of early castellated architecture in Scotland. There is no reason to assume that in Scotland things are not what they seem.

Continuity of development and the persistence of an indigenous tower architecture are facts which forced themselves into a story which does not logically stop with the last of the curtain-wall castles which characterise the thirteenth century. The tower-house, typical castle of the Scottish late Middle Ages, which proliferated in such striking contrast to its predecessors, is in fact derived from the great gatehouses which distinguish their last phase. Thus the first part of the long story with its mediaeval European background merges in the late fourteenth century into the second part in which native propensities prevail and foreign influences are accepted with reservations.

Although sharing distantly and belatedly in the intellectual activity of the European Renaissance Scotland did not take that movement to heart. The spirit of the Renaissance was feeble in a prolonged mediaeval environment. Nor was it fortified by climate, religion, or cash-in-hand. Although enlightened courtly patronage, the influence most likely to affect tradition in architecture generally, was uncommonly vigorous and infused with imported Renaissance ideas in the 1530's and 40's its inspiration came to nothing. The *tour de force* of Falkland and the highly original and imaginative treatment of Stirling are declarations of taste, not the milestones in progress they deserved to be. Indeed, nothing demonstrates more forcibly the native independence and conservatism of the Scottish mason and his patron than this repudiation of the royal works and the subsequent reversion to the old-style tower-house of mediaeval antecedents in the building revival which followed the Reformation and the return of conditions more propitious to architecture. Scottish castles admirably illustrate the truism that architecture is a reflection of its social environment and the spirit of the age, for mediaeval building is vertical building, and tower-houses appropriately express a continuing mediaeval way of life. Renaissance notions are evident in minor parts capable of independent treatment, on window pediments, door and window surrounds, moulded plaster and painted timber ceilings and the like, but the motifs were usually employed with little and frequently with no comprehension of their true significance or use.

In the middle of the seventeenth century, as the last few tower-houses were being erected in the traditional manner with no more than a sidelong glance at defensive requirements, new and alien fortifications appeared upon the Scottish scene. Little more has been done here than to draw attention to the fact of their existence. But that is something, for they have been strangely neglected. As works of architecture and as subjects for archaeological classification in military history the artillery fortifications of the Cromwellian and Hanoverian episodes have received little notice hitherto. Perhaps they have been considered modern and of no relevance to castles. But the youngest is over two hundred years old now, and all are legitimately part of the story of the curtain-wall, drum-tower and arrow-slit, the crossbow, long-bow, and stone-throwing engine of the Middle Ages. They bring the story to an end, by continuing the evolution of Scottish castellated architecture from the time when tower-houses were still being erected to its conclusion when warfare ceased in Scotland.

No comprehensive review of Scottish castles can be or will be written without frequent reference to the historic five volumes of Drs MacGibbon and Ross. Written some seventy years ago with a scholarly caution which is reassuring but never unhelpful they are unsurpassed for the reliability of their factual statements and the perspicacity of their observations. The wonder of it is that so long ago, with so little published material and photographs to assist them, MacGibbon and Ross worked out a classification and a chronology of Scottish castellated and domestic architecture which by and large will never be upset. How they did this, apparently visiting every site, and turning out the five volumes in as many years with an abundance of plans, sections and sketches to illustrate their text, and with a model index and exhaustive classified lists to amplify it is a mystery, and an achievement which compels the most profound respect and admiration. Nor is it all. There are three uniform volumes of Scottish ecclesiastical architecture. These eight books comprise a corpus of national architecture which is probably unequalled. The reader seeking an account of an ancient and historical building in Scotland is confidently referred to "MacGibbon and Ross".

Our debt to Dr W. Douglas Simpson is evident in the appended bibliography, restricted though it be to relevant matter. I am grateful to him for generous encouragement and for much useful information besides, including the use of an unpublished paper on Ruthven barracks, all readily given with his customary enthusiasm and love of the subject of which he is our pre-eminent exponent.

I am also indebted to my colleague Mr Iain MacIvor, who has kindly read the proofs of the last two sections and assisted me with advice and criticism of those parts.

S.H.C.

Foreword

SINCE the first edition was published in 1960, the growing and widespread interest in archaeology in all its aspects has continued with an impressive increase in the number of visitors to Ancient Monuments and historic buildings. On that account alone a new edition can be justified. As well as this there have been since that date, books, articles in learned journals, sundry critical and helpful comment, and reviews: all of these demand attention.

I am happy therefore to take the opportunity provided by the publishers of this new edition to revise and amplify the text and bring it otherwise up-to-date with the following short select list of books and articles which between them cover all the periods of the history of Scottish castellated architecture, from the first-century broch, which some would say is not a castle at all, to the eighteenth-century bastioned fort which some would say is not a castle either.

I am unrepentant in continuing to include both, while admitting the definition persuasively argued by Professor Brown in his *English Castles*, that the true castle is feudal and possessed of a dual nature, that it is both a residence and a fortress, that it is a fortified residence. Neither broch nor bastioned fort is that, and neither is feudal, yet it seems to me that Scottish architectural history requires a wider horizon, even if only to include the broch. This phenomenon is truly architectural and in my opinion conceived and constructed for defence and shelter in time of trouble. It occurs only in Scotland moreover. If it cannot be included in our castellated architecture, where else? The bastioned forts of the eighteenth century on the other hand bring to a logical finish the story of the development of two principal ingredients of castle architecture, the wall and the flanking tower, even though they exclude the residential qualification, at least in its domestic sense.

For that unique *tour de force* the broch there is Mr J. R. C. Hamilton, *Excavations at Clickhimin, Shetland*, (HMSO, 1968); and for recent historical research on mottes "Charter evidence and the distribution of mottes in Scotland" (*Château Gaillard*, Caen, 1972) by Drs Grant Simpson and Bruce Webster; and "Norman settlement in Clydesdale" (TDGAS LIII, 1977), and "Norman Settlement in Galloway" (in *Studies in Scottish Antiquities*, forthcoming) by Mr C. J. Tabraham. The official *History of the King's Works*, (HMSO, five vols. 1963-continuing), includes a chapter on late thirteenth-fourteenth century Scottish castles by the General Editor Dr H. M. Colvin (vol. 1, 1963, 409-22). This is an historical and factual account of royal castle-building and repair derived from contemporary documents such as payrolls and memoranda of intentions and instructions issuing from conferences etc. Observations such as "six carpenters going on strike for three days 'because they did not have their wages as they wished';" and "as many as 140 women were employed with the ditchers, receiving 1½d. a day in comparison with their 2d." suddenly bring the subject to life. Also published by HMSO since 1960 are Reports, or Inventories, of the Royal Commission (RCAMS), of which especially relevant are *Stirlingshire*, (vol. 1, 1963, for Stirling Castle), and *Argyll*, (vol. 1, 1971, "Kintyre", for Skipness, and vol. 2, 1975, "Lorn", for Dunstaffnage).

My debt to Dr Taylor is evident in the List of References and Abbreviations. The list is unchanged with regard to Dr Taylor, but a later paper of his, although not dealing specifically with Scottish castles, must be mentioned here, for it reveals with abundant authentic record "some of the indispensable preliminaries, namely the administrative planning, the organisation of labour and the supply of materials which were the foundations of medieval building achievement." ("Castle-building in Wales in the later thirteenth century: the prelude to construction," in *Studies in Building History*, 1961). Likewise helpful in a better understanding of castles is the above-mentioned *English Castles*, (1976), wherein Professor Brown illuminates the English and Welsh castle scene with historical accounts of tactics and what we may call the organisation and method of medieval siege warfare. Scotland is consciously omitted, being "a separate story", but the facts apply, as Dr Colvin demonstrates.

The weaponry and the technicalities of attack and defence in siege warfare are discussed in *Weapons and Fortification*, (ed. D. H. Caldwell, forthcoming). Mr Iain MacIvor who contributes to this has also written "The Elizabethan Fortifications of Berwick-upon-Tweed", (Ant. J. 1965, 64-96), *Fort George,* (HMSO, 1970), "Craignethan Castle, Lanarkshire, an experiment in artillery fortification" (in *Ancient Monuments and their interpretation*, 1977, 239-261); and in a further account of such later manifestations of castellated architecture Mr Andrew Saunders extends his study of coastal fortifications ("Tilbury Fort and the development of artillery fortification in the Thames estuary"), (Ant. J. XL, 1960, 152-174), with "The Defences of the Firth of Forth" (*Studies in Scottish Antiquity*, forthcoming).

S.H.C.
Edinburgh 1981

Acknowledgments

Thanks are due to the Controller of Her Majesty's Stationery Office for permission to reproduce the following Crown Copyright photographs: Plates 1, 2, 3, 4 above, 5, 6, 7, 8, 9 left, 10, 11, 12, 13 above, 14, 15, 16, 17, 18, 19, 20, 21, 22, 23, 24, 25, 26, 27, 28, 29, 30, 31, 32, 33, 34, 35, 36, 37, 38, 40 above left and below, 41, 42, 44 above, 45 above, 47 above, 48. Acknowledgement is also due to Messrs B. T. Batsford Ltd (pl. 4 below), Dr J. K. St Joseph (pl. 9 above), Aerofilms Ltd (pl. 13 below) and *Country Life* (pls. 31 and 38).

I am indebted to Mr R. A. Sayce, the Librarian of Worcester College, Oxford, and to Dr W. Park, the Keeper of Manuscripts in the National Library of Scotland, for their assistance in photographing the following original Cromwellian and Hanoverian drawings: pl. 43 above (Worcester College); pls. 43 left, 44 below, 45 below, 46, 47 below (National Library of Scotland).

The line drawings are by Mr John Cartwright. Simplified and in some instances altered according to the text of this volume, they are based upon official surveys and drawings published in other works, for which acknowledgments are due to: The Controller of Her Majesty's Stationery Office (figs. 1, 2, 6 (*a*) 7 (*a*) and (*b*), 11, 12, 14, 16, 17 (*a*) and (*b*), 18, 21, 22, 23, 25). Figs. 4, 5, 6 *(b)*, 15, 19 *(a)*, 20, are based on plans in MacGibbon and Ross (1887-92).

Thanks are also due to the Controller of Her Majesty's Stationery Office for permission to reproduce a passage in the author's Ministry of Works' Guide-book *The Brochs of Mousa and Clickhimin* (1951). I would also like to thank Dr A. J. Taylor for permission to quote from his published works.

For the first edition the late Dr W. Douglas Simpson permitted quotation from his published works; the use, for redrawing, of line drawings therein, and the use of a photograph (for pl. 40, above, right). Grateful acknowledgement is rendered to Mrs Simpson for renewed permission to repeat such use of his material.

Contents

List of Plates

List of Illustrations in the text

I

The Earliest Castles

THE BROCH

ON the shore of a small uninhabited island lying off the east coast of the mainland of Shetland, eleven miles south of Lerwick, there stands a solitary stone structure, massive in size, peculiar in appearance, and still more peculiar in character. This tower-like structure is the celebrated Broch of Mousa which by reason of its unusually good state of preservation exemplifies an architectural phenomenon found only in Scotland and of the greatest interest and historical significance (pl. 1, and fig. 1).

A broch is (or was) a lofty circular tower of dry-built masonry some 40 feet high. Its wall is immensely thick, as much as 20 feet at the base in some examples, and encloses a central courtyard space 30 to 40 feet in diameter. Save for a single low entrance there are no external openings. The inside face of the wall is vertical but the outside presents a slow curved batter which thickens the wall at the bottom and gives the building its distinctive and graceful profile. The lower part of the wall is structurally solid, although beehive cells and a narrow gallery are not uncommonly within it, but above it is without exception of hollow-wall construction. The void between the inner and outer walls is spanned at regular vertical intervals of about 5 feet by galleries formed of single flagstones laid side by side across it. The floor of each gallery is thus the roof of that below. These galleries run round the entire circumference of the broch. Each is interrupted by a stair, also contained within the hollow of the wall, which begins usually above ground-floor level and winds round about half of the circumference to the wall-top. Within the courtyard space of the tower evidence is found of domestic occupation and usually a deep well. Two or three tiers of small openings look into the courtyard. Their purpose like that of the galleries is probably structural as they surmount the lintels of the ground-level doorways. It is not known whether or not the brochs were roofed, as none is complete to the wall-head.

Associated finds so far recovered from brochs in various localities and considered to belong to the period of the original occupation indicate that the broch was fully developed and had reached its fullest geographical expansion by the first century A.D.

Although recent archaeological excavation and study of these monuments has clarified to a certain extent the domestic economy of the broch-dwellers and thrown some light upon their derivations, no convincing example of an architectural prototype has yet been discovered and no convincing evolution can be demonstrated. They appear in great numbers, sometimes singly, sometimes in groups, in a restricted area and in perfect development. As examples of fitness for purpose in military architecture they have rarely been surpassed. Built obviously for defence and shelter, frequently behind ramparts and ditches, they would present to an enemy an impregnable front of solid high walling. From the wall-top the defender would have advantage of look-out and fighting position, and at this height the incoming arrow or sling-stone would be rapidly losing power. The immense thickness of the wall rendered them safe from undermining. No fire could drive the inhabitants out. The vulnerability of the entrance was reduced to a minimum. The only access was through a passage, long, narrow, and low, leading to the courtyard space. Some half-way along it checks or jambs were provided against which a heavy door (probably a stone slab) could be placed and barred. A guard-chamber on one or both sides of the passage gave further protection behind the door.

No weapons of war are found among broch relics. Only domestic appliances and the implements of husbandry and weaving reveal the customary pursuits of the inhabitants. Hammer-stones, pounders and scrapers, whet-stones, pointed bone tools, spatulas for hand shovels, querns and coarse hand-made unglazed cooking pots are common.

Such subjects of daily and indeterminate use might be found in any community engaged in a primitive livelihood. The distinction of one early community from another and the affinity of one with another relies however not on commonplace artifacts but on more specialised relics which confer individuality upon their makers and users. Of greater significance therefore is the distinctive complex of weaving implements, triangular crucibles, dice and ornaments, which relates it to certain pre-Roman cultures of south-west England, especially that known as the Glastonbury Lake Village culture. This was overwhelmed by invaders in the middle of the first century

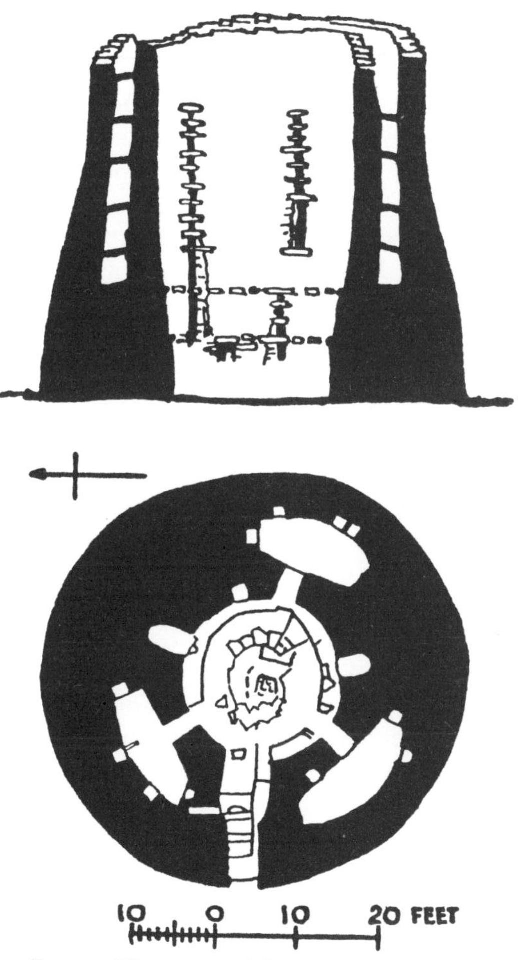

FIG. 1. Mousa, ground floor plan, and section

A.D. and it may well be that the Glastonbury people were compelled to emigrate north, where they settled and developed the broch as the stronghold of a conquering aristocracy. In the light of this explanation the broch is the castle of an intrusive petty chieftain built to subjugate and control an older native population.

But there is another possible explanation of brochs which should

be mentioned, because it seems to be more consistent with their appearance and distribution. They are always to be found near arable land, either still cultivated or plainly cultivated in the past. They are seldom far from the edge of the sea. They are strong towers capable of passive defence, but in no sense offensive structures. In a word, they appear to be refuges used by peaceful cultivators in the face of grave peril from the sea. Their enemies seem to have been possessed of unusual warlike equipment, perhaps scaling ladders against which the brochs were built high, and battering rams—hence the single narrow entrance and deeply recessed doorway. These enemies did not seem to have coveted the crops or flocks of the natives, since there is no room in the brochs for any accumulation of these possessions in safety. The conclusion seems to be that their object was to obtain the persons of the broch people, in other words to enslave them.

There is yet very little evidence which bears on the precise date of the brochs, but few will dispute the statements that they are unlikely all to be the product of one generation, and that many of them, perhaps all, were in existence in the first century A.D. When, therefore, one considers the question of seaborne slave raiders, as one must in accordance with this alternative explanation of the brochs, one naturally thinks of the expanding Roman Empire which needed more and ever more slaves.

Tacitus, writing late in the first century A.D., mentions slaves as one of the prizes of Roman conquest in Britain, and it is of interest that the same writer narrates that Agricola's fleet in A.D. 83 or 84 "discovered and subdued previously unknown islands, called the Orcades (Orkney)".[1] Orosius, moreover, describing the Emperor Claudius's annexation of Britain in A.D. 43 implies that Orcadian chieftains sent envoys to the Roman conquerors to make formal submission and to foster a Roman alliance as a move in inter-tribal politics. However much or little truth there may be in this latter statement, it at least suggests that the Roman power was known and feared, or at least respected, many hundreds of miles away from its then furthest expansion. It might even suggest that the Orcadian chieftains in question sought by submission to Rome to save their people from enslavement, since even a powerful conqueror would hardly raid for slaves in a land from which he obtained submission and perhaps tribute.

[1] Agricola, c. 10.

The suggestion is, therefore, that from the time of the Roman conquest of Gaul in the middle of the first century B.C. slave raiders, whether Roman or middlemen, such as the Belgae of southern Britain amongst whose remains slave chains have been found, were in the habit of ranging far and wide in search of slaves. In the far north of Britain the natives resisted manfully and evolved a defence admirably suited to the occasion. Eventually the Roman armies succeeded in conquering most of the habitable parts of Britain south of the Great Glen. It may well be significant that brochs occur almost exclusively in the areas outside the direct Roman sphere of control, i.e. north of Inverness on the east coast, in the western islands, and in the extreme south-west of Galloway.

Another aspect of the broch culture is observable in most examples. This is the complex of secondary buildings within and around the broch tower. It has recently been proved during excavations at the remarkable site of Jarlshof, at Sumburgh Head at the south end of Shetland, that the secondary buildings are later but not much later than the broch.[1] Inferentially, the broch had collapsed comparatively soon after erection and at a time when the threatening conditions and the need for impregnable defence no longer obtained. This is consistent with the hypothesis that the brochs were erected by the natives in a critical period of comparatively short duration, say fifty years or a century, and thereafter ceased to be strongholds.

The grouping of independent brochs in close proximity may be explained as the result of supply and demand: a skilled and organised labour force is implied and there is no reason to suppose that it could not erect brochs according to the size of the population demanding security. Some communities in rich and fertile land supporting many families would require three or four broch towers; for others less numerous one alone would suffice.

Although incapable of the more aggressive and serviceable achievements of the mediaeval castle-builder, the broch-builders did yet achieve a castle of a sort. It is consequently not merely the remarkable and unique architectural features of the brochs that arouse our interest but equally the social problems and customs of the communities which erected them. The mystery of their origin and of the people by whom they were made and occupied, and against whom they were intended, add greatly to the interest which they

[1] J. R. C. Hamilton (1956), 40, 90.

possess as early architectural works of outstanding merit. The origin of the style is wholly constructional, and the style so arresting as to imply a preconceived notion. It was an idea before it was a fact—the idea of a highly original mind.

The remains of about five hundred have been identified. By far the greater number are in Caithness, Orkney, Shetland and the Western Isles. While it is difficult to formulate a definite and unvarying description that may be entirely applicable to each example, in the essential features of plan, construction and arrangement they are all the same.[1]

Thus Mousa insists on more than archaeological recognition in any comprehensive account of Scottish castles, just as that phenomenon of the Orkney Bronze Age, the chambered burial mound of Maes Howe, cannot be disregarded as religious architecture. A powerful personality is commemorated in both. Yet although Maes Howe is superb in scale and in its suggestion of some prehistoric genius struggling with the problem of erecting a dome upon a cube, which exercised the constructional ingenuity of Byzantine architects 2,000 years later, it is for all that but an example of a type of structure widespread throughout Europe and the Mediterranean. The broch on the other hand is a unique and enigmatic phenomenon. We must wait upon the advent of the Normans in the eleventh century for the beginning of a continuous castellated tradition. The subject of brisk controversy since the earliest days of Scottish antiquarian speculation the broch is inexplicable still, but its defensive purpose cannot be denied, and no explanation is adequate which does not address itself to the elucidation of that purpose. It is the most remarkable ancient castle in Europe.

THE MOTTE

The typical Norman castle, known as a motte, called for a different constructional skill. It was a work of carpentry. The past tense is advisedly used in reference to it, for none have survived in anything like the same extent of the more ancient stronghold, whose most substantial representatives are imposing structures still. Of the structures of the mottes nothing now remains. Only the earthen mound which gives the type its name, and the surrounding banks

[1] c.f. J. R. C. Hamilton *The Brochs of Mousa and Clickhimin*, HMSO, 1970.

and ditches which assisted in its defence, remain to indicate the fact of their existence rather than to indicate the form they took. According to this evidence that can only be conjectural. Happily conjecture is supported by art, an embroidery, woven to relate the story of the Norman Conquest within twenty years of the events it so vividly records. The Bayeux Tapestry, as this work is inaccurately called, illustrates upon its 232 feet of pictorial history the castles of Hastings, Dol, Rennes, Bayeux and Dinan. They are seen to be large earthen mounds surrounded by a ditch and bank. A timber tower occupies the summit, enclosed by a palisade around its edge. A flying bridge of timber crossed the ditch and rose from the outer bank.

To this strong-point a more extensive enclosure, likewise protected by ditch and bank, was frequently attached at a lower level, to make a motte-and-bailey castle affording greater accommodation for more than temporary and emergency occupation. The towers and palisades of these castles have to-day entirely vanished. Only their post-holes, yielding to skilful excavation, reveal their presence.[1]

A word-picture of the castle of Somerled of Argyll, composed about 1209, when mottes were still the characteristic baronial stronghold, confirms the evidence of spade and needle, and makes its own contribution to our knowledge of this early type of castle which will never be seen in reality in Scotland or anywhere else. The tower upon the summit was built of neither stone nor lime, but of earth, i.e. probably clay.[2] It was crenellated, battlemented, and the fortunate Somerled within had no fear of escalade or engineer.[3] But he may have feared the burning arrow, unless his timber tower and palisade were hung with wet hides or shields which the Bayeux Tapestry suggests in its coloured pictures of the castles of Dol and Dinan. A sculptured capital in Westminster Abbey is another possible illustration of this, and Mersier illustrates a timber tower draped with shields.[4] Doubtless all these vulnerable timber structures were protected by cladding of some sort. The embroidery also suggests that the towers were stilted, raised upon corner posts over an open ground floor. This is consistent with the pattern of postholes recovered at the Motte of Abinger,[5] which yielded the holes of

[1] B. Hope-Taylor (1956), 223-49.
[2] For the use of clay in castle-building see W. M. Mackenzie (1934), 117-27.
[3] See *Roman von Guillaume le Clerc*, ed. E. Martin (1872) especially lines 304-13. This tale, written *c.* 1209 for Alan son of Roland of Galloway, is quoted and discussed by R. L. G. Ritchie (1954), 307-9. "Le Castiel de Dunostre" (Dunottar) which figures in this romance as the scene of marvellous events was a motte castle.
[4] A. Mersier (1923), 117-29.
[5] B. Hope-Taylor (1956), 236.

extra-large corner posts, and reminds one of the "wonderful carpenter work" of the motte of Arnold the lord of Ardres, which was erected about 1117 and excelled all the houses of Flanders. Its first storey was raised upon the top of the motte hill for cellarage. Over this were two floors of domestic apartments: hall, solar, servants' quarters, a sick room, garret bedrooms and a decorated chapel.[1]

Mr Hope-Taylor advances a theory that the towers were raised high upon massive corner timbers against whose lower parts the earthen mound was heaped, i.e. the towers were not erected upon the mound, but the mounds were heaped about the towers. This theory is not entirely convincing. The mound is composed of the upcast from the encircling ditch. Therefore the stilted tower would exist before the defensive ditch was begun, which is questionable. Nor is it necessary for skilled carpenters to bury their towers in order to stabilise them. Half-timbering was commonplace in the eleventh century and twelfth century, when the land was "filled full of Castles". Cross-braced and strutted the free-standing tower would be safe enough.

We have a statement of 1130 worthy of consideration in this connection. The well-known description of the motte at Merchem near Dixmüde says that upon the crest of the mound a close stockade of squared timbers was erected with as many towers as were possible in its circuit, and within this at its centre a house or citadel (*arx*) which overlooks everything. "It is the custom of the nobles of that region, who spend their time for the most part in private war, in order to defend themselves from their enemies to make a hill of earth, as high as they can, and encircle it with a ditch as broad and deep as possible. They surround the upper edge of this hill with a very strong wall of hewn logs, placing towers on the circuit, according to their means. Inside this wall they plant their house or keep, which overlooks the whole thing. The entrance to this fortress is only by a bridge, which rises from the counterscarp of the ditch supported on the double or even triple columns, till it reaches the upper edge of the motte".[2]

This suggests that the timber works were erected upon the completed mound. The truth may be that variations of method would occur with soils of different strength, density, cohesion, and angle of rest. Loose and doubtful soil, providing insecure founda-

[1] Walter de Clusa, quoted by Ella S. Armitage (1912), 89-90.
[2] Johannes de Collemedio, quoted by Ella S. Armitage (1912), 89-90.

tions for superincumbent weight could well cause such a procedure as Hope-Taylor ingeniously suggests, just as the angle of rest, or the inclined face of the mound, could be secured by a surface layer of clay, as he discovered in his excavation of the Mote of Urr in Kirkcudbrightshire. Investigation at Farnham Castle (Surrey) has produced remarkable results. The present edifice, a shell-keep of twelfth-century date, consists of a thick circular wall, with projecting turrets, which rises from near the foot of the long slope of an earlier motte and wholly surrounds it. Excavation has revealed the base of a stone tower, about fifty feet square on the outside with walls 18 feet thick enclosing an open interior, embedded in the centre of the mound from its summit down to the presumed ground level. At the top the wall projects as a sort of flange that overlies the mound. The mound and its embedded tower were made at the same time. There is little doubt that the embedded tower was designed to carry a motte tower (possibly stone) and that it was placed to serve as a well-shaft at the same time.

Mottes occur most numerously in the south-west. Clustered in the river valleys along the north shore of the Solway their distribution extends far inland, particularly up the river valleys of formidable name and history, Nithsdale, Annandale, Eskdale and Liddesdale. It is characteristic of these districts to use naturally defensible sites and to improve upon them by art, heightening and modifying the slopes. A peculiar feature of three in Dumfriesshire, at Lincluden, Lochwood and Garpol Water, is a terraced slope, which at Lochwood seems clearly to have had a parapet upon its terraces.

North of the Forth mottes are less numerous. Although by no means uncommon—there are many in Aberdeenshire and the adjacent country—they are nowhere thickly studded upon the ground as they are in the valleys of the southern Dee and Nith for instance, and *a priori* they are later than the mottes of the south. This is an historical inference, yet to be tested by systematic excavation which alone will yield the evidence of their chronology. Early enfeoffments dating from the reigns of Edgar and Alexander I (1097-1124) were in the south of modern Scotland (in Lothian and Cumbria, not then considered to be in Scotland proper). Territorial awards to incomers supporting the Crown with military service were there most easily granted. The process of infeudation, accelerated by David I in pursuance of his policy of reproducing the pattern of feudal tenure prevailing in the Normanised England he knew so well, was continued by his successors throughout the twelfth century and spread far north of the Clyde-Forth line to the Celtic realm.[1] Charters of enfeoffment indicate a steady feudalisation of the Celtic earldoms, and the existence of mottes, themselves the outcome of a feudal tenant's military obligations of castle-building and castle-guard, afford archaeological evidence to supplement the written record.

Two instances of this correspondence of history and archaeology may be cited, for the mottes which exist are outstanding examples. A charter of William the Lion,[2] of a date 1166 – 1172, confirms to William son of Freskin, a Fleming, for a fee of two knights' service, lands in West Lothian and Duffus and elsewhere in Moray "which his father held in the time of King David". This enfeoffment dates from the subjugation of the last native mormaer by the king in 1130, when Moray was annexed by the Crown,[3] and the great motte hill of Duffus, near Elgin, upon which a massive stone tower was later erected[4], probably dates from this time if not to the time of the confirmation charter. Again, the feudalisation of the exclusively Celtic district of the Garioch in Aberdeenshire was hastened by the granting of a fief to David when Earl of Huntingdon by his brother the king between 1179 and 1182.[5] The *caput* was established at Inverurie where David founded a burgh and, it is only reasonable to suppose, erected the castle whose motte-hill and outer bailey survive to this day, known as the Bass of Inverurie. (pl. 1.)

Mottes are alien works, the imported castles of Normans, erected by them and by native barons following fashion as they did in Wales in similar circumstances. They occur throughout the feudalised parts of the country, following in the wake of the Norman, Breton and Flemish baronial infiltration which was encouraged by the royal house of Canmore. They mark the spread of the feudal system.

[1] G. W. S. Barrow (1956*a*), 1-31; (1956*b*), chs. VIII and XV.
[2] *Cartae Variae* (MS. in SRO), fo. 299, quoted by G. W. S. Barrow (1956*a*), 4.
[3] G. W. S. Barrow (1956*a*), 4. [4] See below, pp. 14, 125-6.
[5] Lindores Charters, No. 1, quoted by G. W. S. Barrow (1956*a*), 18.

2

Early Stone Castles

It might seem, by the nature of its introduction, that the motte would mark the beginning of a new development in military architecture, as it was the symbol of an alien presence and the visible sign of conquest. In fact it did nothing of the kind. It marks the end of a development—the end of the prehistoric system of fortification by ditches and earthen ramparts surmounted by palisades.

Indeed, no architectural evolution is possible in a defensive system principally comprising a small timber tower upon a restricted summit of an artificial hill, and although the motte-castle provided a local stronghold and a base of operations in the subjugation of a hostile population it had in fact no architectural future: it could lead to nothing but larger mottes or more mottes together. To develop and to increase in strength and complexity of defences, to contain apartments suitable to a lord and his household (often on a palatial scale and greater than the requirements of a garrison whose warlike activities were in any case spasmodic), and to become "the material expression of the pride and pomp of a ruling class", the castle had to quit the hill and stand upon the ground; and for security, particularly against fire, timber had to give way to stone.

These things came to pass, yet even as they did the two basic components of the motte-castle, the tower and the palisade, preserved each its own separate importance throughout the Middle Ages, and were employed separately or together. The timber tower on the motte hill became the great tower or keep, the timber palisade and the earthen rampart became the curtain wall of stone. The history of mediaeval stone castles is a history of the tower and the wall.

The perfect synthesis of tower and wall was achieved in the Edwardian castles of Wales in the last quarter of the thirteenth century, by which time the Crusaders had returned home after further education in military science in the Levant. These castles, the final and perfect achievement of the mediaeval castle, are characterised by high curtain walls disposed one outside the other in concentric fashion, with lofty projecting towers, and by massive frontal gatehouses.

In the face of shortcomings in the historical record and an almost total lack of authentic commencing and finishing dates it is impossible to date most Scottish castles of early type with any degree of precision or even within close limits. To do so invites a charge of dogmatism unsupported by sufficient evidence. Consequently, when confronted with castles as things of uncertain individual history, the writer inevitably brings the apparatus of archaeological assessment to bear upon the problems of dating and development, and tends to regard each as a demonstration of some phase in a steady progression from early simplicity to late elaboration. The general picture thus composed is doubtless accurate enough, but the inferences to be drawn from it should not be overstrained. No particular building can be incontrovertibly placed merely according to a theoretical development in which its general type is adequately accounted for. This is especially so in Scotland, where written records, the necessary complement and check to observation in the field, are so sadly defective, as compared for example with the extensive and detailed contemporary building accounts of the later thirteenth-century Welsh achievements of Edward I. No more can it be placed by accepting its first recorded date in history as a *terminus post quem*. A sense of frustration consequently attends the analysis of many of our finest monuments. Their history will never be known, for in the long run the written record is the last word; all else is supposition.

It seems advisable, indeed inevitable, to review early stone castles in Scotland in groups according to type. But typology can be misleading. There is invariably an overlap, with earlier types persisting alongside later, according to which of many factors predominantly influenced design and construction. A castle is a functional structure. Its form varies with the changing demands of military or domestic requirements, with the terrain, with the nature of the challenge it is intended to meet, and with the notions and material resources of its builder.

It is the simpler castles, devoid of closely datable detail, which present the most awkward typological problems, because simplicity of conception, even when allied with a corresponding severity in execution, does not prove an early date, although these characteristics afford *prima facie* evidence of one. For example, the form of the simple curtain-wall castles of the western seaboard is largely determined by the nature of the terrain and the extent to which it is used to facilitate resistance. A simple basic conception of defence by high walls is applied with telling effect to conveniently rocky and naturally strong positions evidently selected with deliberation. On the other hand, in studying the plans and beholding the mass of Inverlochy, Kildrummy, Caerlaverock, Bothwell and others to be described, which if later are not much later than those of the western seaboard, we feel that we are in the presence of a fully accepted standard model, preconceived according to established principles and executed in conformity with them on flat or at any rate amenable ground. The design came first. These works are not expedients of fortification adjusted to local conditions, but the embodiment in stone of the contemporary idea of a superior castle, unequivocal, well understood, and executed with skill and experience. The terrain or *assiette* is secondary and does not greatly influence the result. In cases like these the siting of a castle can be significant: those which consciously exploit natural features to increase their defensive efficiency, and which lack datable features of construction, ornament, or military technique, are inferentially earlier than those which relied for security solely on the strength of their structure and the expertise which fashioned it; but failing reliable historical evidence the chronological sequence and the development must remain conjectural and general.

There are four basic types of early stone castle to consider. Some of them have variants and these will be noted. The main types are: the isolated tower or keep, the enclosure or curtain-wall castle, the curtain wall with towers, and the curtain with massive frontal gatehouse.

THE KEEP

Massive rectangular keeps, or great towers, as they were called by contemporaries, are in popular conception the very embodiment of the Normans. Yet most were not erected until a century after the Conquest, by Henry II (1154-89), and only two, the Tower of London and the Keep at Colchester, are known to have been raised in the eleventh century; the Keep of Pevensey was begun in 1101. They usually stand alone and are invested with an immense defensive strength. They have exceedingly thick walls and broad pilaster buttresses of slight projection. As the ultimate strength and refuge of a conquering aristocracy in an alien locality they perpetuate the timber tower of the motte in their function and essential form. But they are emancipated from the hill and raised upon the ground, because, by the dead weight of their masonry, such structures could not be erected upon earlier mounds wholly or partly artificial. Such heavy substitutions of stone for timber were in fact made, although rarely, as at Skenfrith (Monmouthshire),[1] where Hubert de Burgh *c.* 1220 built a perfect example of a small castle of the period, using an existing motte hill as the base of a round tower and enclosing this strong-point within a quadrilateral curtain wall provided with projecting corner towers, a lay-out to which there will be occasion to refer when reviewing curtain-wall castles. But the expedient generally proved to be unduly optimistic, as is demonstrated at Duffus Castle near Elgin, a stone tower erected by Reginald le Cheyne in 1305 upon a motte hill of twelfth-century date. The erection of such a ponderous structure as this tower upon forced soil has resulted in the collapse of the entire north-west corner, which has separated from the main mass and slid downhill *in toto*, testifying to the excellence of the lime mortar if not to the wisdom of the builders.

Alternatives contemporary with the motte tower and its surrounding bank and palisade were simple earthworks of different character. Such are ring-mottes, comprising areas often small and circular, sometimes irregular and large, which are defended by a single bank and ditch.[2] They are to-day of an archaeological rather than architectural interest, and less to our purpose than the last variation on the motte theme, the shell-keep, which was the refortification in stone of a motte and bailey castle.[3] The Peel of Lumphanan in Aberdeenshire, and the Doune of Invernochty, also in Aberdeenshire, that county par excellence for castles of all types and periods, are good examples of the type.[4] Without the concentration of weight upon forced soil, to its detriment, the shell-keep was a safer structural proposition than a superimposed stone tower could be. The defensive necessity of difficult access, previously fulfilled by elevating the tower upon a mound, were in the keeps met by raising the entrance, making it at first- or even second-floor level, and reached by an exterior stair or retractable ladder.

[1] C. A. R. Radford (1954), 2.
[2] B. H. St J. O'Neil (1946), 131.
[3] B. H. St J. O'Neil (1946), 134.
[4] See below, pp. 27-8.

The majestic scale of the great towers of London, Rochester and Richmond is not typical of contemporary castellated architecture in England. These are exceptional works. Structures of such grandeur appear never to have been erected in Scotland, the most northerly comparable examples being distributed across the border marches at Carlisle, Wark, Norham, Bamborough and Newcastle upon Tyne. Others following close behind, at Appleby, Brough, Brougham, Richmond, Barnard and Conisburgh, to name but a few, provided an impressive weight of military architecture to sustain the Norman power in the turbulent north of England. Beyond the Border however this calibre of Norman keep is totally absent; not even from documentary records can it be inferred, although motte hills occur frequently as far north as Inverness-shire, and are very numerous in the south-west country, as we have seen.

This conspicuous absence of one of the most spectacular manifestations of the late eleventh- and twelfth-century Norman penetration, which is rivalled only by the abundance of surviving ecclesiastical building, has prejudiced influential opinion about the dating of early stone castles in Scotland. In appraising remains of apparently early type we are confronted and misled by this prejudice. There is an unquestioned assumption that no twelfth-century stone castles exist in Scotland, and few of the thirteenth save those which are high, mighty and unequivocal. As an example of this, with reference to certain curtain-wall castles of early type, which are later to be described, we have it on good authority that: "Of this simple type there are several examples in the West Highlands and Isles, which accordingly have been attributed to this early period. In these districts however this is a dangerous logic. At a time when memorial effigies in the south were being cut in a complete outfit of plate armour, those in the west show only the ancient quilted coat with cape of mail. So too in the case of the western castles. They do not necessarily fit into any chronological scheme elsewhere. Their simplicity of type is no certain indication of antiquity. Nine castles however and two towers are named by the chronicler, John of Fordun, of the second half of the fourteenth century, as existing in the isles. But even inclusion in that list does not warrant us in taking the existing structure to be of that time."[1]

In these and other similar observations we sense that the possibility of early date is considered with alarm and dismissed with relief,

[1] W. M. Mackenzie (1927), 42.

and we feel the author's growing confidence as he transfers his attention to features of unquestionably later date. MacGibbon and Ross, whose attribution is doubtless that referred to in the aforesaid quotation, in their monumental and historic work only classified tentatively. Prudently cautious, they did not assert, as we can do to-day with some confidence, that in point of fact there is no reason why these early types should not be what they seem. There is in fact no justification for the assumption that in the twelfth century there could not be stone castles in Scotland. That there might be none to survive is an all-too-natural possibility, but the implication that there were no men of advanced ideas and wide experience to conceive them, nor masons capable of erecting them is inadmissible: the castle of King Edgar (d.1107) at Invergowrie was of stone.[1]

Furthermore, favourable political and social factors and influences were at work. The remarkable Canmore dynasty had introduced, endowed and fostered the Anglo-Norman element whose possessions and influence in England and Wales were consolidated by a swift and numerous creation of motte-castles, stone keeps and stone curtain-wall castles. Less so in Scotland where circumstances were different. The Norman conquest of Scotland was peaceful and gradual, the Scottish Crown secure. "There is no indication that it regarded castle-building, . . . as essential props of royal authority."[2] The effort was towards church building and ecclesiastical reform. The late eleventh-twelfth century reformation of the Church in Scotland is not wholly irrelevant. "The impetus given by Queen Margaret to the process by which the older Scottish church was transformed into the *Ecclesia Scotticana* and the prodigality of her youngest son, King David I, to a wide variety of religious orders, were prominent aspects of what was really a family enterprise. The establishment of English and continental monks and canons north of the Scottish border in the late eleventh and early twelfth centuries was in strikingly full measure the exclusive work of the royal house, a work, moreover, which the ruling members of this house seem to have undertaken with a conscious sense of dedication and unity of purpose."[3]

Upon the marriage (*c.* 1070) of Malcolm Canmore with Margaret of the Saxon line, a refugee of European upbringing, there began a systematic and methodical reorganisation of the Scottish Church to bring it into line with the general remodelling of the

[1] Boece, xii.262. [2] G. W. S. Barrow (1973) 280. [3] Barrow, *op cit*, 165.

Plate I

above Mousa Broch, Shetland, first century

below The Bass (motte) of Inverurie, Aberdeenshire, *c.* 1180

Church then current in western Christendom. Her policy was continued by her sons Alexander, Edgar, and especially David. Although St Margaret's first foundation at Dunfermline (*c.* 1070) was a diminutive church, its successor, whose nave dates from 1150, is one of the finest romanesque survivals in Scotland. Turgot, prior of the Benedictine Durham and Margaret's spiritual adviser, a strong protagonist of the Roman order, was installed in the episcopal throne of St Andrews about 1107. At the death of David I in 1153 no less than nine cathedrals and fourteen abbeys or priories of the reformed monastic order had been founded.[1] The Augustinian canons, the very vanguard of the monastic reform introduced into England at St Botolph's about 1100, were introduced to Scotland at Scone by Alexander I as early as about 1120. The Tironensians, founded in 1109, were introduced directly from France to Selkirk by 1113, and this was their first footing in Britain. Not only that, but their great abbeys of Kelso, Arbroath, Kilwinning and Lindores far surpassed their English houses. Dunfermline was colonised by monks from Canterbury, Scone from Nostell, Cistercian Melrose and Dundrennan from Rievaulx in 1136 and 1142, Cluniac Paisley from Wenlock in 1165, the Augustinian Holyrood from Surrey, Cambuskenneth from Arrouaise. St Andrews was begun in 1160, Kelso 1128, Arbroath 1178 and Jedburgh about 1139 and so on.

These works, to illustrate but major projects, prove that in conception and execution, mass and detail, the Scottish churches of the twelfth century were in the full floodstream of European ecclesiastical activity. It is clear that these far-seeing Canmore rulers, especially David, who had spent many youthful years in the English court of King Henry, were alive to the significant religious and political influences at work in their day. Twelfth-century Scotland was no cultural back-water, and an awareness and reception of contemporary English and continental architectural trends and influences must have continued until the end of the thirteenth century, when the Wars of Independence disrupted the social, cultural and diplomatic connections of Scotland with her neighbours at home and abroad.

In the temporal field one of the most spectacular architectural performances, which, it is possible to infer, is a result of Scottish connections with France in the thirteenth century, is the immense donjon of Bothwell, the grandest and most accomplished piece of mediaeval secular architecture in Scotland, to be compared not

[1] On this see G. Donaldson (1953), 106-17.

unfavourably with the best work of England, Wales, or France. The most striking parallel to this handsome round keep is in fact the colossal stronghold of Coucy, built between 1225 and 1242; and the two Scottish castles which can legitimately be classed with Bothwell in the preponderance of a round donjon in their *ensemble* are Kildrummy, whose lay-out bears a remarkable resemblance to that of Bothwell, and Dirleton, which was erected about 1225 by John de Vaux, seneschal to Marie de Coucy, Queen of Scotland, daughter of the builder of the justly celebrated Coucy.[1]

If massive Norman keeps are wholly absent and lesser towers less frequent than the presence of the Normans might lead one to expect their scarcity is due to reasons other than inability or ignorance. If there were masons to build stone churches, there were masons to build stone castles too. It is essential, therefore, to review our early stone castles with a fresh eye, untroubled by time-lag complexes. However reasonable the presumption of time-lag may sometimes be, it has a questionable validity in the present context.

In the north and west of modern Scotland, in Caithness, Orkney, Shetland, Argyll and the Hebrides, influences other than feudal created an environment encouraging to castles. The Norse earldoms of these areas, from the early tenth century to the mid-thirteenth, were the fruit of conquest no less attractive to the Viking than was the fall of Saxon England to their Latinised kinsmen the Normans.

Norway of the twelfth century was not a feudal country of the continental pattern. No mottes were raised there, nor were other castles common.[2] But Magnus Barelegs, King of Norway and overlord of the King of Man, visited that island in 1098 and according to a record of *c.* 1260 erected forts there. These were probably mottes, for he caused quantities of Galloway timber to be imported for the job, stone being scarce in Man then as it is now.[3] In this he probably exemplifies the Norse rulers and expeditionary leaders of the Viking and Middle Ages who must have secured, with the energy and adaptability characteristic of their race, their uncertain and interrupted colonisation west-over-seas by the erection of strongholds they did not use at home. Not until the reign of Hakon Hakonson (1217-63) did castles assume a native importance in Norway. *Kongespeilet* or *The King's Mirror*, written about 1250,[4] proves that by

[1] See below, pp. 40, 83.
[2] G. Fischer (1951), 320.
[3] B. H. St J. O'Neil (1951), 1.
[4] See below, p. 32.

the mid-thirteenth century the Norse castle-builders in the homeland were well acquainted with the best of contemporary military architecture and theory elsewhere.

Words and phrases descriptive of castles and their equipment, siegeworks, engines of war, and other defensive contrivances then current in western Europe, are in this cautionary guide to the art of war seen to have been absorbed into the technical vocabulary and rendered into Norse. Yet the contemporary European castle was originally a foreign conception to the Norse, as the borrowed descriptive saga-word *kastali* implies, for it is an alien term, derived from *castellum* and coined by Norse chroniclers to describe the new type of stronghold. It is never used of their native fortifications.[1]

In Hakon's Saga, composed by the Icelandic historian Sturla Thordson about 1265, reference is made to several Hebridean *kastalar*. No identification has been made with existing structures. The only material evidence of the long Norse occupation of the whole extensive area of the earldoms is derived from the grave-goods of burials and the exposure of settlements, such as Freswick in Caithness and Jarlshof in Shetland, which were pacific.

In the Orkney and Shetland islands and throughout the Hebrides and Inner Isles pagan deposits in considerable number and of a great richness attest widespread colonisation in the Viking Age. The settlements uncovered at Jarlshof prove a continuous Norse occupation of the site from the early ninth until the thirteenth century.[2] They were peaceful here, yet it seems improbable that in the wide area of colonisation and in their long occupation of it the Norseman should nowhere have erected castles of stone, for their activities were by no manner of means always peaceful and stone was the material of the country. Among the southern islands of the earldoms the group comprising Colonsay, Oronsay and Islay has produced the most distinguished Viking finds in Britain. They have for long been recognised,[3] but what has not been recognised as possibly Norse is the castle of Duniveg on the south coast of Islay. It comprises a bailey, enclosed within a curving curtain wall, which contains the grass-grown foundations of long buildings recalling those excavated at Jarlshof and Birsay of ninth- and eleventh-century date. A stone tower protected by the bailey and its curtain on the landward side is perched high upon rock rising from the sea. A stone garderobe

[1] J. S. Clouston (1931), 3.
[2] J. R. C. Hamilton (1956), 3.
[3] H. Shetelig (1945), 10.

chamber overhanging the water from the upperworks is of sixteenth-century date, according to the moulded stone corbels which support it, but the tower is clearly of more than one earlier period.

This is conjecture based on ruin and grass-grown foundation; more conclusively the Orkneyinga Saga refers with precision and circumstantial detail to a Norse castle on the island of Wyre, Orkney, which on internal evidence can be dated to about 1150: "At that time [1143 × 1148] there lived in Wyre in the Orkneys a Norwegian called Kolbein Hruga, and he was the most outstanding of men. He had a fine stone castle built there; it was a safe stronghold."[1] A later incident, mentioned in Hakon's Saga, also refers to this castle on Wyre: in 1231 Earl John Haraldson was murdered at Thurso; his assailants made off across the Pentland Firth to Wyre, which castle they provisioned and successfully held against the murdered earl's avengers. The saga relates that they fared to Wyre "and placed themselves in a castle which Kolbein Hruga had caused to be built". . . . "But it was difficult to effect an attack there."[2]

There is a ruined castle on the small island of Wyre. It stands upon a ridge near a twelfth-century church and is not far distant from a farmhouse called the Bu of Wyre, which is believed to be the homestead of Kolbein Hruga. The castle is called Cubbie Roo's. This name is certainly a corruption of Kolbein Hruga, Kubbe or Kobbe being a Norse term of familiarity for Kolbein. The castle was a small tower, a miniature keep, internally only 15 feet square, with walls 5 feet thick, rising to-day to a height of 6 feet. There is no entrance to the ground floor, which has two slit windows. The window jambs are splayed to the outer face of the wall and the cills are stepped. A water tank or water reservoir is sunk into the rock floor. The castle is enclosed by ramparts, and there are other buildings, of later date. The material throughout is the hard and sharp local flagstone. It is beautifully built, but has no feature by which it can be instantly dated.

The island of Wyre is a very small island and supports but two or three farms, and it contains no other site likely to be that of the castle of Kolbein Hruga. The architectural features of the existing ruin are primitive: the thick walls, the slit windows with wide splay and stepped cills, the absence of entrance to the ground floor, the proximity of the Bu, and of the twelfth-century church,

[1] A. B. Taylor (1938), 275.
[2] *Hakon's Saga*, quoted by A. O. Anderson (1922), II.482.

both of similar material and build, all combine to present an array of material evidence which consistently asserts an early date and has nothing which denies it. Furthermore the absence in the historical record of another personage who could have built this castle, and the absence of another site which could have been the castle, seem to place its identity beyond dispute.

The probability is enhanced by a close parallel at Dolwyddelan Castle (*c.* 1170) in Caernarvonshire,[1] where a small rectangular keep of two storeys was originally surrounded by a timber stockade, and in Provence,[2] by a group of small towers of eleventh- and twelfth-century date which Norse Crusaders might have seen when Earl Sigurd and his host made their journey across Europe to the Holy Land in 1116, when Earl Hakon about 1118 made his penitential pilgrimage to Rome and Jerusalem,[3] and when Earl Rognvald made his crusade in 1152 with many of his Orcadian vassals, one architectural result of which is the Round Church at Orphir, modelled on the Temple of the Holy Sepulchre at Jerusalem.

There are sundry other saga references to Norse castles in the Orkneys. A castle at Damsay was certainly in existence in 1136. Cairston castle near Stromness was attacked and almost captured by assault in 1152,[4] and existing ruins of a small square courtyard, now involved in a farm steading, are said to be remains of it, and could be; but it is little more than an archaeological site, and reliable inferences to be drawn from the masonry and conclusions as to the nature of its form are impossible. The stump of a tower at Westness on Rousay[5] bears much resemblance to Cubbie Roo's, but without supporting history cannot be confidently ascribed to an early date—or indeed to any date—for the hard Orcadian flagstone which has been local building material throughout the ages imposes such restrictions upon building technique that works widely separated in time cannot but be very similar, and without complementary evidence in support definite ascriptions are inadmissible.

For some stone towers on the Scottish mainland an early date may be hazarded. The Fore Tower of St Andrews Castle (Fife)[6] embodies part of the basement of a stone tower built in superior dressed ashlar, long in the course, and with tight joints, all characteristic of superior thirteenth-century work. This doubtless represents the castle or

[1] C. A. R. Radford (1946*a*).
[2] RCAMS XII.ii (1946), 237.
[3] J. S. Clouston (1931), 13.
[4] J. S. Clouston (1931), 17.
[5] J. S. Clouston (1931), 27-33.
[6] S. H. Cruden (1954*a*), 5, 7.

bishop's palace erected by Bishop Roger about 1200 as a place of residence more becoming to the dignity of his office than had hitherto been provided in the cathedral precincts. It would have earthen ramparts and palisades, removed to make way for the later work which now forms the curtain. The Castle of Old Wick[1] stands upon a rocky promontory. It is cut off from the land by a ditch and is naturally defended on all other sides by a precipitious fall of cliff. The masonry is some 30 to 40 feet high, the ruin of a simple keep which may well be Norse. There is no ground-level entrance, and the walls of the ground floor or basement were lit and ventilated only by a narrow slit window: entrance must have been by an external stair to an upper floor. At Dun Creich on the north shore of the Dornoch Firth the foundations of a small square stone tower stand within the ramparts of an Early Iron Age vitrified fort and may well be the ruins of a tiny mediaeval fortress.

The aforesaid castles present some presumptive evidence for the existence in widely separate areas of stone towers in the twelfth and thirteenth centuries. It is not suggested that stone structures were common or even characteristic; indeed the worn earthworks of Dunscaith, opposite the town of Cromarty, which was founded by William the Lion in 1179 indicate that this was a motte castle.[2] Yet these works have a family likeness and common characteristics of early type. Their finished appearance is not difficult to imagine: small square towers; thick walls, lit by but a few narrow windows, rising through two or three storeys to a saddle-back roof, and having a first-floor entrance by outside stair or ladder. With Castle Sween we move, to remain, on firmer ground.

On the east shore of the sea loch of Sween in Argyll there is a castle of that name. It stands high upon rock rising from the water, and it is one of the most remarkable and unexpected monuments in Scotland. It possesses architectural characteristics of the late eleventh century in a marked degree and with uncompromising simplicity, unmarred by destruction or later addition. It has a reasonable claim to be the earliest existing castle in Scotland (pl. 2, fig. 2).

Its four walls comprise a large quadrangular enclosure 70 feet by 50 feet, originally without towers. But against the two corners of the north side there have been added two later towers, one round, the other square. The curtain walls are 7 feet thick and rise to a height of some 40 feet all round. Within the open courtyard there

[1] J. Anderson (1890), 161.

[2] W. M. Mackenzie (1927), 9.

is no building, but some fragmentary foundations, and a well. The round tower is a later work, probably sixteenth century; the square tower is a massive building of thirteenth-century date, with narrow lancet windows such as occur at Mingarry and slit-windows with splayed cills and lintels on the ground floor.

The curtain of the great castle stands foursquare and without apertures save for the main entrance in the middle of the south front, and a sea gate, now broken, in the west. There are no windows.

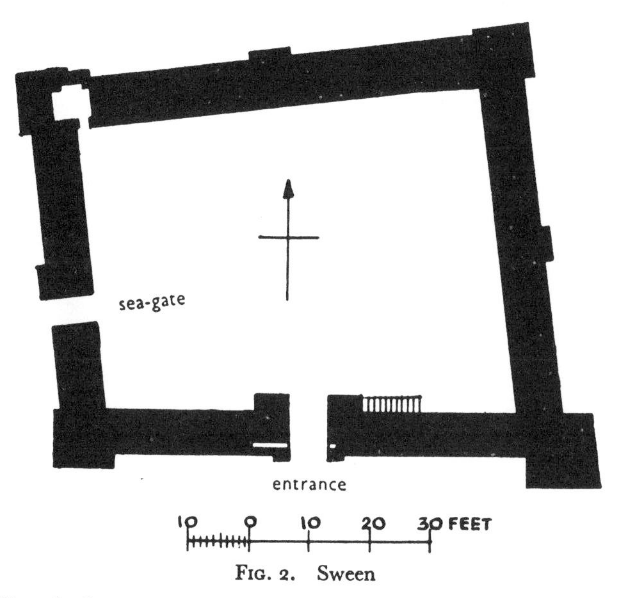

FIG. 2. Sween

The walling is featureless save for flat clasping buttresses which grip each corner and a flat pilaster buttress projecting from the middle of each side. The main entrance is through the mid-buttress on the south wall. The buttresses have but slight projection from the wall face and are of equal projection from bottom to top, save where it is reduced by a short splayed intake. Broad clasping buttresses such as these are unmistakable characteristics of early Norman work, and the piercing of a buttress by a doorway or window is just as much so, being paralleled at the Jew's House, Lincoln (*c.* 1150) and at a window in the second storey of the keep at Newcastle (1171-5). The entrance is a round-headed opening of the simplest sort. The voussoirs of the arch are well-contrived in dressed ashlar, but unmoulded. The jambs are checked for a door. This was secured by a draw-bar housed in long slots in either jamb. There are no other defensive features attendant upon this entranceway. The entrance passage is barrel-vaulted and extends into the enclosure beyond the inner face of the curtain. On the right-hand side of the entrance, in the south-east corner of the enclosure, a stone stair against the inner face of the curtain rose straight to the wall-walk over the entrance. The projection or thickening of the curtain inside the court, made to carry the stair, thus provided extra length for the entrance passage-way.

This occurs in identical fashion at Tioram in Moidart, and at Mingarry in Ardnamurchan, and it is a perfectly simple, straight-forward and effective arrangement. But whereas the details of the Tioram stair are uncertain and complicated by the ruins of what appear to be two mural chambers within the stairway, the scheme at Sween is perfectly clear in its essentials. The steps, crossing the inner end of the entrance passage, went straight up to the wall-head, where they finished in a small square chamber or cap-house with slightly rounded interior, now much ruined. At this point a small projecting bretasche might have overhung the outer wall face to defend the entrance, as it does at Tioram, Mingarry and Kisimul.

The wall-walk was provided with a parapet wall on its inner face as well as on the outer. In the north-east corner of the wall-walk there is a small square chamber entered from the adjacent walks by a lintelled doorway without rebates or checks. Two small narrow windows lit this chamber: both exist, one in each face of the two clasping buttresses which contain it. These windows are original features. Each has a flat cill and a deep splayed ingo and a high stepped lintel sloping upwards from outside to inside. Along the east walk the outer parapet preserves the cills and broken jambs of three openings. Their outline is ragged, and it is impossible to say whether or not these openings are of windows or of crenellations. Their cill level is that of the windows in the corner chamber, which suggests a range of windows continuing along this front, but the openings are on the other hand 4 feet wide, which is more suggestive of battlementing. The wall-head of the south curtain at the west end shows signs of blocking and partial dismantling suggestive of crenellations, but this may be fortuitous.

Round the inside or courtyard face of the curtain runs a deep chase or channel. It is continuous round the east, north and west sides, and round the south as far as the stairway projection, where it stops. It is deep into the wall, and carefully made to house the heavy timber of a floor. Its course round three quarters of the interior, and its absence in the quarter where the stair is situated, and where there has been no alteration to provide a reason for its absence, is highly significant.

In interpreting all the evidence we are forced drastically to revise first impressions of the original castle. The impression of an open courtyard is illusory, owing to the absence of the buildings which occupied three quarters of the structure. It was not in fact a courtyard castle, or curtain-wall castle. It was a keep, with an open stair and entrance well, such as we find on the Isle of Man at Castle Rushen, which was probably erected by the Norse King of Man, Godred II, in 1153-87.[1]

The name Sween is a corruption of the Gaelic *Suibhne*, occurring in Adamnan's *Life of Columba* as *Suibneus*. The first mention, in connection with Scotland, of a noble named Suibhne is in the Annals of Ulster under the year 1034. During the thirteenth century Knapdale was controlled by the MacSweens, who took the English side in the War of Independence. In 1301 John "son of Suffne" went with Sir Hugh Bissett and Angus of Islay to Bute and Kintyre with a fleet in the service of Edward I to find Sir John Menteith and John of Argyll in armed possession. In 1310 Edward II encouraged John MacSween of Argyll and his brothers to recover lands lost in Knapdale.

This summary history is given by Watson in his notes on a poem relating to the castle.[2] It is his opinion that the poem was written about 1310 with reference to the events of that year. The poem is in Gaelic, and it relates in conventional and mannered heroic verse the tryst of a fleet from Ireland against Castle Sween, and how welcome is the adventure in Inis Fail; the warriors are noblemen and Norsemen (*lochlannaigh*), "golden heroes from Ireland", and John MacSween it is who leads this fleet on the sea's surface, a hardy leader; and there are quilted hauberks and shields hung from the long sides of the ships. The references to the castle are nominal, none help to date it or even to identify the existing ruin with the object of the expedition, but such an identification is very probable.

The allusion to quilted hauberks and long ships is important. Knights thus apparelled and girded about with a long sword, one hand grasping the belt, the other a knightly spear, and wearing a pointed helmet, are stock figures on late mediaeval sculptured stones

[1] B. H. St J. O'Neil (1951), 4.

[2] W. J. Watson (1937), 6-13, 257-9.

of the west Highlands. The restricted distribution of this very notable Scottish art corresponds closely with modern Argyll and the Islands. The stones occur abundantly in churchyard groups, as gravestones, or exhibit their distinctive forms upon upright crosses. With the knight is frequently associated a long-shafted calvary cross with floriated head, a long sword with depressed quillons, panels of debased interlacework, and an extremely Norse-looking galley or long-ship, single-masted and with towering stem and stern. The reference to shields hanging from the long sides of the ships recalls the long-ships of the Viking Age thus dressed in harbour to denote rank and importance. Without a doubt the galley remained for long in use by the chieftains of the western seaboard. The sculptured stones date mainly from the late fifteenth to the mid-sixteenth century, according to those which bear inscriptions, but the earliest possible date is of the fourteenth century for two similar stones, one on Iona, the other on Islay.[1]

The peculiar survival of accoutrements and vessels of an earlier age has been cited as evidence in support of a similarly late date for a western seaboard group of castles of early aspect and history. Nevertheless, a detailed analysis of these western curtain-wall castles of early character reveals nothing inconsistent with a thirteenth-century date, and one may well ask, if they are not early, where are the early castles; for there are no other candidates.

CURTAIN-WALL CASTLES

The mediaeval idea of a castle was somewhat different from our conception of a mediaeval castle. It might have been a tower—a building so to speak—but this was not essential. A high curtain wall was sufficient to constitute a castle, and indeed mediaeval chroniclers frequently made specific distinction between tower and curtain wall. A petitioner to Alexander III in 1262 had a house within the precincts of Elgin Castle (*cum sua domo in castra de Elgyn*)[2]; the *Heimskringla*, referring to the *kastali* which King Sigurd the Crusader erected at Konghelle in 1116, describes it as of turf and stone, surrounded by a great ditch, and having within it a church and several houses[3]; Robert de Bedeford, master carpenter with the in-

[1] R. C. Graham (1895), 26. The Iona stone bears an illegible inscription which has been interpreted as commemorating either Angus Oig, who died shortly after Bannockburn, or John son of Angus who died in 1380. The Islay stone is not inscribed but it is a close artistic parallel which must be a near contemporary.

[2] APS I.91.

[3] J. S. Clouston (1931), 5-6.

fantry of Edward I in Scotland, was in charge of the erection of houses in the castle of St Andrews in 1303-4, when preparations were made there for the accommodation of Edward and his queen.[1] Mackenzie gives examples of the distinction between tower and wall which occurs in written descriptions and references in early records,[2] and concludes: "It follows from this specific distinction that a castle might exist which had no tower or towers, might indeed be but a lofty enclosure within which its occupants were housed."

Typologically the earliest curtain wall of stone replaces the palisade of a motte: such is the shell-keep. Not uncommon in England and Wales, the type is seemingly rare in Scotland. Only one example exists in height, at Rothesay (Bute), but there are two other imposing earthworks, the Doune of Invernochty and the Peel of Lumphanan, both in Aberdeenshire, which can confidently be identified as the sites of stone-walled shell-keeps.

The Doune of Invernochty was the capital messuage of one of the five great feudal lordships of the province of Mar. It is one of the most impressive of the many Norman earthwork remains in Scotland, not exceeded in size or interest by the great mounds of the mottes of Urr, Duffus, or Inverurie, to mention but a few. The oval summit is more extensive than those of the aforesaid mottes, measuring 250 feet by 120 feet, and it is girdled with a stone wall of 6 feet thick, now reduced to a maximum height of 4 feet. There is one entrance at the south end, and within the curtain wall are the foundations of two rectangular stone buildings: one, square and near the entrance, was probably a tower; the other, oblong, probably the chapel. This has yielded a part of a basin designed as a Norman cushion capital with scalloped sides, and another stone fragment worked in romanesque technique.[3] These relics are numbered among the few recorded examples of Norman stonework on a motte-castle (a twelfth-century respond capital from the church within the Peel of Linlithgow is exhibited in Linlithgow Palace). The mound, 60 feet high, is encircled by a wide and deep ditch with an outer bank. The ditch was flooded by means of a great earthwork dam running from it to high ground some distance away. Marsh was thus converted into reservoir. A series of sluices permitted a controlled flow of water to enter the ditch, or to leave it, a most remarkable piece of early military engineering.

[1] J. Harvey (1954), 27. [2] W. M. Mackenzie (1927), 37-9.
[3] W. D. Simpson (1936), 177.

Earthworks, ditches and water defences distinguish also the castle mound of the historic Peel of Lumphanan. This splendid mediaeval earthwork, rivalling Invernochty in size and surpassing it in historical interest, consists of a large circular earthen mound about 120 feet by 150 feet rising 30 feet above the level of a surrounding ditch. The ditch is about 50 feet wide and is contained by an earthen bank 10 feet high and 8 feet broad across the top. A stone curtain wall 3 feet thick girdles the summit of the mound and is erected on its very edge. The lower courses of the curtain are visible all round. On the summit, within the enclosure, the top of the ruined wall is almost flush with the grass level, but, the ground level having risen, 2 to 3 feet of wall doubtless remain to be exposed. The foundations of a long hall building, approximately 50 feet by 12 feet internally, are clearly to be seen butting against the curtain, but whether contemporary with it or not cannot be said without excavation. Here and there on the flat summit of the mound, beneath the long thick grass, one suspects the presence of masonry, but the indications form no coherent plan. There is an outer ditch also, 10 feet wide but shallow; the earthen bank is breached on the west side and here may have been the entrance. The mound, its stone curtain wall, outer bank and ditches are complete all round, and the whole presents a first-class type-site. Small mottes, some with earthworks and baileys, are common enough, especially in the south-west country, but this type with its spacious flat summit, stone built hall, and enclosing curtain of stone is exceedingly rare.

The site is an important one in the early mediaeval history of Scotland, in the formative period when Malcolm Canmore was fighting his way to the crown of feudal Scotland. Under the nominal sovereignty of Macbeth the Norse power over Scotland was at its greatest, but Macbeth was overtaken by Canmore "in the wood of Lumphanan" and was here slain by him at a date variously given as 5 December 1056[1] and 15 August 1057.[2] Shakespeare, following Hollinshed, identifies the scene of Macbeth's death as Dunsinane in Perthshire, but this has been plausibly explained away as literary licence.[3]

In all probability the castle of Lumphanan was the scene of the submission of Sir John de Malvill (Melville), "donées a Lunfanan",

[1] John of Fordun, v. *c.* vii.
[2] W. F. Skene (1867), 152; F. J. Amours IV (1906), 258-9, 300-1.
[3] J. Robertson (1845), 1082-5.

to Edward I in July 1296, when that victorious monarch was making a triumphant progress to the north, receiving homage on the way. There is a continuing if intermittent documentary record throughout the fifteenth, sixteenth and seventeenth centuries. In the late eighteenth century and early nineteenth century memory is said to recollect walls and gables of the structures upon the mound. In 1829 the sluice of the water ditch was revealed and the position of the drawbridge was discernible.

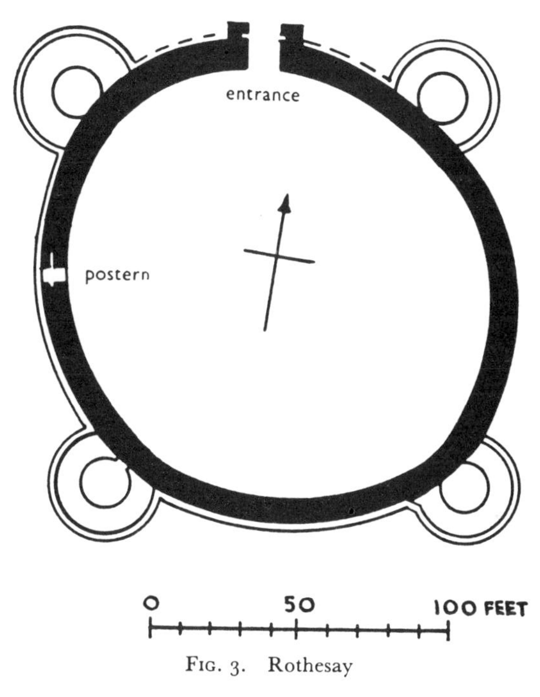

Fig. 3. Rothesay

The first stone castle of Rothesay was a shell-keep of great size and regularity (pl. 4; fig. 3). It survives as a circular curtain wall with four projecting round towers added to it in the thirteenth century. It stands upon the spacious summit of a flat-topped circular mound which is surrounded by a water moat. The curtain is 9 feet thick and 30 feet high and constructed of ashlars more square than long, an early characteristic recalling romanesque work. The towers, equidistant round the circuit, advance boldly upon long spreading bases into a wide berm which surrounds the curtain. They rose higher than the curtain. Two are much reduced in height. The original arched entrance was flush with the curtain, of the simplest sort, without architectural pretension, a mere aperture in the wall for entrance and exit. In the early thirteenth century a buttress-like jamb was placed on either side to lengthen the entrance passage by 10 feet and accommodate a portcullis and gate. The entrance through this modest forework was a lofty pointed arch springing from a squared and chamfered impost of early type not likely to have been hewn after about 1220. Erected against this and advancing far beyond it into the waters of the moat a more prominent forework of late-fifteenth to mid-sixteenth century date latterly combined the functions of entranceway, great hall and barbican. Save for the main entrance and a small postern in the west quadrant of the curtain, there were no external openings in the early castle.

The curtain was raised by some 6 feet, in rubble similar to that of the lowest part of the later forework, presumably when that edifice was erected. This operation, so often destructive, was happily not so in this instance. On the contrary it has preserved the finest and one of the few surviving examples of mediaeval crenellation in Scotland (pl. 5). When the curtain was heightened the crenellations of the quadrants on either side of the entrance were neither levelled nor destroyed, but were sealed up, immured in the later walling, where they are discernible with the square put-log holes of an overhanging gallery or hoarding.[1]

The castle is thus remarkable enough as a ruin. Its dating has caused conjectures to be advanced which add greatly to its interest, and the probability that it is the "castle in Bute" besieged by the Norse in 1230 invests it with added significance, for the description of this siege in Eirspennill's Hakon Hakonsson's Saga (1263 × 84)[2] is the earliest authentic and detailed account of such a military operation in Scotland. If the evidence of the structure can be satisfactorily explained, and if an objection on the grounds of feasibility, advanced by Mackenzie, can be met, there will remain little doubt that the existing castle incorporates that besieged by the Norse.

The saga relates that the Norse hewed through the soft stone of the wall. The ships sailed afterwards south off the Mull of Kintyre and so into Bute. And there sat the Scots in castles, and there was a steward at their head, one of the Scots. The Northmen ran in to the burg and made a hard assault on it. But the Scots defended

[1] Cf. Skipness, where there is a perfectly preserved merlon with a cross-slit loop embodied in a later heightening of the wall, and Craigie, an embattled hall-house upon whose parapet a rib-vault was raised (see below, pp. 56, 94).

[2] A. O. Anderson (1922), II.476.

themselves well, and poured down on them boiling pitch and lead. Then fell many of the Northmen and many were wounded. They bound over them "flakes of wood" (obviously as a protection against the burning liquids), "and after that they hewed at the wall, for the stone was soft; and the wall crumbled before them. They hewed at it on the ground . . . Three days they fought with the Burg-men ere they got the burg won." The version in *Flateyjarbók* expands one passage to the effect that "the Norwegians hewed the wall with axes, because it was soft".

This is an authentic and detailed account of the greatest value, all too rare in Scotland. Such a narrative, with its abundance of circumstantial detail, having regard to castles involved and tactics employed, is rivalled in interest, style and value only by Walter of Exeter's eyewitness account of the siege of Caerlaverock by Edward I in 1300, and by Barbour's lively passages in *The Bruce* of the sieges of Kildrummy in 1306 and of Berwick by Edward II in 1319, which latter must be received with caution, for Barbour was born between 1320 and 1326 and could only have written from hearsay about the events he so vividly described in 1376. Furthermore, the saga story permits us to speculate upon the date of the castle in the light of a precisely dated historical event. Before proceeding to conclusions it is however necessary to identify the castle, in whole or part, with that referred to, to determine what if any of the existing structure could be of 1230, and what later. There is little doubt about the site being the same.

The placing of the existing castle into the narrative depends upon a single crucial interpretation, that of the saga reference to the hewing at the wall because it was soft. Mackenzie totally rejects the identity of the existing castle with the besieged castle on the grounds that it would have been impossible to hew through stone however soft with the tools then available, which he says would have been weapons of war, that the castle besieged by the Norse must have been of clay; and to conclude his thesis that the castle of 1230 was of clay he dismisses the saga word *steinn* on the analogies of German *backstein* ("brick"), and "stone-ware" for pottery.[1]

The question of feasibility being crucial, let us then turn aside a moment to consider thirteenth-century siege technique and methods of withstanding it in order to set the vivid narrative of Hakon's Saga against the general background of contemporary military exercises.

[1] W. M. Mackenzie (1934), 117-27.

It has already been observed that the Norse were by no means backward in warfare. They travelled much, they ventured to the Crusades, and they did not travel with their eyes shut. *The King's Mirror*, already referred to,[1] presents to the aspiring young knight the fact and theory of attack and defence, the conduct of a siege, and the proper methods of counter-attack. It is an essay in the art of war, fully up-to-date, including in its descriptions the machines and contrivances mentioned in the following summary account.

Although the western nations in the early Middle Ages had not been ignorant of the heavy mechanical devices, such as the ballista, employed in the later years of the Roman Empire, they did not greatly use them. Incendiary projectiles, the sudden onslaught, escalade by ladders and then close fighting, were the normal and rarely varying methods of attack. Against the timber motte-castle of the west these methods were sufficient, but confronted with the new strength of the stone castles of the East they were not. The first Crusade, of 1096, and those which followed in the twelfth and thirteenth centuries, consequently worked a revolution in western military technique.

The essence of the change was the development of mechanised warfare. This inevitably affected the design and construction of castles. Massive timber towers, moving upon rollers and protected by a skin of wet hides, closed upon the curtain walls of the besieged castle over a causeway made in advance by filling in the ditch or moat with any material available. From the upper platform of these towers or belfries a direct onslaught upon the wall-head was possible if the defenders upon the wall-head were stricken by the covering fire of the attacking artillery in the form of massive throwing engines capable of casting projectiles at a high trajectory.[2] Operated by the mechanical application of the principles of torsion, tension and counterpoise, these catapults comprised the main armament of a major action. Costly and laborious to construct, they could be brought accurately into play only against a static target, and were preferred only when more direct and less complicated attempts to reduce a castle had failed or when the provocation was great, as on the occasion when King Stephen was barred from his castle at Newbury by his own marshal and was urged to cast the marshal's

[1] See above, p. 18.

[2] On this see R. Allen Brown (1976), ch. 7, and E. Viollet-le-Duc (1879*a*), *passim*.

Plate 3 Dunstaffnage, Argyll, early thirteenth century

Plate 4

above Rothesay, Bute, twelfth and thirteenth centuries

below Sappers breach a stone wall. Illuminated MS., fifteenth century

prisoner son into the castle as an inducement to surrender.[1] The destructive power of these engines was considerable, and it was usually directed against the upper-works of the target, to facilitate escalade and the establishment of a bridgehead from the belfry, and against the body of the curtain wall to breach it, or to assist sappers to do so.

The sappers had their own protection, the *masculus*, which Caesar describes at the siege of Marseilles. Known to mediaeval soldiers as a "gate", "chat" or "cat", it was a mobile gangway or tunnel, open at both ends, constructed of timber, faced with metal plates or hides, and moving upon rollers. It could be pushed, as the belfry could be, over a causeway to the base of the castle walls. Under its protection the "mouton" or battering-ram and the sapper with his tools could work to effect a breach in the wall.

The construction of these machines, the mustering of the men and materials on the site, and their preparations for use, was an undertaking of considerable magnitude. It demanded a high degree of specialised skill and experience, even when the engines were prefabricated and completed components assembled in their firing positions, as they presumably were on many an occasion. At the siege of Ayr in 1298 Thomas de Houghton and Robert de Holmcultram sent engines to Ayr from Carlisle by sea,[2] and at the onslaught upon Bothwell in 1301 a leading role was played by "le Berefrey", a prefabricated wheeled tower of great size and ingenuity which was conveyed some 20 miles in 30 wagons to the scene of its operation. At the even more spectacular siege of Stirling Castle three years later there was an English siege engine called "Bothwell".[3] Such militant carpentry doubtless explains the numbers of highly skilled carpenters who were drafted to Scotland during the Edwardian campaigns, and the record of their presence and employment north of the border need not imply, as it has been taken to do, that these men were employed only on timber fortifications.

This summary account of siegecraft suggests that the breaching of a wall, however formidable an undertaking it might appear to be, was not beyond attempt. Contemporary illuminated manuscripts illustrate the point in lively fashion (pl. 4). Here we see sappers or pioneers caught in the very act of hewing through an undeniably stone wall. Picks in hand they are at work on the core of the wall, having already removed the facework, their hardest task. Around

[1] A. Bryant (1954), 187. [2] J. Harvey (1954), 136. [3] See below, pp. 70, 102, 200.

them the assault rages in its various ways.[1] Therefore, as the castle of the siege, the existing castle of Rothesay cannot be ruled out of court because it is of stone, and there is no other reason, save for the apparently later date of the towers. There is no doubt that the castle we see to-day substantially represents that stormed by Uspak and his Norsemen in 1230.

The main objection to an early date resides in the towers with their slits and spreading bases of late thirteenth-century type. The structural evidence is incomplete and demands close scrutiny and interpretation; unanimous agreement is therefore not to be expected. The significance of the crenellations so fortunately preserved cannot be overlooked for they present one of the most interesting and significant subjects of study in the castle, stepping up as they do to the flanking towers with the stair which rose from the curtain wall-walk to their upper floors. They have put-log holes, and the merlons are wider than the embrasures, which are thirteenth-century features. The rise of the crenellations serves to identify the curtain with the towers. Now the towers have splayed bases and an interesting type of loop or arrow-slit. It is long and narrow. This is not in itself unusual. Long and narrow slits with spade-, shovel-, or stirrup-shaped terminations are of the late thirteenth century. They occur in the thirteenth-century towers of the celebrated Crusader stronghold, Krak des Chevaliers, and there is a perfect and closely dated example (c. 1290-1300) over the first-period entrance to Caerlaverock Castle in Dumfriesshire. At Rothesay the spade-shaped oillets open out not through the vertical face of the tower but through the splay of the spreading base. This mannerism occurs nowhere else in Scotland.

As the rise of the crenellations towards the towers connects curtain with tower, and as the slits are original features of the towers, it would seem that the castle is substantially of the late thirteenth century, posterior to the siege. Yet the original entrance through the curtain is earlier than the first small forework, which, by the evidence of its impost cannot be later than about 1220, i.e. before the siege. On this evidence the curtain is earlier than the towers. Now there is nothing in the saga narrative or in later history to suggest that the castle besieged in 1230 was demolished then or thereafter.

[1] The Exchequer Rolls for 1453 record payment for the construction of a "sow" to protect the quarrymen engaged in hewing their way through the walls of the great tower house of Hatton (Midlothian) when it was besieged by James II (cf. ER v.606-7).

On the contrary, as investigation has shown the curtain was consolidated and the towers were added to it. The postern, the only other opening, a round-arched barrel-vaulted passage contemporary with the curtain it penetrates, was blocked by the spreading base applied to the foot of the curtain on the outside. This reinforcement of the curtain wall is an interesting example of medieval resourcefulness. Investigation has revealed that the original wall went straight down, and that in forming the spreading base the face stones of the old lower courses were withdrawn and reused in the new base.

An explanation for the addition of towers is not hard to find. Improvement in defences to meet improvement in attack is only to be expected, and a close parallel instance is to be found in White Castle, Monmouthshire, a twelfth-century curtain-walled structure which received projecting towers about 1220.[1] An explanation of the addition of the spreading base is more diverting, and best expounded in the following brief conjectural history of this immensely interesting and valuable castle, to which it has been thought necessary to devote some detailed analysis in justification of surmise and conclusion. The difficulty in interpreting ancient and incomplete buildings is to account for all the evidence in one argument. An account of parts and periods, however perspicacious, without explanation or at least recognition of other parts perhaps incompatible with it is hardly good enough, and dogmatism is not justified by brevity when the facts admit of doubt. The following summary reasonably accounts for the evidence as a whole, although not all the details of interpretation are beyond dispute.

The first stone castle consisted of the circular curtain wall with an entrance at the north and a postern at the west. This was a shell-keep of the twelfth century. The curtain was sunk into the earthen bank of a pre-existing fort, thus superseding an earlier timber palisade. This would be a natural enough development, for which a particularly close parallel exists at Restormel, Cornwall, where this occurred about 1200[2] and at Exeter, for example. At Restormel the exposed base of the stone curtain is rough core-work which is set back from the ashlar above: the curtain was erected upon the ground, in place of the inner half of an earthen bank. The outer half of the bank remained: it assisted stability and defence and did not get in the way: it acted as a splayed base to the new stone wall. But it was not permanent. It was removed or drifted away to leave

[1] C. A. R. Radford (1946*b*). (Recent discoveries date it *c.* 1260.) [2] *Idem* (1947), 2.

exposed the core-work of the curtain along the bottom of its outer face. Similarly the inner face of the Rothesay curtain, being exposed from the time of its construction, is ashlar in its whole height.

What happened at Restormel demonstrates precisely the evidence at Rothesay save that, at Rothesay, the weakened and overhanging base exposed by the removal of the outer bank was made good by masonry flush with the curtain (in the east quadrant) or by the application of the spreading base to replace the outer slope of the earthen bank. It is to be noted that the spreading base of the south-west quadrant does not run well with the coursing of ashlar above, and that the lower courses of the walling of the north-east quadrant which descend to the ground follow a wavy course. These irregularities tend to confirm the assumption of a previous earthen bank: it would be somewhat uneven along its crest. The new stone wall overlapping the crest would conform more or less to this unevenness, and the repair work, consequent upon the removal of the outer slope of the bank, would naturally conform to the coursing of the ashlar just above it.

These alterations antedate the first small forework of the entrance, which was built not later than about 1220 upon the spreading base.[1] The towers were added in the last quarter of the thirteenth century, when the wall-head was remodelled to take the crenellations. In the late fifteenth or early sixteenth century the great forework was added to complete the castle as we see it today.

There is some suggestion of an even later history: the wide berm outside the wall should have an outer bank. Its unusual width and lack of bank may be due to a Cromwellian reconstruction of the outer works in 1650, including the provision of gun-platforms in rounded bastions at each of the corners dominated by the mediaeval towers. The reduction of mediaeval towers for gun-emplacements occurred at even earlier dates elsewhere. Fifteenth-century military theory, of which more hereafter, deprecated high walls, and Dürer (1471-1528) altered low round towers into bastions (*basteien*). At the towers there is an outward swing in the regular curve of the mound, and here Lord Bute, in his restoration of 1872-9, made flower beds, which is just the sort of thing he would do: finding evidence he could not restore or explain, he would preserve the evidence in this way.

[1] The three stages—exposed core, spreading base, and early forework—are clearly revealed in section in the small chamber in the later forework, on the east of the entrance.

Meanwhile the defence had not been idle. Lofty curtain walls and projecting towers were evolved to combat these appliances of attack. Illustrations in contemporary manuscripts depict castle and tower walls crested with overhanging timber galleries thrust out from the wall-head in time of need, to be withdrawn when not in use. These galleries were protected from fire by hides draped about them or were "*hourdés*" by a thick coating of loam or clay, from which treatment the descriptive term hoarding or hourds is derived. From these galleries, well provided with firing loops and apertures in their floors, the defenders commanded the base of their walls. The holes for the timber supports of the hoardings are still occasionally to be seen in masonry, particularly in French work and the Edwardian castles of Wales. Giotto's fresco "The Devils cast out of Arrezzo", painted before 1300 in the upper Church of St Francis at Assissi, depicts the city walls embattled and provided with put-log holes for the reception of timbers to support the hoardings, and other contemporary illustrations are numerous. The long sloping batter at the base of the walls thickened them and increased stability, gave the miner more work to do, and held him out at arm's length, his cat and belfry the more exposed to the overhanging timber galleries. The narrow slits, which appear when considered singly to be inadequate for bowshot, were not provided to enable the defence of a beleagured fortress to bring down a rush of men. They were for light, ventilation and viewing; and for converging bowshot to keep the enemy at a distance by hindering him in settling down, assembling his weighty engines of war, and bringing them up for close-range assault.

In Scotland the defensive needs met with so much ingenuity and skill were to a certain extent served by the rocky ground so abundantly provided for the castle builder, particularly in the west country. Here remoteness would render the construction of engines the more tedious, and the rocky terrain would gravely inconvenience their operators, while the greatest danger of the mine and the sapper was sufficiently resisted by the very rock upon which the castles could be situated. Accordingly there was less need for a systematic arrangement of towers with covering fire such as would be advisable in a countryside which did not in itself offer obstacles to attack. Defence against the sudden rush was sufficient. In such an environment we might expect to find local versions of the most advanced contemporary achievements, exhibiting all stages of the absorption of new influences and the retention of those outmoded, according to the circumstances, resources and requirements which make for a truly native architecture. And this in fact is what we have in a certain group in the west Highlands.

CASTLES OF THE WESTERN SEABOARD

Of quite unusual interest and little renown is a closely related group of curtain-wall castles in the west Highlands. They are all of irregular plan, and are situated, each and every one, upon abrupt rocky outcrops or on the edge of sea rock. They follow the outline of their site, and, with one exception, they have no projecting towers. Their siting, general characteristics, and some particular features, strongly suggest contemporaneity and the work of the same school of military architects, a supposition which is strengthened by their distribution. They are Kisimul in Barra, Mingarry in Ardnamurchan, Tioram in Moidart, and Dunstaffnage near Oban.

All are substantial ruins and claim the attention of students of military architecture and historians alike. They reveal in a state of remarkable completeness the towering conception of the curtain wall and in varying degrees preserve the evidence of the hourds in a manner unparalleled in Scotland, save at Rothesay. They have other features of early type and they testify eloquently to a compelling need for major strongholds on the western seaboard at some critical period of the Middle Ages.

Two dates are feasible, and both are concerned with connected efforts to disengage the Norse hold on the west. The first was the pacification of the Isles by Alexander II after his reduction of Ergadia (Argyll) in 1222, when the royal power reached the Atlantic and the Norwegian supremacy was challenged. The Chronicle of Man records his professed determination to "set his standard on the cliffs of Thurso and reduce under himself all the provinces which the Norwegian monarch possessed to the westward of the German Ocean".[1] The enterprise was arrested by his death on Kererra in 1249. His son Alexander III resumed the struggle and provides a later probable date. He defeated the Norse at Largs in 1263, subdued Man, and received the homage of Magnus at Dumfries. Thereafter, in 1264, he sent a large force under Buchan, Marr and Dorward to reduce the island chieftains still loyal to Hakon.

ER I.lxii. [2] ER I.lxv.

It may well have been this second phase of the campaign which caused the castles.

Later (1290-1300) Dunstaffnage was of continuing importance. In the campaigns and policy of Edward I it commanded, with the castles of Inverlochy, Urquhart and Inverness, the route through the Great Glen. In pursuance of these policies, the Alexandrine reaching-out and the Edwardian penetrating-in, Dunstaffnage would hold a position of vital strategic importance. With Duart (now modernised) and Mingarry, it could control the Sound of Mull, a principal channel of communication between the mainland and the Isles, and would function as a base of operations at sea and on land.

There is then no lack of authentic history to justify an ascription to the thirteenth century for this western seaboard group. But while the inherent military and political probabilities suggest the first half of the century closer dating is historically inadmissible. Nor do the architectural characteristics permit of greater precision. The lancet windows with simple chamfered arrises of Mingarry and Dunstaffnage, so like those of the later square house attached to Sween, are undeniably of thirteenth-century type, but devoid of more closely datable detail. The long fish-tailed slits of Dunstaffnage occur at Inverlochy, a conventional thirteenth-century castle which is attributed to about 1280 by analogy with Flint, Harlech, Pevensey and other English and Welsh parallels, and curtain-wall castles such as these and Duntroon, Duart and Dunollie are closely paralleled in Wales, e.g. at Newcastle Bridgend,[1] which is dated to the first half of the thirteenth century.

In point of fact, close dating is imprudent with such simple castles whose architectural style is of local rather than national significance. It is sufficient to place them firmly in the thirteenth century and to refute the assumption that they must be outlandish survivals just because their documentary history begins in the fifteenth century or later. There is neither historical nor architectural justification for rejecting a thirteenth-century date or for regarding them as mere outlandish survivals of an early type in a later period. Nor is there reason to doubt that their builders and their sponsors were well acquainted with contemporary military practice and achievement and could put their knowledge to good use. Experience and assistance of one kind or another was doubtless available in good

[1] B. H. St J. O'Neil and H. J. Randall (1949).

measure. The prosperity of the Scottish kingdom during the reigns of Alexander II and his son, and their successful establishment of royal authority over the western Highlands, were largely due to their good relations with the English crown.[1] Relations with France were also friendly, and important French influences on native castle-building in the thirteenth century have been inferred from the fact that the wife of Alexander II and the mother of Alexander III was Marie de Coucy, daughter of Enguerrand de Coucy, lord of one of the most imposing mediaeval castles in Europe, from which parallels can be drawn to Dirleton and especially to Bothwell. Such splendid works are not to be expected in the remote Highlands, but our castles of the western seaboard are none the less extraordinarily impressive and efficient. They must surely be a part, and a vital part at that, of the enterprise which has been called the most solid achievement of these reigns, and which at long last brought the Viking Age to an end.

By reason of their intrinsic significance and outstanding scenic advantage these castles rank among our finest monuments and can fairly claim to be one of the most important groups of secular structures of the Middle Ages in Scotland. They are of inestimable value. Nowhere else is there such a closely related group. While the documentary evidence and architectural detail are lacking which are essential for absolute dating, their general characteristics are distinctive and shared by all, and in the survival of the evidence of their wall-head defences they are particularly valuable, for so much has been lost of these features elsewhere, wall-heads being particularly vulnerable to destruction.

Dunstaffnage Castle (pl. 3) is perched upon an abrupt rocky eruption on a low-lying promontory which juts into Loch Etive near Oban. The castle is roughly quadrangular. The walls are 10 feet thick and closely adhere to the irregular outline of the rock, from the edge of which they rise precipitously to an overall height of 60 feet above the general ground level, or 30 feet above the level of the courtyard they enclose. A forework projects from one corner to contain the entrance which is elevated some 20 feet above the ground. It is a high pointed arch, without mouldings, and partly blocked and altered. At the foot of the jambs there is evidence of a drawbridge structure which suggests the Kisimul arrangement of a lifting-bridge

[1] F. M. Powicke (1953), 585.

working on a permanent timber erection. A seventeenth-century tower-house is built over the entrance passage.

Diagonally opposite this tower-house, in the north-west corner of the enciente, and erected upon the highest point of the site, there is a large tower. By its elevation and position of reserve, being withdrawn from the entrance, it could have been the keep. It is rounded to the outside and partially disengaged from the adjacent curtains by being recessed into them, an expedient forced upon the architect by the restricted and precipitous site prohibiting full outward projection. Within the courtyard the tower boldly projects as a square with a rounded corner. Its ground floor is 6 feet above courtyard level, entered by an outside stair. Within the entrance passage there is access to a curving mural stair ascending to the floor above. The basement was secured by door and draw-bar. The uppermost of the keep's three floors was entered from the battlements. In the north-east corner of the enceinte there is another tower, rounded and partially projecting to the outside, square and fully projecting to the inside. It is ruinous. The third round tower projects not at all within the enceinte and not much to the field, being little more than a round swelling of the corner. The curtain and round towers have long fish-tailed slits which have widely splayed internal jambs with deep square embrasures; the slits have been blocked and reformed with shot-holes for musketry. The wall-heads have been mutilated but retain evidence of their crenellations and put-log holes. On the east and north-west curtains there are pairs of thirteenth-century lancet windows.

About 200 yards from the castle there is a ruined and roofless chapel. It is unaisled and without transepts or tower. Mouldings, capitals and enrichment of first-class design and execution place it securely in the first half of the thirteenth century, if not in the first quarter, and provide corroborative evidence in support of an early thirteenth-century attribution for the castle itself, for this chapel must surely have been attached to it.

There are only two other mediaeval ecclesiastical buildings of note in the district; one is the cathedral of Lismore, of which fragmentary remains are embedded in the parish church on that island; the other is the ruined Valliscaullian priory of Ardchattan, founded by Sir Duncan MacDougall of Lorn in 1230[1]. In this we have a direct connection with Manx history, for the MacDougalls of Lorn

[1] OPS II (1854), 149; W. D. Simpson (1955), 2.

were of the royal house of Man; and Bishop Simon, who began to build Peel Cathedral there, was from Argyll. His episcopacy was from 1226 to 1247, and for part of that period it contained the diocese of Lismore. Affinities between the ecclesiastical buildings of Loch Etive and Man in the mid-thirteenth century may therefore be expected.

Kisimul Castle occupies the whole of a small rocky offshore island in Castlebay, Barra. At high water it seems to rise straight from the sea. From shore it appears to be complete and undamaged.

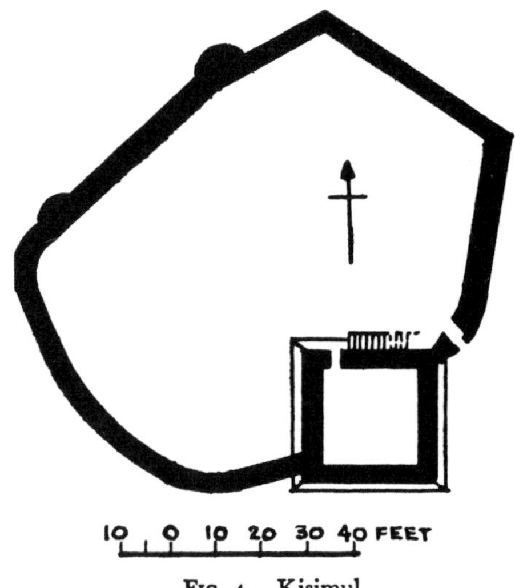

FIG. 4. Kisimul

The walls rise sheer to their battlements; much of the hard skin of harl with which the walls were freely plastered still survives; and a strong square keep rising high in one corner of the irregular enceinte conveys an added air of strength and resistance.[1] It is a most agreeable ruin to satisfy the lover of the picturesque, and it is of considerable archaeological importance (pl. 5; fig. 4).

There is no record of its existence before the early part of the fifteenth century, when the island became the chief patrimony and home of the MacNeills, and it has accordingly been attributed to that period, features of unquestionably early type having been dismissed as outlandish survivals.[2] But the evidence of the structure cannot thus

[1] Mr Sidney Toy (1953), 131, states that the south face of the keep has a "true prow" i.e. that it is in two planes which come forward to meet in a sharp vertical edge or keel. This is not so. The wall-face is perfectly flat.

[2] RCAMS IX (1928), xlv; W. M. Mackenzie (1927), 42, 163.

lightly be denied. The whole work is consistent with an early date, and although its general characteristics are simple and lacking in closely datable architectural detail they preserve in good measure a characteristic defensive feature of twelfth and thirteenth century wallheads. That is the put-log holes for the hourds, which by the beginning of the fifteenth century had been replaced by permanent wall-head works in stone.

There are neither windows nor slits in the curtain. The defence was wholly conducted from the wall-head which is crowned with deep crenellations. Below them a row of holes about nine inches square penetrates the walls of the towers as well as the curtain. These holes have been mistakenly identified as weep holes to carry water from the parapet walk.[1] This is impossible, for they are too high in the merlon, and there is no parapet walk. Now the battlements could not be used, nor the hourds erected and manned, without a wall-head walk of some sort, and if, as seems certain, there has been no stone wall-walk removed, we are forced to the conclusion that the wall-walk was a permanent timber erection. In time of peace no doubt (but not necessarily) the hourds overhanging the outer face of the curtain would be withdrawn.

This explains the scarcements, otherwise a puzzling feature, for they are not wide enough to walk upon. They must be structural. The most likely explanation, and one which is entirely consistent with a wall-head arrangement, is that they were offsets to receive the timbers of a permanent erection, a scaffolding or half-timbered structure rising from the ground with horizontal members bearing upon the offsets or, alternatively, a gallery overhanging the summit, supported below by brackets rising from the offsets.[2]

The keep rises from a broad splayed base which the curtain wall does not have. This base returns round the tower within the enceinte, the curtain is built over it, and there is a straight joint between the tower and the curtain with the curtain set back an inch or two from the outer face of the tower. The keep was erected first. The curtain followed soon after, the island site being doubtless considered sufficiently safe during the building of the all-important tower. The same sequence of tower preceding a contemporary curtain can be observed in the great Plantagenet castle of Conisburgh in Yorkshire. Similarly the early thirteenth-century castle

[1] RCAMS IX (1928), 127.
[2] J. G. Dunbar, (Glasgow Arch. J. 4, 1976), advocates a 15th cent. date for Kisimul.

of St Andrews was a stone keep with a timber palisade, later superseded by the stone curtain which runs into the keep on either side.[1] The keep is severely square, and of no great size in plan. It rises through four floors to high battlements similar to those of the curtain. It is lit below by the minimum of small slits, and in the second floor, which was evidently the hall, by small windows in wide embrasures, one to each wall. It has a high entrance in the courtyard side approached by a flight of stone steps against it. The present flight is late, and crosses an original entrance to the basement. They rise to a platform over the entrance to the courtyard through the curtain. From the platform the ascent turned back across the wall of the tower and rose to its elevated doorway in a way which can now only be conjectured. Presumably it was a timber erection incorporating a lifting bridge, which when drawn up would leave an impassable gap between the platform at the top of the stone stair and a small entrance platform of timber projecting beyond the doorway (a somewhat similar arrangement is to be inferred at Dunstaffnage). An intruder happening to gain admittance despite these unwelcome difficulties of access was now confronted by a choice of stairs; one straight down to the first floor in the thickness of the wall, the other twisting round in the corner of the tower to the second floor, where the hall was. From a window embrasure in the hall a further mural stair ascends to the wall-walk. Communication between first floor and basement must have been by hatchway and ladder.

The entrance to the courtyard from the beach was as usual but a piercing of the curtain wall, with the short passage thus formed prolonged internally by the walling which supported the outside stair and platform. The present entrance to the courtyard may not be original, but it is beneath the corbels of an overhanging bretasche. A few yards to the north of the entrance two straight joints several feet high suggest an earlier doorway now blocked up. This possibility is strengthened by indications of a blocked doorway on the inner face of the curtain at this point. Above the position of this possible earlier doorway, in floor of the platform, there is a long slot, which could be that of its portcullis. The platform does not continue round the curtain. As at Castle Sween it is a landing at the top of the stair, over the entrance passage. At Sween it was built in as a small caphouse; here it could be the floor of a timber-framed portcullis chamber, placed tactically in the corner contained by the

[1] See above, pp. 21-2.

curtain and the keep, controlling the entrance passage through the curtain by a portcullis and the ascent to the keep by doors.

From the evidence of the structure and the defensive features we can confidently attribute this most interesting Hebridean castle to the thirteenth century and even suggest that the keep is a twelfth-century structure of the type discussed above. Houses in the courtyard, now ruinous, were built and rebuilt in the seventeenth and eighteenth centuries.

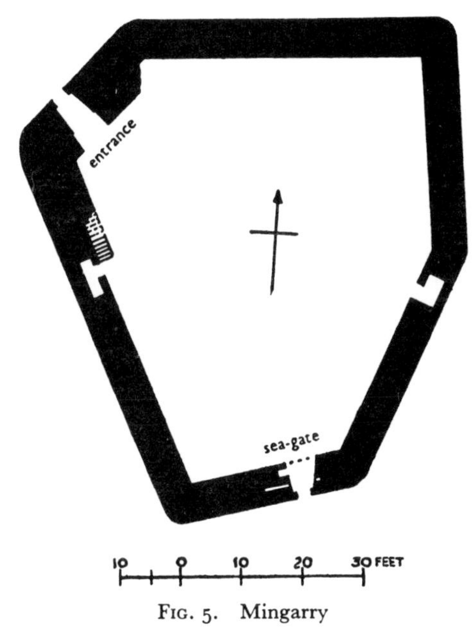

FIG. 5. Mingarry

Mingarry Castle in Ardnamurchan (pl. 6; fig. 5) is situated at the west end of that peninsula, upon the shore, overlooking the waters of the Sound of Mull. The original conception, whose external appearance is unaffected by later work within, was simply that of a massive stone curtain enclosing an irregular courtyard. The walls are 6 feet thick, 30 to 40 feet high, and make a rough hexagon with rounded corners. This rises from the rocks on the seaward side and is cut off from the landward by a deep and wide dry ditch. There are two entrances, one overlooking the ditch, the other from the rocks, which would be approached by sea only (still the easiest method). The sea entrance is approached by a flight of rock-cut steps. The doorway was defended by a draw-bar housed in the jambs of the passage through the curtain, and later by an iron yett, a swinging openwork grille of interlacing iron bars, a contrivance of peculiarly Scottish occurrence frequent in the tower-houses of later date and here a later insertion.[1] The landward entrance, from across the ditch, was covered by a machicolated overhanging timber bretasche, of which the supporting stone corbels and two access doorways high up in the curtain remain. One of the doorways is a pointed arch of truly mediaeval appearance. Outside the entranceway at the bottom of the opening is an original hollowed corbel for a drawbridge trunnion. The entrance passage is prolonged to a depth of 9 feet by an inward thickening of the curtain wall made to carry a stone stair rising over it to the wall-head as at Sween, Kisimul and Tioram.

At the bottom of the stair there is a mural chamber within the thickness of the curtain; it has a garderobe flue and a hatch in the floor giving access to a pit below. The wall-head is crenellated, with long loops in the merlons of the west side and loops below in the north. Beneath the cills of the crenellations are the put-log holes of the hoarding. In the north elevation, overlooking the ditch, there is an astonishing series of narrow lancet windows with splayed arrises. The windows are on two levels, and two of the lights are paired, both heads being wrought in the one stone, as are the heads of the single lights. The heads, jambs and cills are hewn in freestone, well bonded into the angular rubble of basalt of which the curtains are built. Behind this wall there has evidently been a hall of some importance. These windows are closely paralleled in the square thirteenth-century house attached to one corner of Castle Sween, at Duart, and in the paired lancets in the curtain of Dunstaffnage. Early thirteenth-century rectangular chapels of the west, such as Keills and Kilmory on Loch Sween, have similar windows, with jambs rebated at the outside corners for the reception of timber window frames; one window at Mingarry appears to be thus equipped.

Against the inner face of this curtain an eighteenth-century barrack-block has been erected, obscuring or destroying in its construction the evidence of the mediaeval hall. The barrack has regular rows of large windows and it is divided within by a scale-and-platt stair extending from front door to back wall. Confined within the restricted and irregular enceinte the plan of this block could hardly be symmetrical, but it is clearly of the standard official army plan to be seen to greater advantage in the complete but

[1] For yetts see D. Christison (1883), 98-135; (1888), 286-320.

roofless Hanoverian garrison of Ruthven Barracks, Kingussie, erected in 1719.[1] The corner roundels are part of late sixteenth or early seventeenth additions.

Tioram Castle (pl. 6), at the eastern neck of the Ardnamurchan peninsula, is clearly a near relation of Mingarry. In unmatched scenic splendour it rises superbly from a prominent rocky eminence at the dry end of a long spit of sand jutting into Loch Moidart. At high water the site is cut off from the shore. Like Kisimul and Mingarry, it is the essence of the curtain-wall defence, adapted to suit its site and occupying the whole of it. The area enclosed is roughly pentagonal, the walls are 8 feet thick, 30 feet high, and characteristically rounded at their outer corners. At the seaward side they rise sheer from the very edge of the uneven rock to a height of some 60 feet above the waters of the loch. Nowhere have they collapsed: all round the wall-head is complete although disfigured, frequent rebuildings and alterations having here and there obliterated its original form.

The embattling had deep and narrow crenellations, the merlons being very broad as at Mingarry and Kisimul. Two types of hole penetrate the wall below the crenellations: one, with projecting spouts, cast water from the wall-walk; the other holes, without spouts, bear no logical relationship to the wall-walk when considered as gargoyles, but when considered as part of the hoarding their significance becomes plain. On the inner face of the two stretches of curtain which are not obscured by later work (the east and west walls) there are two narrow scarcements precisely of the sort which occur at Kisimul, and doubtless for the same reason. There were two entrances, through the north and south walls; the southern is blocked, the northern is that in use. It is crudely arched in small voussoirs and was covered by a bretasche supported upon stone corbels, a diminutive one-man chamber entered directly from the wall-walk. Two stumps of timber beams attest the provision of a timber stair and platform giving access to the blocked postern in the east curtain, above which a patching of the masonry suggests another bretasche. In the north-west corner of the enclosure, on the right-hand as it is entered, there is a stone stair mounting alongside the curtain, returning round the corner, and thus ascending to the wall-walk over the entrance passage in the manner characteristic of these castles. As at Sween, the wall-walk had an inner

[1] See below, p. 236.

parapet. At the foot of the stair is a small chamber, with a breach through the curtain, as though a window or door had been torn out.

A massive rectangular keep with walls 6 feet thick rises high above the curtain. It has a vaulted basement and comprises four storeys and a garret. It is patently later than the curtain, but affords presumptive evidence of early date in put-log holes, in an access door for a chamber probably half timbered which overhung the courtyard, in slab-stone corbels crudely supporting a stone-built chamber of slight projection, and in the ghost of crenellations filled in when the wall was heightened. A high tower with corbelled angle turrets was erected about 1600 as part of a domestic range built against the south wall.

The curtain-wall castles reviewed above are of the simplest sort. The group is small and even within itself not without variety; but the similarities are more significant than the variations, and the members insist on being considered together as a family. They are distinguished alike by their distribution, siting, and crude architectural detailing. They occur nowhere else but the western seaboard: one and all they bestride sites which leave nothing to chance, and each occupies all the site, be it island, rocky eminence, or cliff. In each the course of the wall is nicely adjusted to the irregularities of the *assiette* to enclose an area of about 70 feet by 60 feet; corners are generally obtuse and on the outside always rounded. They present to the field a series of unbroken flat walls whose defence was conducted solely from a wall-head hoarding. Only Dunstaffnage proclaims a more aggressive attitude, with its business-like loops and embryo rounded towers. Doorways are but apertures in the walls, primitively fortified by bar-hole and bretasche, the existence of which latter feature at Kisimul, Mingarry and Tioram makes characteristic an appendage so often only to be presumed. Crenellations with deep merlons, merlons with loops, put-log holes, and inner scarcements, all afford archaeological data of the greatest interest and value, while the corner stair to the wall-head, contrived to prolong the entrance-passage, is another notable characteristic unparalleled save at Sween, which is of earlier date but likewise of western provenance.

The building technique is in all cases identical. The walling is beautifully constructed of large, hard and intractable stone, polygonal and with sharp corners. Necessarily of random rubble, this

Plate 5

above Kisimul, Barra, Outer Hebrides, early thirteenth century

below Rothesay, Bute: early thirteenth-century battlements

Plate 6

above Mingarry, Ardnamurchan, Argyll, early thirteenth century, turrets later

below Tioram, Moidart, Inverness-shire, early thirteenth century, turrets later

masonry is brought to a level course every 6 feet or so, by flat pinnings. This style of masonwork is a consequence of the restrictions imposed upon the mason by the material at his disposal, and undue significance should not attend its occurrence. It occurs in castles of a different type elsewhere, at Lochindorb, Inverlochy and Moulin for instance, yet still in a thirteenth-century context, and it is not unreasonable to regard it as a thirteenth-century technique employed where the preferred freestone is lacking.

In addition to those described, which are substantial and free-standing ruins unaffected by collapse or modern work, the following should be included: Duart on the Sound of Mull, Dunvegan in Skye, Duntroon on Loch Crinan, all modernised, and Skipness, to be described below.[1]

MAINLAND CASTLES

Castles so uncompromisingly "curtain-wall" in conception are not restricted to the western seaboard. Elsewhere, however, the curtain defines a more regular shape than do those of the west; the reason for this is that the rocky perch is no longer available or preferred. The ordinary and straightforward quadrilateral enclosure is the usual form, and it has a wide distribution.

Several have a family resemblance to one another but the characteristics are less individual and less marked than are those of the western group. Ardchonnel, on a small island off the east bank of Loch Awe, Roy at Nethybridge, Achanduin on Lismore, and Skipness in Kintyre, are all square or nearly square enclosures, about 70 feet across, contained within high curtain walls. None have elaborate defences but each has a single rectangular corner tower of modest projection. Doorways were secured by bar-holes and perhaps a portcullis; the entrance passage may be prolonged outwards by the doorway jambs advancing slightly from the wall-face, as at Skipness and Achanduin. Ardchonnel has a curtained base-court before the entrance. Save for a small garderobe chamber worked into the curtain, as at Achanduin and Roy, or a stairway within the thickness of the wall these castles have no architectural details of note. Yet Ardchonnel recalls Tioram with its straight open stairs to the wall-walk on the right hand of the entrance.

It possesses features of detail, however, which urge a late fifteenth-century date, and none which suggest a thirteenth-century

[1] See p. 55.

one. The aforesaid straight stair in the courtyard does not return round the corner to cross over the entrance passage upon a thickening of the curtain in the manner characteristic of the western seaboard group, and the typical rounded bull-nosed external corners of this early group are conspicuously absent. The detailing of chamfered door and window openings, which include a flat arch and a three-sided one, is consistently fifteenth-century in character, as is the lofty chimney stack with offsets on its internal wall-face.

The interior wall-face of Roy has a chase cut in it for the timbers of the courtyard buildings, which presumably were of wood as there is no indication of stone buildings against the curtain. The masonry has the characteristics noted: it is of rubble, polygonal and difficult to use, but beautifully handled and brought up to a level course every 5 feet or so by the clever use of small pinnings. In all probability the whole exposed surface of the walls, without as well as within, would be lime-washed or plastered, as it still is at Kisimul. The entrance is to-day a high pointed breach in the curtain, robbed of all distinctive masonry. A high and wide pointed arch doorway with ashlar voussoirs is suggested by the profile of the gap and the restricted use of ashlar at the mural garderobe chamber. Such an entrance admitted to the courtyard of Dunstaffnage. A complete and undisturbed example of a simple pointed entrance whose arch rises smoothly from the jambs without capital or impost, such as this might well have been, is to be seen in Loch Doon Castle, described below.

Kinclaven Castle (Perthshire) is an exceedingly large enclosure about 130 feet square now sadly ruined and overgrown. Each corner had a tower projecting from it, seemingly square, but nothing of them remains except their narrow entrances from the enclosure. A dog-leg entrance passage evidently protected by a tower admits to the interior of the courtyard in the centre of the south side.[1] The castle was a royal residence in the time of Alexander II, and in 1264 the Exchequer Rolls record the payment of the carriage of wine to it, and mention it in connection with the repairs of a boat.[2] Edward I stayed in the castle, during his first campaign, in June 1296; in 1297, according to Blind Harry, it was taken by Wallace.[3]

Large as Kinclaven is it is nevertheless exceeded by the Banff-

[1] The castle of Ballymoon (Co. Carlow) is a close parallel to Kinclaven and dates from about 1220; see H. G. Leask (1941), 74, and his fig. 44.

[2] ER 1.3, 26.

[3] D. MacGibbon and T. Ross (1887), 1.69.

shire stronghold of Balvenie, a great quadrangular enceinte 150 feet by 130 feet in area. The curtain wall is 7 feet thick, over 25 feet high for the most part, and achieves 35 feet on the entrance front. The walling again is of massive coursed rubble. Some evidence of a parapet wall survives, but none of the hourds, nor of any bretasche-work. Of the original entrance nothing can be said, for it has been usurped by a sixteenth-century domestic range. The curtain rises from a spreading base not unlike that of the ruined thirteenth-century castle of Coull.[1] There are no towers, save incipiently at one angle, where a sort of extra-large clasping buttress does duty for a tower by containing a small vaulted garderobe chamber at first-floor level. At the other end there is some evidence of a greater tower, and the only loop, a plain narrow slit with weathered sand-stone dressings and wide internal splay. Stone buildings are ranged round the curtain, within the enclosure. Of exceptional interest is the wide flat-bottomed ditch which enclosed the castle on three sides (the ground on the fourth falls steeply away). A berm 30 feet wide separates the curtains from the ditch, which is 40 feet wide 12 feet deep and faced with good masonry.

Hume Castle (Berwickshire) and Kincardine Castle (Kincardine-shire) have each a history going back to the twelfth century. The reconstructed walls of Hume stand high round a large court, like Kinclaven about 130 feet square. What is of most value in these two castles, the one much restored, the other much ruined, is the plan, which shows that the simple curtain-wall type, most of the surviving examples of which are to be found in the Highlands or Islands, is to be found also in the Lowlands.

An aberrant type, unique in its plan, is Loch Doon Castle in Ayrshire, which stands to-day where it ought not, upon the western shore of that loch.[2] Its eccentricity is due to the configuration of its original island site in the middle of the loch, to which the lay-out was closely adjusted. It comprises a curtain of masonry of work-manship far superior to anything yet encountered in this survey, comparable to the highly accomplished masonwork which falls to be discussed later. The ashlar is raised upon a splayed plinth some six to eight courses all round, save at the entranceway. A raising of

[1] W. D. Simpson (1926), 132-48.

[2] Before the waters of the loch were raised the castle was dismantled by the Ancient Monuments Department of the Ministry of Works, and, shorn of its later work, re-erected on its present site. The re-erection was a very careful operation—each stone was numbered before it was moved to the new site.

the ashlar progressively towards the entrance, where it is at its highest, suggests a predominating structure here. The facework exhibits a minor feature which it is worth noting. This is the checked or rebated joint, a technical mannerism by no means of common occurrence, but where occurring frequently, as it does here, it is in work attributed to the early fourteenth century, e.g. Torthorwald and Lochmaben in Dumfriesshire.

The enclosure is eleven-sided, the longest side 60 feet in length, about twice the length of any of the other sides. The courtyard area is about 90 feet by 60 feet, and the walls are about 28 feet high and unbreached. They average 8 feet in thickness and rise from the splayed plinth which runs all round but stops short of the main entrance on either side of it. There are two entrances, the main entrance 9 feet wide and a postern 2 feet 8 inches wide. The main entrance is a simple but imposing pointed-arch opening of two chamfered orders. Between them, on either side and at the bottom, there is a bold chamfer stop, a simple and effective concession to the urge to decorate an important feature, wholly in keeping with the massive simplicity of the structure. A heavy timber door of two leaves closed the opening. It was secured by two draw-bars across the back and by a portcullis in front. Save for the door the entrance-way is complete and affords a valuable, instructive and rare example of this simplest of all types of entrance, an aperture through the curtain with self-contained essentials and no added architectural pretensions, however useful.

The portcullis chamber above the entrance has gone, lost in a later rebuilding of the upper part of the curtain, which is clearly to be distinguished in the change in mason-work round the entire circuit. As a consequence of resiting the castle the main entrance is on the lower ground level outside, and the access from it to the court-yard level is awkward, by a slope cut into the uneven ground. The postern is also complete, original and unchanged. It is elevated above outside ground level to afford direct access to the entrance three or four feet higher than the outside. It is a pointed arch opening with broad chamfers. The door was secured by a draw-bar. The passage of the postern through the curtain is a pointed barrel-vault of well-wrought ashlar similar to the facework of the curtain. The interior facework of the curtain on the other hand is of unwrought rubble throughout, save at the corners where the obtuse angles are made in hewn ashlar. Within the enclosure are evidences of later work difficult to interpret in their fragmentary remains.

The castle is a particularly important source of information because of the completion of the curtain's circuit, the excellence of the masonwork, and the unaltered survival of the doorway openings. This is a rare occurrence, and doubly fortunate, for it affords precise information on vital parts invariably altered, restored or reduced to shapeless gaps by stone robbers; and furthermore they present the best and strongest possible examples of this simplest of entrances. Wyntoun includes the castle in the six strongholds which held out against Baliol when all others were in his hands, the other five being Dumbarton, Urquhart, Lochleven, Kildrummy and Lochmaben.

Lochmaben is a much ruined curtain-wall castle, strictly rectangular and seemingly without projecting towers. Placed at the end of a promontory extending into the loch it is cut off from the landward approach by no less than four ditches and banks, the outer of which, dog-legged in its course, runs right across the neck of the promontory and would originally be flooded with water from the loch. Within this outer ditch and some distance from it, not integrated with it in a defensive scheme, are two ditches together, probably also filled with water originally. They define the limit of an extensive outer bailey. This is separated from the castle walls by the fourth and innermost wet ditch cutting across the promontory. From the bottom of this inner ditch rises the long spreading base of the frontal curtain, faced with good ashlar still. In the middle of the frontal wall was the entrance, reached by a turning-bridge across the ditch. The pit for the counterpoise of the bridge is well preserved and of first-class dressed ashlar work. Opposite the pit, on the outer bank of the ditch, the foundations of the bridge abutment have been revealed.

This inner ditch is, with the Kildrummy chapel,[1] one of the most puzzling and intriguing details of mediaeval secular building in Scotland for it passes beneath a forward extension of the two lateral walls of the castle. These rise 40 feet above the water level and stop vertically against the outer bank of the ditch. They do not seem to have returned across the front, along the outer margin of the ditch, as John Clerk of Eldin's etching of 1780 is said to suggest.[2] If there were a return wall across the front it would enclose the ditch and make it, as it were, an internal moat or service canal, an intriguing

[1] See below, pp. 77-8.

[2] RCAMS VII (1920), 149.

possibility. Unhappily all the face stones of the lateral extensions have been robbed, and it is impossible to do more than conjecture the nature of the thing. The lower courses of the lateral extensions and the sloping facework of both sides of the ditch are in excellent ashlar, axe-dressed with diagonal strokes, a technical point not by itself conclusive but strongly indicative of the thirteenth century. A double-splayed plinth with profile similar to that of the west curtain of Caerlaverock (*c.* 1290-1300) runs straight into the earthen bank and has no suggestion of a return across the front.

The curtains are high, and within the entranceway, which seems to have been a more substantial affair than in the others of this group of castles, there is on either side of the passage, at its inner end, a broad and solid platform of corework, shapeless because of the lack of its facing stones, but suggestive of stairs to wall-head and gate-house. The far-flung outer ditch of dog-leg course and the manner in which the lateral extensions of the walls of the castle are embedded into the outer bank of the inner ditch without proper finish or return (as far as one can see) suggest that there is a system of earthworks earlier than the stone castle. The outer bailey, a flat plateau above the general level of the promontory, may precede the masonry, may in fact be the enclosure which Edward I made strong with a palisade after his success at Falkirk in 1298.[1]

The Royal Commission cautiously dates the stone castle to the fifteenth century, but an earlier date is quite justifiable. There is little enough left to go on in all conscience but what there is indicates the late thirteenth or early fourteenth century. The splayed plinths could be early in the century and the plain ashlar walling contained many a checked or rebated joint, a technical mannerism occurring elsewhere in a reliable early fourteenth-century context, as has been discussed in connection with its occurrence at Loch Doon.

In all likelihood the stone castle of Lochmaben was erected in the early fourteenth century, its plan having been laid down in the last years of the thirteenth century, when Edward erected his peel. It is evident from Welsh documentary sources relating to his castle-building operations there that the erection of a timber stockade or *magnum palicium* was the normal procedure during the first stages of the erection of a stone castle; it formed in the outer bailey a temporary defence and home for the garrison and labourers while the *murus lapideus* was under construction.[2]

[1] J. Stevenson (1870), II. 404. [2] J. G. Edwards (1946), 23.

The outer walls of the enclosure, although standing high in parts, have been wholly robbed of their face stones and are now shapeless fragments. Stone buildings came away from them inside the court, but what form these structures took and whether or not they surrounded the court it is impossible to say. The lack of these interior buildings leaves the outer walling standing high and free in the manner characteristic of the curtain-wall type. Obviously the evidence can be misleading if overstrained to produce conclusions requiring the corroboration of less durable evidence. Doune Castle in Perthshire (*a.* 1400) is another cautionary example of the same kind. There, although tall lancets were provided in the south wall, and tuskers in the kitchen tower for a range against the west wall, nothing else whatever indicates the existence of these buildings, and in view of the unusual completeness of what has survived of Doune, including these south and west enceinte walls which are complete to their parapets 40 feet high, it is perfectly reasonable to conclude that the courtyard ranges were never built. In fact, no other conclusion is reasonable. From the outset Doune was conceived as a courtyard castle, and as such it is described below.

Another instance which it is relevant to include here is Skipness in Kintyre (pl. 7).[1] A long rectangular hall-house, with walls over 6 feet thick upon a splayed base, and upper windows only, constituted the original castle.[2] It is an early thirteenth-century building, erected in all probability, architectural and historical, in the first quarter of the century, perhaps just after 1222, when Alexander II subdued the house of Somerled in pursuance of the policy referred to above. Associated with this strong hall-house was a separate chapel 60 feet away, dedicated to St Columba. Both hall and chapel were partly demolished and their remains incorporated in later thirteenth-century buildings ranged about the courtyard, which is now enclosed only by the outer walls. The entrance into the courtyard extension of the first castle is by a pointed arch and a passage through a wide flat buttress which advances but a foot or so in front of the curtain, instantly recalling the buttress-entrance of Sween. Above the passage was a portcullis chamber, small but nevertheless rib-vaulted. Crosslet or cruciform loops in the re-entrant angles of the entranceway covered the curtain on either side of it.

[1] For "hall-houses", including this, see pp. 91-9 and see also RCAMS, *Argyll* vol. 1, "Kintyre", (1971), 165-178.

The west curtain remains a splendid thing to-day (pl. 7). It is of two periods. The northern part is the west gable wall of the original hall-house, the southern part is the outer façade of a superior building which can only have been a great hall over a storage undercroft, the later thirteenth-century successor to the original hall-house of lesser size, which would doubtless become its solar when the castle was extended and radically altered in conception. It is 70 feet long and rises from a double-splayed base which steps down according to a slight fall in ground level. Along the first floor it is pierced by a regular level row of crosslets with wide arched embrasures, without window seats, in its thickness. One of these distinctive loops is to be seen in the north wall of a tower-house which was added to the east end of the original hall-house in the late sixteenth century. It is to be seen, moreover, in a merlon in a short extent of battlementing at the second floor level of the tower, immured by a raising of the tower upon an earlier crenellated wall-head. Crosslets and simple narrow slits are the only window openings in the later enceinte wall, and nowhere were there such window openings at ground level save in the early chapel, where three rounded windows were blocked by the later curtain raised against its outside face in the later thirteenth-century reconstruction.

Skipness is of quite unusual interest because of the extensive survival of the enclosing curtain and the amount of early datable features which are still embodied in it, notably the blocked-up but complete crenellations, the fine series of crosslets—which, as far as the present writer is aware is the only systematic display of this type of arrow-slit in Scotland[1]—and the rare but undoubted existence of an early thirteenth-century hall-house.[2]

CURTAIN WALLS WITH TOWERS

The defensive apparatus of the simple curtain-wall castles described was on the wall-head. Even arrow or crossbow slits in the walls are rare, only Dunstaffnage being thus equipped to an effective degree, and that castle is distinguished furthermore by embryo protecting round towers at the corners. Wall-head hoardings were vulnerable to fire and the smashing impact of stone-throwing

[1] It appears haphazardly in a thirteenth-century tower at Bothwell, and at Dirleton and Rothesay in fourteenth-century walls. Several Aberdeenshire tower houses of late fifteenth- to late sixteenth-century date contain loops for hand guns or small cannon which revive this, by then, unpractical design, a local mannerism referred to on pp. 216-17.

[2] See below, pp. 91-2.

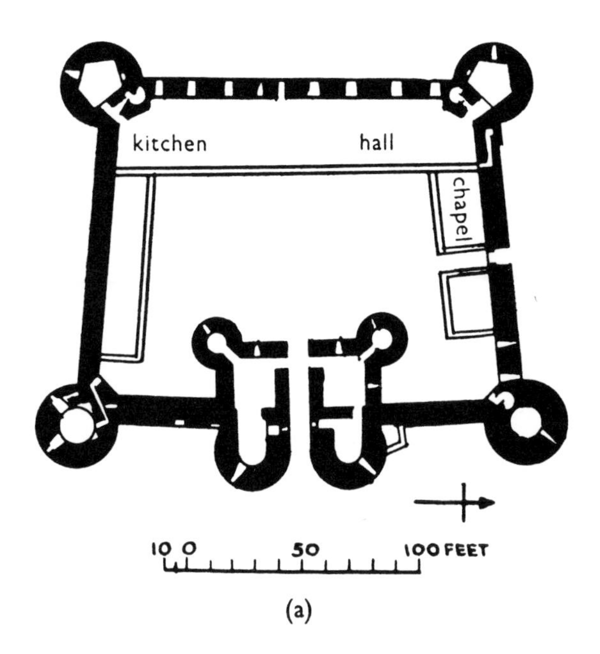

(a)

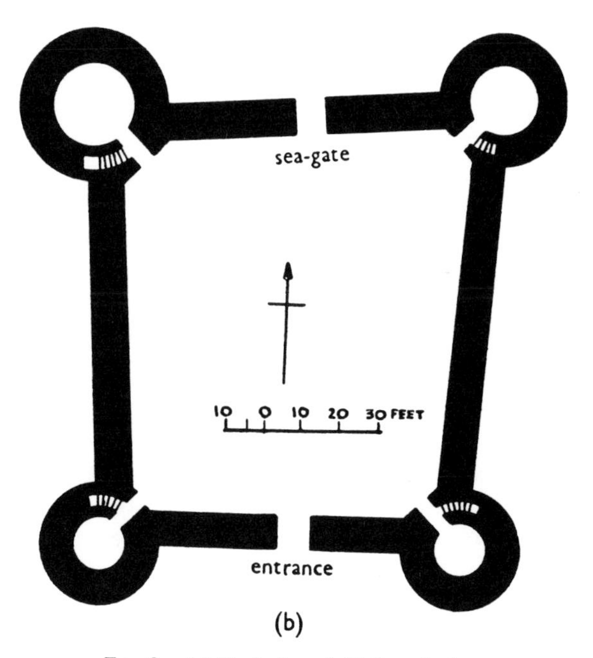

(b)

Fig. 6. (*a*) Harlech and (*b*) Inverlochy

engines. The range they provided was either vertically downward to the base of the walls or obliquely to the field. To cover the length of the curtain adequately boldly projecting towers were introduced into the defensive scheme. Placed at the corners of the enceinte they provided a field of fire along the face of the curtain as well as directly outwards. Should the curtains be so long that complete coverage was not provided by the corner towers, intermediate towers were erected.

There are no castles with true mid-wall towers in Scotland. The intermediate towers of Kildrummy and Bothwell are placed obliquely in the curtains at the angles of their polygonal circuits. But in Inverlochy Castle (Inverness-shire) there is a first-rate and rare example of the quadrangular castle fortified with round corner towers, a type not uncommon in England and Wales and there dated securely to the last quarter of the thirteenth century, e.g. Kidwelly (*c.* 1275), Flint (1277) and Harlech (1283).

Inverlochy (fig. 6) is a simple square courtyard contained by four high curtain walls. A massive round tower projects boldly from each corner, one, the donjon, being larger than the others. The enclosure so formed has two entrances, plain pointed-arch openings, without foreworks or gatehouse, through the centre of two opposite sides. The entrance is but a doorway in which hung a heavy two-leaved door secured by a draw-bar and protected by a portcullis. The curtain is surrounded by a wide ditch and outer bank concentrically disposed about it. The ditch is silted but is clearly definable round three sides. The fourth side, confronting the River Ness, was not ditched. The entrance through this side was the water-gate; before it there would be no doubt a channel from the river, and a small harbour or dock, such as still exists at Beaumaris in Anglesey, an Edwardian castle which was begun in 1295. Water from the river was introduced to the ditch round the other three sides.

The curtain and towers stand to a height of about 30 feet. The towers were floored and each is equipped with long narrow loops with fish-tailed cills resembling those at Dunstaffnage. The floors were each served by a mural stair within the thickness of the wall. It does not rise as a wheel or spiral stair characteristic of later building, but as a slower curve within the arc of the wall, which is unusual in Scottish architecture but occurs in the keep of Dunstaffnage. The wall-head is much broken, and on the south side the crenellations have been remodelled in recent times.

The donjon tower is closed to the courtyard by a straight gorge wall which cuts obliquely across the corner of the enceinte. At ground level there is an entrance from the court which penetrates the wall to the interior of the basement of the tower; its door was secured by draw-bars housed in deep holes in either jamb. On the left hand of the deep entrance passage a doorway admits to the bottom of the mural stair which rises as far as the second floor. The first-floor chamber is entered directly from this stair. The floor itself was supported upon a wide scarcement which has been repaired and finished with an inward slope, doubtless to cast off rainwater falling through the roofless ruin of the tower, which gives a misleading indication of vaulting. The embrasures of the long narrow loops are wide, double-splayed and straight-lintelled, just as in the curtains and towers of Conway Castle, for example, erected by Edward between 1283 and 1287. In the corner, where the tower meets the west curtain, there is a mural garderobe chamber, dog-legged in plan, and blocked on the outside where the masonry of the curtain is thickened to accommodate the garderobe chute. The second floor of the tower has no less than three doorways: one from the stairhead, one from an adjacent garderobe chamber, and one through the centre of the gorge wall. The garderobe chamber overhung the curtain at its junction with the tower, as it does at Caerlaverock and Rothesay. Two deep channels in the wall-walk testify to the presence of deep-seated projecting timbers or stone corbels. Of the chamber nothing remains.

At second-floor level the gorge-wall is reduced in thickness and the ledge thus formed serves as a passage or gallery across the corner, connecting the wall-walks of the flanking curtains at a slightly lower level. The parapet walk of the south curtain steps down from the wall-head to the second-floor level of the tower, crosses the straight rear face of the tower to the west curtain, and by another short flight of steps carries one to its wall-walk. From here a flight turns sharply back towards the tower and climbs steeply to the leads. The merlons stepped up with it, as at Rothesay, where this interesting aid to mobility on the *chemin de ronde* is still to be seen, embodied in a later heightening of the wall. From the leads a hoarding of the tower overhung the wall-face. Over the elevated entrance to the tower there are two ashlar corbels; these carried the curving overhang of the tower which above the passage level resumes its circular form.

The continuation of the curtain wall-walk across the corner, by-passing the tower as it were, permitted quick circulation and security, two requirements difficult to reconcile when a tower straddled a curtain or was interposed at the junction of two. Access from one curtain to another through the interior of an intervening tower increased its vulnerability by the unavoidable necessity of two doors; on the other hand completely to isolate the tower from the curtains stopped access from one to another at wall-walk level, where the rapid and even precipitate movement of men and materials from one part of the wall-head to another was an activity to be provided for. But again, in the event of a curtain being taken, it was greatly to the advantage of the garrison if a number could retreat from the captured wall-head into a tower, there to rally, re-emerge and drive the intruders off. Consequently, where there existed a likelihood of a curtain being taken, there was need for towers capable of both independent resistance and direct access to the adjacent curtains, not obstructing free passage nor being obliged to open their doors to provide it.

The Inverlochy solution of this wall-head problem, as we are able to study it in the donjon tower, is a sound and ingenious one. It provides admittance to the second floor of the tower and a refuge therein directly from the wall-walk, and that by only one door. Now, movement within the tower was by the mural stair, which finishes at this level, and it was probably only through the tower and up this stair that the wall-head was reached from ground level. This is both safe and convenient. Furthermore, should the door be necessarily secured against the wall-walk, rapid and unimpeded movement round it would still be possible. A somewhat similar passage serves the same purpose behind the mural towers of the outer curtain at Beaumaris. Like the Inverlochy passage it is lower than the flanking parapets and reaches them by a short flight of steps at each end. It is not offset in the tower wall as the Inverlochy gallery is; it is an oversailing walk corbelled out from the wall of the tower.[1] At Harlech (1283-90) and upon the castle walls of Conway (1283-9) there is a similar method of ensuring mobility, but the *chemin de ronde* maintains its level course upon the wall-head, and the interiors of the towers thus by-passed are not always provided with direct access

[1] The history of the outer curtain of Beaumaris is disputable. J. G. Edwards (1946), 24-30, argues the matter comprehensively for a period 1295 to about 1323, but J. Harvey (1954), 236, gives it as in and after 1316.

to it. The method is of interest rather than importance; the princely Caernarvon, for instance, does not have it, but goes to the extremes of providing access through the interiors of the towers which straddle the walls and, on the other hand, completely stopping wall-head movement by running the parapet walk straight into the solid wall of intervening towers, where it stops. But Caernarvon had other methods of ensuring mural circulation within the thickness of the walls and at different levels.

Everything about Inverlochy proclaims the thirteenth century and nothing contradicts it. The simple quadrangular layout, the high curtain walls and projecting corner towers rising from long spreading bases, the pre-eminence of one tower as the donjon, the long fish-tailed slits in the towers and the total lack of openings in the curtain, the simple entrances in each of two opposite sides, and the form of a ditch are all unmistakable thirteenth-century characteristics. With its primitive entrances in an architectural context of good quality, which implies that the castle is as good as its builders could make it, Inverlochy is hardly likely to be later than 1280, say about 1270-80. A naval engagement was fought outside its walls in 1297.[1] As a first-rate transitional work its importance can scarcely be exaggerated.

There are few close parallels in Scotland; two, Lochindorb and Auchencass, survive to some considerable extent; and a third, the Black Castle of Moulin (Perthshire), a closer parallel, is greatly ruined. Lochindorb is an island castle on the border of Moray and Nairnshire. Its enclosure is larger than that of Inverlochy and the corner towers are smaller. An outer curtain at one end, apparently a later work, has a portcullis gate and encloses the one part of the island excluded from the principal enclosure, the doors of which were fortified by draw-bars only. The walls of the enceinte are comparatively thin and the towers have no great projection nor stairs within, access having been presumably by ladder and trapdoor. Two diagonally opposite towers, the north-east and south-west, have long fish-tailed slits, heavily plunged downwards, which suggest a date in the second half of the thirteenth century. The castle is first mentioned in connection with the death of John Comyn, Lord of Badenoch, who is said to have died there in 1300.[2] In 1303 Edward I stayed in the castle and may be responsible for the outer curtain, a distinctly superior work. The main enclosure is probably of the late

[1] J. Stevenson (1870), II.190.

[2] Andrew of Wyntoun, v.239.

thirteenth century. It was destroyed by the king's command in 1455-6.[1]

Auchencass (Dumfriesshire) is a quadrangle with a round tower at each corner and one entrance which is dog-legged.[2] The lower parts of the towers are solid,[3] recalling the solid mid-wall towers of Kisimul and Doune, Conisburgh and Skenfrith, of which the last named had a chamber furnished with loops in its upper parts.[4] As we have observed in the discussion of Kisimul, solid mural towers probably represent the earliest attempts to provide flanking fire along the face of the curtain. The most remarkable feature of Auchencass is its outer defensive system, to be discussed below with "concentric" defences. The castle's written history, like Lochindorb's, begins in the first decade of the fourteenth century; inferentially therefore the castle dates from the last quarter of the preceding century, a conclusion justified by style and history.

The Black Castle of Moulin, Pitlochry, now a sadly decayed and tumbling ruin, bears witness to a similar rectangular lay-out with corner drum towers. The proportions of its plan closely resemble Inverlochy.

The plan of Inverlochy is a most satisfying one to study. Simple and direct, it conveys the impression that here is nothing fortuitous. The symmetrical disposition of the towers and entrances, the projection and weight of the towers in relation to the lengths of curtain they contain, and the slight convergence of the east and west walls such as occurs at Harlech, all combine to make it a plan of quite unusual distinction. It is a classic example of the early curtain wall and tower type, technically far in advance of anything we have yet considered, with the exception of Rothesay, which is fundamentally the same, with the square made a circle as it were. But whereas Rothesay is a hybrid of disputable architectural pedigree, Inverlochy is closely related to a highly respectable family with unimpeachable connections.

The quadrangular enclosure with high curtains and round corner towers boldly salient is the basic plan in England and Wales in the later thirteenth century. Developing in the course of time, as we shall see it did in Scotland also, it occurs as early as 1220 at Skenfrith, where however the enclosure is an irregular quadrilateral and the

[1] Annie I. Dunlop (1950), 178, giving references; ER VI.I, cxxxvi, 486, etc.
[2] For this type of entrance see R. Fedden and J. Thomson (1957), 51.
[3] R. C. Reid (1926), 117.
[4] C. A. R. Radford (1954).

defence is still pre-eminently the keep upon a mound. The corner towers do not control the curtain, the lay-out spreads (a weakness of Lochindorb also), and there is room for improvement. Again, at Pevensey,[1] within a large and irregular Roman enclosure wall there is set a polygonal and more formal curtain of about 1250,[2] fortified by projecting rounded towers which are equipped with long slits and have a profile and overall appearance very similar to the towers of Inverlochy.

In the last quarter of the thirteenth century, under the direction of Edward I's master masons, to be numbered among the most accomplished in Europe, the simple plan of Skenfrith is pulled in and becomes tighter, foursquare, and stereotyped. The inner ward of Kidwelly (*c.* 1275) is a square enclosure contained by a high curtain with four fully rounded towers, one at each corner. Another early example of this logical and basic type is Flint,[3] which, like Bothwell, Kildrummy and Inverlochy, preserves the early characteristic of the superior size and strength of one tower as the donjon or keep. This is one of the last keeps or donjon towers to be erected in England or Wales. The successors to the motte-castle, they were themselves superseded by the elaborate frontal gatehouse, such as that of Harlech, erected by Edward in 1286. Begun by him in 1277 and finished in 1280, Flint was the first of his chain of northern Welsh castles to be systematically erected in accordance with campaigns and policy designed to contain and subdue the Welsh.

Master James of St George, of whom more will be said, was in charge of this work from 1278 concurrently with a similar undertaking and responsibility at Rhuddlan.[4] In 1290 he was Constable of Harlech, then nearing completion. The plan of its inner ward, excepting the gatehouse, bears a strong similarity to Inverlochy, extending even to the convergence of the two opposite curtains which do not have entrances. Harlech furthermore presents with Inverlochy an instructive comparison of dissimilars.[5] It has a massive frontal gatehouse. Inverlochy has no sort of gatehouse at all.

[1] C. Peers (1952). [2] C. Peers (1952), 11. [3] W. J. Hemp (1929).

[4] A. J. Taylor (1949); J. G. Edwards (1946), 32-7.

[5] A comparison of the great Edwardian castles of North Wales reveals nothing more striking than their dissimilarities. Among these more or less contemporary works, which were erected under the same direction, close parallels are strangely hard to find. Their absence is of little significance in dating, as Edward's strictly contemporary first two castles, Flint and Rhuddlan, forcibly demonstrate. They are quite dissimilar. Building sites available and deliberate intent could account for much variation among the castles of this group. Certainly no enemy familiar with the lay-out and the tricks of one would find his knowledge of much advantage in attempting to reduce another.

Harlech presents a new idea. Inverlochy perpetuates the old. While demonstrating the two basic defensive ingredients, curtain and tower, at an advanced stage of development, Inverlochy retains the entrances as mere openings in the walls, and it also retains the early superiority of one tower over the others.

Towers and curtains having been brought to a high pitch of efficiency and use, it remained for the English mediaeval military architects to direct their genius to the problem of securing the ever-vulnerable entrance. It was inevitable that this would be done. With truly remarkable *panache* it was done. The great school of royal military architects of Edward gave to the entrance a new significance. They invested it with an architectural prominence which surpassed even that of the mural towers in scale and complexity, and in doing so they achieved for English secular architecture of the Middle Ages a distinction no less than that accorded to its ecclesiastical. Herein resides the essence of the subsequent development of the mediaeval castle in Scotland.

It was rapid along those lines, and in the greater Edwardian works in North Wales at Rhuddlan, Conway, Harlech and Beaumaris the evolution was accompanied by a multiplication of walls and of mural towers, so that the basic plan, that of Inverlochy, which is the essence of the Edwardian castle and the core of the concentric system, is apt to be overlaid and lost to sight. It remains unchanged within itself, save in one significant respect, and that is the reduction in size and importance of the donjon tower, the architectural corollary of the increasing significance of the gateway.

CONCENTRIC CASTLES AND THE INFLUENCE OF EDWARD I

In 1274 Edward I returned to England from his Crusade, having tarried awhile on the way at the Castle St Georges d'Espéranche, a residence then in course of construction belonging to the Duke of Savoy, who did him homage there.[1] In Edward's entourage was Otto de Grandison, a Burgundian, a friend and a counsellor, a commander of forces in the subsequent Welsh war who was entrusted with general supervision of Edward's vast castle-building programme in North Wales, for which formidable enterprise the Master James of St George has acquired a just and lasting fame as its architect. This is the same James the Mason who worked at the court of Savoy

[1] A. J. Taylor (1953), 33-47.

Plate 7
Skipness, Kintyre, Argyll, early thirteenth century
above entrance front *below* west exterior

Plate 8 Caerlaverock, Dumfriesshire: the gatehouse, late thirteenth century; machicolations, early fifteenth

Plate 9

Caerlaverock, Dumfriesshire

above air view from north-west

left the Renaissance range, 1634

Plate 10 Bothwell, Lanarkshire: the donjon tower, *c* 1280

from 1261 to 1275, and who, thirty years after, is employed by Edward in Scotland.[1]

The Edwardian castle is the climax of European military architecture in the Middle Ages. It is characterised by masterly design and masonwork and is the supreme exploitation of the gatehouse in combination with towers and curtains; and it is further characterised by the use of a system of concentric defences which was employed in Byzantine fortifications of the twelfth and thirteenth centuries. The Crusading architects from the west adapted and improved upon this system during the last quarter of the thirteenth century, and in all probability it was introduced into England by Edward on his return from his Crusade. Such defence-works are designed completely to surround a castle, which, being itself an enclosure, provides the inner line of defence. The innermost curtain overtops its next outside; this in turn is higher than that which is outside it. Consequently each defence, rampart, or curtain of stone can be brought into play at once, the inner discharging its fire safely over the heads of those outside: *per contra* the outer defences, if taken, are exposed to continuing assault from those within.

Advanced and elaborate concentric fortifications were not erected in Scotland. The evolution of the single curtain, its towers, and the gatehouse is the thirteenth-century history of the Scottish stone castle. But several testify to a recognition of the concentric principle, for example, Auchencass (Dumfriesshire), a square enceinte with corner towers, which is surrounded by a deep and wide ditch. Containing this ditch a broad earthen bank, doubtless once palisaded, constitutes a concentric defence. At the middle of three sides (the extent of bank along the entrance front is much disturbed) the rampart swings out to include a rectangular plateau within its course, thus making three separate outer wards beyond the ditch.

There are two separate fully concentric castles at Caerlaverock (pls. 8, 9) (Dumfriesshire). There is the so-called question-begging "old" castle of grass-grown foundations and earthworks of unknown date situated in a wooded marsh; and there is the substantial ruin 200 yards to the north of it, which was erected most probably between 1290 and 1300. Its position, on the north shore of the Solway, suggests that it was a bridge-head of an English invasion, partly sea-borne, but it may be a Scottish work designed to impede just

[1] For James of St George see W. D. Simpson (1928*a*), 31-9; A. J. Taylor (1950), 433-57; (1953), 33-47; J. Harvey (1954), 235-8.

such an invasion. Certainly in 1299 the head of its Scottish constable, Robert de Cunynghame, was impaled in retribution upon the tower of nearby Lochmaben by the English commander there,[1] and it was besieged by the English in 1300 from Carlisle, after the fall of Stirling,[2] and it was taken after a brisk but brief resistance. Among those present at the siege was one Walter of Exeter, whose rhyming account of the event has survived to be one of the most interesting narratives which has been preserved of any mediaeval castle in Britain.[3] The text is glossed with the arms of the earls, barons and knights present, and includes memoirs of personages taking part, among whom are Gascoigns and Flemings with their troops.

The castle is one of the most impressive in Britain, and in a lovely and unspoiled country setting. The mediaeval curtains and towers stand high, and within the courtyard, against the east curtain, is perhaps the most accomplished and sophisticated Scottish Renaissance building south of the Earl's Palace in Kirkwall (pl. 9). The enceinte is unique in Scotland, being triangular. There is a round tower at the two basal angles, and an imposing twin-towered gatehouse at the apex, all the more dominating as its flanking curtains recede rapidly and obliquely away from it on either side, to leave the front all tower (pl. 8). The gatehouse is built upon a rock outcrop in low-lying land, and the castle is entirely surrounded by a wide water moat contained by an immense earthen bank following the course of the curtains. It is not so conspicuously triangular however. On the south side it is dog-legged about its centre, which is thus about twice the average distance away from the curtain. But the water of the ditch or moat maintains its average width round the curtain even on the south side. Consequently, on this side, between the outer edge of the wet ditch and the rampart, there is a wide, flat earthen platform or ward, higher than water level, which recalls to mind the outer wards of Auchencass similarly situated between moat and bank.

These outer wards may have been included in the defences as launching platforms for stone-throwing engines and other apparatus impossible to operate accurately from behind lofty stone curtains, and by vibration and concussion inadvisable to work upon their

[1] R. C. Reid (1954), 62; J. Bain (1884), II. 1101; RCAMS VII (1920), 151.

[2] F. M. Powicke (1953), 692-3.

[3] The poem in mediaeval French (*Le Siège de Karlaverock*) has been translated and published by Nicolas Harris Nicolas (1828). For full-dress accounts of the castle see B. H. St J. O'Neil (1952); W. D. Simpson (1938*a*), 180-204; (1953*a*), 123-7; G. P. H. Watson (1923), 29-40; RCAMS VII (1920), 11-24.

wallheads. A similar explanation suggests itself to account for the smaller circular earthen platforms which project from the ramparts, from the centre of each side and from the basal angles reminiscent of the platforms of the besieging engines at Berkhamstead Castle.[1] But they might have some connection with the construction of gun batteries in 1594 or 1640, or even with the dumps of a modern clearance of the moat. Excavation is necessary to explain them.

Recent excavations undertaken to elucidate the defensive system prove, as is so often the case, that even the most straightforward and uncomplicated structure is not so simple as it looks. The original outer defences consisted of a wide ditch all round with about 2 feet depth of water, contained by a low earthen bank. The poem says the ditch was filled to the brim with water and, far from being hyperbole, this was the literal truth. The ditch was crossed at the entrance by a simple drawbridge to an outer abutment having no barbican to protect the bridgehead. This scheme lasted long and is shown thus in a map in the King's Collection in the British Museum, which is dated 1563. On the occasion of the artillery siege of 1640, for which documentary evidence indicates considerable modifications and improvements to the defences including the placing of gun-batteries upon the ramparts, the mediaeval bank was raised to its present height, the short outer ditch was laid across the front or apex of the site, and the approach was diverted to run obliquely to the gatehouse entrance, a long passage penetrating the towering frontal mass to the triangular courtyard within.

This is the earliest keep-gatehouse in Scotland, ante-dating Tantallon and Doune, the rival claimants for this distinction, by some 50 years or more.[2] Gathering to itself all the principal domestic accommodation and main defensive strength of the castle as well as the security of the gate it thrusts itself magnificently forward as well as upwards. It is analogous to the mid-tower of Tantallon with the flanking walls pushed back, so to speak.

Two drum towers, rising from spreading bases built upon rock, flank the long and well-defended entrance passage, on either side of which are guardrooms. Above was a fine hall, originally covered by a stone ribbed vault springing from the side walls and without central piers. Admittance to this floor was originally by a timber stair from the courtyard; thereafter access to the upper floors and

[1] C. Peers (1947); M. Kendall (1923), 39.
[2] For the "keep-gatehouse" see pp. 83-91.

wall-head was by a wheel stair in the south-west angle. The portcullis chamber, still with evidence of the provision made for winding gear and chains, was entered from the second floor. The internal arrangements of the gatehouse have been considerably altered, and the external aspect is predominantly of the fifteenth century, when there was a major reconstruction which included the heavy overhanging machicolations which cover not only the front but also the courtyard walls of the gatehouse. They occur also upon the south-west basal tower, which has a window of curious and early type, square, above and part of a long slit with a fish-tailed cill. Such distinctive combined windows and arrow-slits occur at Clifford's Tower, York Castle, of the mid-thirteenth century.[1]

The "old" castle is a site for excavation. No walling is now visible, but low foundations have been revealed to indicate the outline of a quadrilateral enceinte with inner buildings and probable round corner towers. The site of this castle is a slightly raised plateau in marshland not much above sea-level and not far from the Solway shore, which in the days of its occupation would be closer than it is to-day. Earthworks in the wood surrounding the site have suggestive shapes and provoke conjectures of harbours and the like. These are matters for investigation; what is significant in the present context is the undoubted wide ditch and massive earthen bank which concentrically surrounds the "old" castle. A thirteenth-century splayed plinth course, wrought in freestone, was discovered *in situ* during clearance work many years ago. It has been suggested, however, that this castle was erected to serve the lords of Caerlaverock after the main stronghold had been rendered unusable in the later Middle Ages.[2]

Not all the castles built by Edward in Wales were on the concentric principle,[3] however, and in seeking to define his influence on Scottish military architecture, and to identify, if it be possible to do so, what works he was actually and directly responsible for in Scotland, when he turned his attention north after subjugating the principality in 1283, it is necessary to seek for more than this.

In relating the Scottish castles which featured in the first Wars of Independence to the historical background of the time, and in pondering by whom were they built and against whom, a persistent

[1] A. J. Taylor (1954), 153-9.
[2] B. H. St J. O'Neil (1952), 8.
[3] See above, p. 63*n*.

question pursues the investigator. That is, what work did Edward do in Scotland: did he build any castles, complete, from foundation to wall-head, as he did in Wales? And if not, what was the nature and extent of his attempts and achievements? When were the major strongholds built which survive to rival Caerlaverock in their aspect of thirteenth-century feudal might, in scale, excellence of masonwork, detail, and application of current principles of attack and defence? These manifestations of thirteenth-century "European" as opposed to "native" military architecture are Bothwell in Lanarkshire, Kildrummy in Aberdeenshire, and Dirleton and Tantallon in East Lothian. Are they native castles erected before the Edwardian impact? Were they built to resist it, or were they planted by Edward's adherents during or after the pacification?

Typologically the last possibility would place them too late, for they possess features of detail, arrow-slits, drum towers on spreading bases, chamfered window and door jambs, portcullises and the like, which would be quite at home in castles of the 1280's in England and Wales. And also, they are known to have defied the English at the turn of the century: Dirleton was besieged by Bishop Anthony de Bec for Edward in 1298; Caerlaverock was taken by Edward in 1300; Bothwell in 1301,[1] and Kildrummy in 1306. Not likely to have been built by the English and taken by Scots before these dates, they seem therefore to be Scottish castles, or at any rate castles erected before "the brooding discontent which King Edward left behind him in Scotland burst out in May 1297 into widespread disorder".[2] On the other hand, all these major strongholds are conspicuous absentees from the list of 23 castles ordered by Edward in November 1292 to be delivered up to Baliol,[3] which suggests that they did not then exist or, if they did, were in safe English or pro-English hands. The crux of the matter is the lack of records relating to building operations at this period in Scotland, such as pay-rolls, household accounts, audits and the like, which are the fruitful sources of so much knowledge of mediaeval architecture elsewhere, and nowhere more helpful than for the castles of North Wales. The dates quoted give only a time at which the castle referred to was in being. An earlier date, a commencing date if possible, is highly desirable, even essential, for a true evaluation.

These major works must be dated and assessed on architectural

[1] F. M. Powicke (1953), 693. [2] F. M. Powicke (1953), 683.
[3] RS I.11, 12. The list is given in full in ER I.xlix.

features and merit, which must be compared with dated castles in England and Wales. In addition reference to authenticated building operations of Edward in Scotland may permit provisional conclusions.[1]

The last of the new castles to be built in Wales was Beaumaris, the climax of concentric building. Master James of St George was in charge of the works there and William de Felton was its constable. Within a year or two (*c.* 1302) both are at Linlithgow, serving the king in the same capacities. In the same year the Sheriff of Northumberland is commanded to draft "30 of the best carpenters he can find without delay" to assist Master James in the construction of the Peel of Linlithgow. These carpenters, and doubtless others beside them, were under Thomas de Houghton and Adam de Glasham, master carpenters.

Thomas de Houghton was at Beaumaris in 1295, at Edinburgh Castle in 1300, and at the siege of Stirling in 1303-4. On this occasion, under James of St George, he was the senior of seven master carpenters, probably engaged upon the construction of siegeworks and the engines of war which played such a conspicuous part in that action. In 1305 he was at Westminster, and in 1306 back again in Scotland at the memorable siege of Kildrummy. Adam de Glasham had been at work on the fortifications of Dumfries Castle in 1299-1300. In 1303-4 he was with James of St George and de Houghton at the siege of Stirling. An account of 1302 lifts for a moment the mediaeval haze which obscures so much of men and motives. Concerning Linlithgow, it relates that James of St George, "Mestre James de Seint George le Machoun", had been instructed to build certain gates and towers of stone, but the king had changed his mind and "would have the gates and towers of timber and the Peel itself to be built of untrimmed logs". Similarly, the Peel of Selkirk was to have a postern "faced with stone"; at Lochmaben a peel was erected when Sir Robert de Clifford was captain; and at Lochindorb there is a possibility of an additional defence-work attributable to Edward.

Further documentary evidence illustrating the movement of skilled technical men from Wales to Scotland in the wake of the English armies relates to Master Walter of Hereford, master mason

[1] For detailed and extensive documentary evidence see the *History of the King's Works*, HMSO, (1963), ch. 7, 409-422.

at Caernarvon 1288-1309.[1] In 1300 he was responsible for the erection of a town wall at Perth, and for the provision of stone ammunition for the siege of Stirling in 1304—doubtless destined for the engines manufactured by his aforesaid colleagues. In this year he was also working on Edinburgh Castle.[2] A writ dated 7 March 1304 announces Walter in another capacity. Mr A. J. Taylor's transcription is worth quoting in full. It is addressed to all sheriffs and bailiffs, and runs thus:

> We have assigned, the King says, Master Walter of Hereford, our mason, to choose and bring into our service in Scotland, for such works as we may intend there, so many and such masons as he shall deem necessary, and as he has been more fully charged on our behalf. To this end the sheriffs are commanded that in selecting the said masons they shall be intendant, obedient, assistant and advisant to the said Walter or his nominee, and the masons so chosen shall, if need be, be distrained. They are to come to Scotland and remain in the royal service there as Walter or his deputy will make known to them more fully on the King's behalf. The writ is to continue in force until Whitsun (17 May).[3]

It is quite clear from these references that when Edward turned his attention to the pacification of Scotland he did so with all the technical resources at his command and with the thorough preparations to ensure success which had characterised his campaign against the Welsh 20 years before. But despite the recorded presence in Scotland, over some four or five critical years, of not a few of Edward's most highly skilled and important masons and carpenters, there is no reference to a major royal undertaking or to the construction of a new stone castle. It is probable that Edward did not in fact erect stone castles in Scotland because, (*a*) when he applied himself to the pacification of Scotland in 1296 he was affected by a grave financial crisis which was to precipitate a constitutional crisis of even greater gravity the next year,[4] and (*b*) there was a sufficiency of good and well-placed stone castles already existing in Scotland, which, once taken, would be well worth maintaining.

These could include the major works not mentioned in the list of 23 castles to be surrendered to Baliol. On architectural evidence they could ante-date the date of this list of 1292 by a safe margin. Their siege and capture by the English in the years just before and

[1] J. Harvey (1954), 126-7, calls him one of the three great Edwardian designers, the others being James of St George and Walter Lenginour. He flourished *c.* 1278-1309.

[2] J. Bain (1884), II. 399, 1536.

[3] See A. J. Taylor (1955), 44-5.

[4] J. G. Edwards (1946), 64.

after 1300 can be accounted for by assuming a change in mind and loyalty of their castellans when the time came in 1297 for the unhappy necessity of taking sides against the overlord to whom they had previously and willingly enough rendered homage for lands held in England. The great Scottish castles of Caerlaverock, Bothwell and Kildrummy stylistically and historically could have been erected between 1275 and 1295 by Scots or English lords who had seen service at home and abroad and were acquainted with current practice and achievement, and who enjoyed Edward's favour at the time of construction (and doubtless his encouragement too, even to the extent of technical advice) but renounced it when the "wide-spread disorder" burst out in May 1297. And Dirleton, as we shall see, might well be earlier.

THE GATEHOUSE

Foundations of later barbicans advancing outwards from both entrances at Inverlochy indicate the need for added strength at these positions. The inevitable solution to the problem of gateway security was the incorporation of the entrance in a tower of superior strength. This was usually built as two projecting towers closely flanking the entranceway which was thus deeply recessed between them. Over it a chamber bridged the gap, connecting the flanking towers and served as a control room and strongpoint wherein the portcullis was housed and operated. Through the floor of this chamber there might be openings, or meurtrières, for the greater annoyance of those attempting to force an entry in the passage below.

Two contemporary castles in the south of Scotland, now utterly ruined but discernible under turf, are closely datable examples of this. Both were English foundations, i.e. founded to sustain the English cause against the Scots. One, Tibbers, was erected in 1298 by Sir Richard Siward, a Scot in English service[1]; the other, Kirkcudbright, is dated by a restricted English occupation period of 1288-1312.[2]

The plan of Tibbers has a close resemblance to those of Lochindorb and Auchencass. It is a simple quadrangle of four curtains adjusted to a restricted site upon a naturally defensible plateau. There is a round tower at each corner, and one of the two which

[1] RCAMS VII (1920), 65.

[2] This site has produced the only piece of French polychrome pottery to be recovered in Scotland, which pottery has limiting dates of about 1275-1300; see S. H. Cruden (1951), 179.

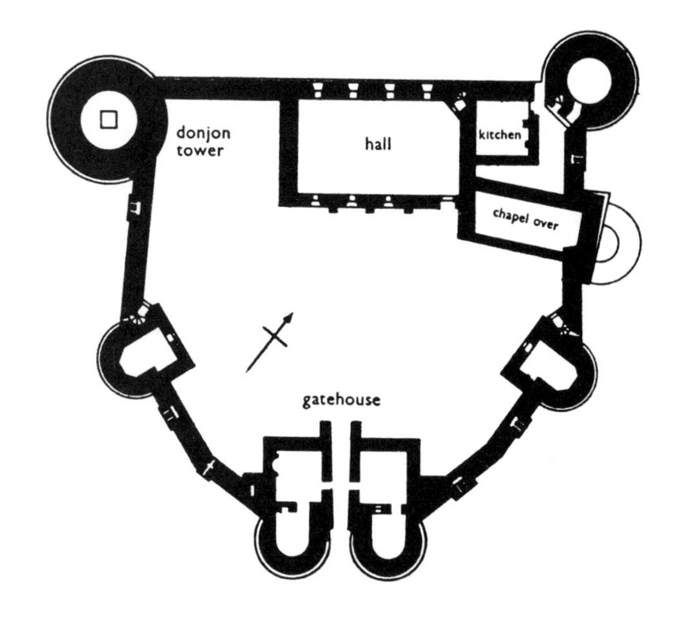

(a)

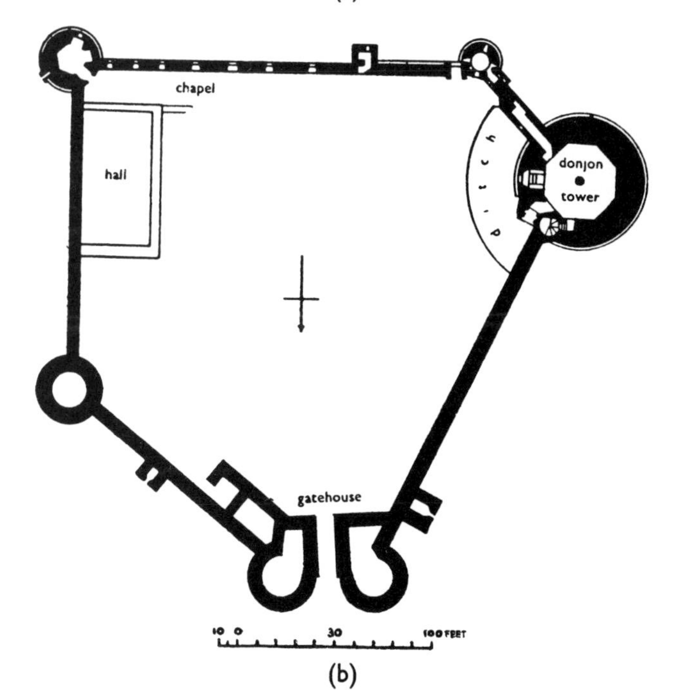

(b)

FIG. 7. (*a*) Kildrummy and (*b*) Bothwell

confront the natural line of approach is made to serve as a gatehouse tower. The entrance through the curtain is hard by it, and an extra tower flanks the entrance on its other side, so that there were three towers facing the front on a comparatively short length of curtain, a formidable frontage. Before it a ditch and bank cuts off the plateau, as the ditches and banks cut off an Iron Age promontory fort and as the rock-cut ditch of Tantallon separates the site of the castle from the mainland.

Two major strongholds of thirteenth-century date, Kildrummy in Mar and Bothwell on the Clyde, illustrate not the least interesting aspect of the typology of castles by maintaining the pre-eminence of a tower as the donjon in a system of defences still basically curtain-wall and projecting-tower while incorporating the improved gatehouse into the scheme. As we have seen in comparing Harlech and Inverlochy, the gatehouse places the former in a more advanced class, if not actually proving it to be of later date.

This conjunction at Kildrummy (fig. 7) of the new, in the shape of a gatehouse, with the old, in the shape of a tremendous donjon, again recalls Harlech, for, as Simpson has observed,[1] the plan of the Kildrummy gatehouse bears a very close correspondence to that of Harlech, so much so that one might conclude that both were the work of the same mind and the same hands. The supposition is supported by the documentary evidence cited above[2] and emphasised by other striking similarities in plan which are referred to below.

The co-existence of an old fashioned donjon and a gatehouse gives the castle a transitional significance, the more valuable as the gatehouse can with reasonable certainty be attributed to one of two probable dates, i.e. *c.* 1285-90 or *c.* 1306. There is some justification for considering it to be an insertion or a later improved rebuilding soon after 1306, when it fell to the English forces under the Prince Edward. It could have been soon after this that the gatehouse was erected, during the Plantagenet occupation (which was certainly over by 1335 when the castle was again besieged by the English), or it could have been a late completion of the enceinte at this time, which would be natural enough, for free passage (unimpeded by

[1] W. D. Simpson (1928*b*), 73.

[2] The correspondence is well-nigh identical. A similar grouping of hall, tower and chapel, with entrance to the tower through the chapel undercroft, is to be found also at Bothwell in early fifteenth-century work which probably perpetuates a late thirteenth-century lay-out. This suggests that an arrangement such as this was standard Edwardian planning.

scaffolding etc.) through the entranceway for heavy wheeled vehicles and other transport would be necessary during preceding building operations at other parts. The presence of Thomas de Houghton at Kildrummy in 1306, to which reference has been made, adds weight to the argument in favour of this date. At Westminster in 1305, his attendance at Kildrummy in 1306 proves that something big was afoot.

But not necessarily a gatehouse. He was a master carpenter, not a mason, and for carpenters a siege itself is sufficient explanation of brisk activity. At these events there was much for them to do, and as they were the artificers of the mechanised arm of besieging forces much depended on them. Skilled and experienced masters are only to be expected among those present outside the walls. The analogies with Harlech point to the earlier date. That castle is securely dated 1283-90. Its gatehouse has fireplaces of a distinctive Edwardian or North Wales type. It is hooded, and the hood lintels are supported on jambs which carry the overhang of the hood by chamfered "shoulders" leaning or projecting into the room. They occur in fireplaces in all the Edwardian castles of North Wales, and with little variation from the basic design. Those in Conway are precisely the same as those happily still in position in the fireplace in the west guardroom flanking the entrance passage of the Kildrummy gatehouse. Conway was constructed between 1283 and 1289, and the parallels between the Kildrummy gatehouse and those two Welsh castles strongly suggest that it was erected in the 1290's, in time for or at the time of the visit of Edward himself in 1296.

The gatehouse now stands at its greatest height some 6 feet, and unfortunately little more remains of the donjon in the rearward angle of the spacious enclosure, but the plan is complete all round the circuit of the curtains which stand to greater heights. The plan is similar to that of Bothwell, which is the more remarkable because of its unconventionality. In both the lay-out is balanced but not symmetrical. The rearward half of the enceinte is rectangular, but the forward part is unusual in that the curtain retreats from the gatehouse obliquely on both sides of it, as it does at triangular Caerlaverock. The Bothwell gatehouse, akin to those of Kirkcudbright and Tibbers, consisted of two projecting rounded towers closely flanking the entrance passage. The doorways were closed by a drawbridge, the inner end of which, when it was raised, was accommodated in a sunk pit, as at Kildrummy and Dirleton also.

Along the rearward or northern curtain at Kildrummy there was a long hall with a dais, a wheel stair leading to the solar and kitchen, and a series of large windows down both long sides looking south into the courtyard and through the curtain to the northern landscape. Half-way along each of the lateral curtains there is a D-shaped tower which straddles the curtain and projects obliquely into the field. Thereafter the curtains converge rapidly towards the frontal gatehouse. A square-ended chapel at first floor level above an undercroft projects through the east curtain. The east gable windows, three in number and of equal size, raised high above the ground over the blank wall of the undercroft, are plain lancets with wide splays, corner shafts, roll-moulded capitals, moulded heads in square orders, and sconsion arches springing from miniature corbels.

The emergence of the chapel gable through the curtain is the most puzzling and intriguing occurrence in Scottish mediaeval architecture. It projects obliquely, is not set squarely upon its own foundations, and has patently been applied to the curtain. Behind the gable the curtain is breached, but its foundation runs without interruption across the east end of the chapel just inside the gable. Outside, the foundations of a massive semi-circular tower project from the base of the gable into the berm or outer ward which is unusually wide along this side of the castle. There are therefore at this point three buildings represented, of different periods: a curtain, a chapel and a tower, most oddly assembled. Their interpretation provides a key to the building history of the castle.

The masonry of the curtains, except that of the northern, is of large rubble. The towers, external garderobes and north curtain are of coursed ashlar. While the difference in finish and technique could be accounted for by assuming different squads simultaneously at work, rough-wallers and free-masons, the towers and garderobes are not bonded into the curtain throughout and could be additions to it. Moreover, while the east curtain antedates the chapel which is by its style of the mid-thirteenth century, the towers are demonstrably Edwardian (*c.* 1285-1300) according to their general characteristics and such closely datable detail as the cusped shouldered-arch of the twin-light windows in the Warden's Tower, which occurs on fireplace jambs in the Granary Tower at Caernarvon (1295-1323). Another shouldered fireplace jamb in the Kildrummy gatehouse has close parallels in Conway of the distinctive Edwardian type referred to.

The correspondence of this gatehouse with that of Harlech has been noted; it is emphasised by another analogy with that castle, also of plan, which makes it all the more significant. This is the disposition of the buildings grouped about the distant right-hand corner towers, as seen from each gatehouse. The tower in each case is flanked by the great hall on the one side and by the castle chapel on the other side, and between them is a small court which admits to the tower, entry to this court being through the undercroft of the chapel. Thus in both castles the units which comprise these groups are similarly placed in relation to each other and to the whole lay-out. Outside Kildrummy the foundations of an outer curtain suggest concentric or earlier existing defences of no great strength compared with the castle walls.

The first stone castle was a plain polygonal enclosure of probably the first half of the thirteenth century, one of the strongholds which were erected for Alexander II "*pro utilitate regis et rei publice*" by the last Scottish saint, Gilbert de Moravia, Bishop of Caithness from 1223 to 1245.[1] This is represented by the stretches of curtain wall. About the middle of the thirteenth century the chapel was erected, and the curtain was first breached through the upper part only, to accommodate it. Now the curtain does not run truly north and south. Therefore, if it were desired to build a chapel against it, piercing it for east windows, the chapel would not be truly orientated. To orientate the chapel correctly we suppose the curtain to have been breached to permit an east-west axis. This was closed by the gable, built close against the curtain but not parallel to it. The breaching of the curtain and the provision of three lofty lancets caused a weakness in the curtain. This was minimised by raising the chapel and leaving the original thickness of the curtain unimpaired below it. The altar would sit upon the top of the lowered curtain. At a later date the undercroft was extended outwards by breaching the lower part of the curtain down to foundation level, as it is to be seen to-day. In 1296 Edward visited the castle, and then, it is not unreasonable to suggest, gave instructions for its improvement. Towers and garderobes were added; the chapel was condemned and the foundations of a business-like round tower were laid against its gable, with the intention no doubt of pulling down the gable once the tower had been completed in front of it; but it never was.[2] Concentric

[1] A. P. Forbes (1872), 355.
[2] In the stubborn way it defies rational and learned explanations this gable is really

defences were worked into the terrain. All the modifications were comprehensively considered and the castle was completely re-fashioned with Harlech as the model. The first work was the donjon, to provide a strongpoint; and work continued round the circuit of the walls to finish with the gatehouse of later style (*c.* 1300 or probably a little earlier).

The Bothwell enceinte, like Kildrummy, was dominated by an immense round donjon tower in one of the rear angles (pl. 10; fig. 7). Its inner half survives complete to the wall-head from a basement sunk in the inner ditch which cuts it off from the courtyard. The outer half was demolished from top to bottom in 1337 by Sir Andrew de Moray (to whom it rightfully belonged) after the capture of the castle from the English, in order to deny it to them. The donjon is cut off from the inner ward by a deep and wide ditch, a defensive measure occurring elsewhere in Scotland only at Urquhart and Duffus.

The contemporaneity of Bothwell and Kildrummy which is suggested by similar and unusual plans, with massive donjons in comparable positions, the assembling of hall and chapel about a corner tower[1] and the provision of gatehouses, is also indicated by a common dynastic connection with the powerful northern family of de Moravia, of which Walter received the lands of Bothwell in 1242 and dated a charter from the castle in 1278.[2] The great mediaeval lordship of Bothwell was founded in the reign of Malcolm IV by a fief granted to David Olifard, a baron from Huntingdon, ancestor of the family of Oliphant.[3] His introduction is another example of the process of infeudation of which mention has been made with particular reference to the mottes of Duffus and Inverurie.[4] Near Bothwell a Fleming named Tancard was also enfeoffed by Malcolm and is commemorated to-day by the place-name Thankerton. Bothwell was a private not a royal castle, built before the outbreak of Edward's war with the Scots, by the Olifards or their successors de Moravia (Moray): second half of the thirteenth century.

In 1298-9, after a siege of fourteen months, it was taken by the

quite amusing, for it makes nonsense of the stern preoccupation with defence which one is apt to assume for such strongholds as this. It is plainly not contemporary with the curtain it projects through: it can hardly be earlier, for it is inconceivable that a master mason would fail to avoid it on a site with room to circumvent it; and it can hardly be later, for in the thirteenth century if a master pushed a chapel with three lancet windows through an existing impenetrable curtain the king would have had his head off, although the bishop might not.

[1] See above, p. 74*n*.
[2] W. Fraser (1847), 110.
[3] G. W. S. Barrow (1956*a*), 9.
[4] See above, p. 10.

Scots, only to be recaptured by Edward I in 1301 in the ebb and flow of warfare. It remained in English hands until their reverse at Bannockburn when it was surrendered to Edward Bruce and thereafter dismantled by him. There was a second English occupation from 1331 until 1337 when it was taken by Sir Andrew to whom it rightfully belonged. Partially destroyed by him as a necessary military expedient it lay in waste until 1362, when a further reconstruction of the twice-dismantled fabric took place. Much of the original thirteenth-century work remains, and fourteenth- and fifteenth-century parts in considerable height and extent (pl. 11).

The castle has yielded the largest assemblage of mediaeval pottery yet to have been recovered from a single site in Scotland.[1] This is comparable in quality, variety and artistic interest with the best English collections. The substantial quantity of archaeological material (23 vessels have been completely restored and as many sizeable fragments reconstructed) is in full agreement with the historical facts and acts as a useful corroboration of them, for while the general characteristics of the ware are perfectly consistent with standard English pieces of the thirteenth and fourteenth century, the closest and most unambiguous parallels are to be found at York, Chester and Carlisle. Nor was it all imported in the baggage wagons of the victorious English troops or by the merchants who would follow them. Abundant wasters and kiln distortions of various kinds prove local manufacture. Evidently potters were settled here, continuing the ceramic styles of these great northern supply bases in the late thirteenth and early fourteenth century.

The style of the architecture is equally unprovincial. The extensive reconstruction of the English occupation of 1331-7 was by John de Kilburne, an English master of note who was also engaged in works at Edinburgh Castle; and the earlier parts about the donjon, the stalwart tower which has been described as the noblest work of secular architecture which the Middle Ages have bequeathed to us, lack nothing in efficiency and grandeur, nor in sheer technical accomplishment.

This tremendous tower has a diameter of 65 feet and rises 82 feet upon walls 15 feet thick. The detailing is bold and strong, maintaining the big effect. Passages and mural chambers, garderobes and the like, are covered by pointed barrel-vaults with massive stone ribs, entered through lancet-headed doorways with broad chamfers.

[1] S. H. Cruden (1952), 140-70.

The entrance is housed in a projection emerging from its courtyard face as a keel or beak, contrived to turn away the approach from the enclosure and give it some protection. It was exposed and rendered vulnerable from above by a machicolated overhanging gallery supported upon corbels of stone, which still remain. Behind the portcullis a mural passage, high and wide barrel-vaulted, proceeds dog-legged to the lord's hall on the first floor. This was an octagonal chamber whose timber floor was borne upon a central pier in the basement below. Two broad segmental bearing arches sprang from opposite sides of the basement to this pier and assisted it in supporting the floor of the hall, a structural method frequently employed in Beaumaris and in the Queen's Tower at Caernarvon. Each side of the octagonal hall is a bay of a vaulting system whose wall-ribs remain, although the cross-ribs and central column do not. The masonry round the wall-ribs is cut back as though to receive boards, and, above, deep vertical channels in the angles are obviously to house stouter structural members. There is little doubt that the hall was timber-vaulted with a central support, probably also of timber, standing upon the stone pier in the basement. From this the ribs arched to their springing in the angle posts.

Imitation vaulting such as this was fashionable in the later thirteenth and first half of the fourteenth century in England.[1] It is not a structural but a decorative contrivance, especially in such a massive and accomplished work as this, which could without difficulty have been stone-vaulted throughout. Not that the deception would be suspected by the onlookers. With its thin plaster and paint the timber imitation would be entirely convincing. What is of particular interest is the purely aesthetic introduction of a rib-and-panel vault in a chamber of quite unusual distinction. The exploitation of the ribbed vault in the thirteenth-century lord's hall at Bothwell is in marked and significant contrast to the rejection of this truly mediaeval feature—perhaps the most typical of all—in the later tower-houses. A fine arched window overlooks the ditch and inner ward beyond it: it has stone benches in its exceptionally deep embrasure, and the high lancet rear arch, opening into the floor space, is defined by filleted corner-shafts. Between the wall-ribs, in the haunches of the vault, the walls rise smoothly in coursed ashlar: of a stone vault there is no sign.

The round donjon at Dirleton (pl. 12; fig. 8), the nucleus of a for-

[1] G. Webb (1956), 186.

'late 11
3othwell, Lanarkshire
ght
he garde-robe tower,
1280
elow
he south-east tower, early
fteenth century

Plate 12

above Dirleton, East Lothian, *c.* 1225

below Tantallon, East Lothian, *c.* 1350

midable cluster of thirteenth-century towers, also makes much of the ribbed vault in two large polygonal chambers placed one upon the other, the lower being the common hall of men-at-arms, the upper the hall of the lord and his intimates. Neither has a central pier and both are genuine stone structures with ribs of deep chamfered section occurring in window embrasures, passages, and small chambers throughout the thirteenth-century part of the castle.

Dirleton seems to be an early work in the debt it owes to its situation upon an abrupt rocky eminence characteristic of the western castles already described. But its natural advantages are enhanced by a remarkable concentration of salient towers, compact and powerful, and of the utmost excellence of masonwork such as would be expected upon a flat terrain more suitable for such grandeur. They are crammed upon the restricted site with telling effect, and combine powerful defences with residential quarters of considerable architectural merit. High curtains follow the irregular outline of the rock outcrop; round towers at the angles covered them, and the composite donjon dominated the whole and protected the adjacent entranceway which was otherwise not particularly well secured. This concentration of towers is quite unique in Scotland and without parallel in England and Wales, although Castell Coch (1260-1300)[1] and the gatehouse of Denbigh (*c.* 1300)[2] represent similar ideas.

This Dirleton scheme of the thirteenth century emphasises the donjon which was originally a strongpoint placed in reserve, distant from the vulnerable entranceway. Here it is brought forward aggressively in the manner of keep-gatehouses described below.[3] The complex of towers comprising the Dirleton forward donjon are to be regarded as a single architectural unit. The internal security arrangements amply confirm this, access to the various passages and chambers communicating with the courtyard and with one another being very poorly defended. The three towers which comprise this powerful group are each large and of superior thirteenth-century work. Of good dressed ashlar, they rise from long spreading bases from the rock's edge. They have long fish-tailed slits opening from wide internal embrasures with massive arch-ribs over them. The largest drum tower has a splendid polygonal lord's hall, stone rib-vaulted, with a hooded fireplace flanked by squat shafted jambs with early thirteenth-century mouldings and enrichment. The window

[1] P. Floud (1954), 5. [2] W. J. Hemp (1926). [3] See below, pp. 83-91.

embrasures are spacious, stone-vaulted with ribs and have stone window benches. Beneath the hall is a garrison post, also rib-vaulted, equipped with loops in deep arched embrasures, garderobes and fireplaces. Another round tower, less large, and a square tower between the two rounds complete the group. Originally there was an interior tower which formed the enclosing range of the small inner courtyard or close in which an outside stair admitted to the lord's hall on the first floor.

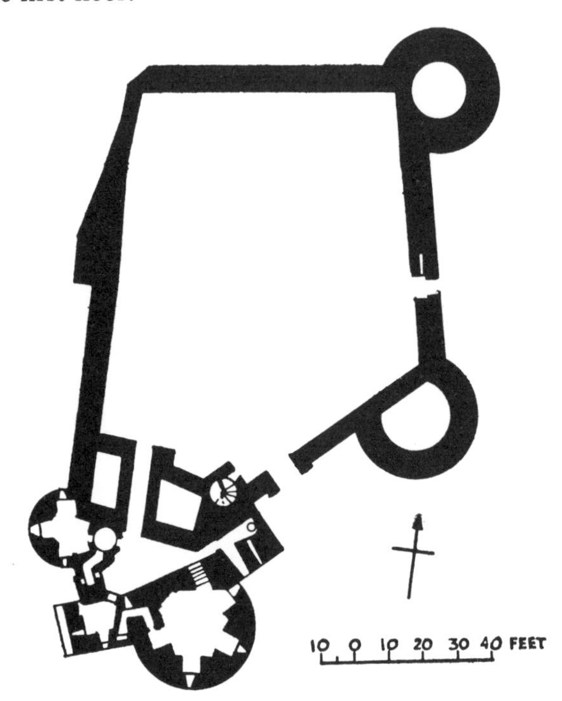

Fig. 8. Dirleton

Beside the donjon, between it and the entrance through the curtain, is an elevated postern, a small lancet-headed doorway. The lack of vulnerable entrances greatly increased the strength of a castle, and every effort was made to reduce their number. It was thus necessary to make provision for entry and exit by raised posterns reached by retractable timber or rope ladders. By these means, in face of blockade, the garrison had access to the bottom of the dry ditch, and those using them were under cover of the protection offered by the donjon as well as the wall-head defences above. At St Andrews Castle (Fife) in a similar position alongside the entrance and high above the bottom of the ditch there is a postern gate of sixteenth-century date. There are thirteenth-century posterns in the wing-walls flanking the donjon tower of Bothwell, opening directly to the field, one being from the moat.

The main entrance at Dirleton was a covered passage slightly prolonged by two projecting jambs. It was fortified by two portcullises and two pairs of heavy timber doors. The timbered deck between the jambs at ground level crossed the pit of a turning bridge and was exposed to a meurtrière in the floor of the portcullis chamber above. The circuit of the curtain has been much damaged and overbuilt and only the splayed bases of the two corner towers remain, but the donjon is substantially complete and presents a splendid example of mediaeval secular architecture in its domestic as well as military aspect.

Dirleton has been attributed to the late thirteenth century, but a *castellum de Dyrlton* is mentioned about 1225.[1] It was a stronghold of John de Vaux or Vallibus whose family had possessed the neighbouring lands since the middle of the twelfth century, and who was perhaps descended from Robert de Vaux the first Norman *vicomte* at Carlisle from 1091. John was the seneschal of Marie de Coucy. From her marriage to Alexander II in 1239 and her connection with Coucy Castle important French influences in Scottish castle-building have already been inferred.[2] We expect her seneschal's castle to be of the first order, which Dirleton is. The word *castellum* is itself indicative of this, and moreover signifies enclosure, which "is the chief idea which the chroniclers associate with the word".[3] Dirleton was besieged by Anthony de Bek, Bishop of Durham, for Edward I in 1298. From its late thirteenth-century history it has been dated. But we prefer to date it to the second quarter of the century, and salute it as an authentic pre-Edwardian castle. Its siting, style and detailing accord well with the earlier historical implications.

THE KEEP-GATEHOUSE

The donjons were to the castles what the castles were to the neighbourhood, a rallying-point, a tower of strength, an ultimate retreat. And they were more than that. They were the material expression of the pride and pomp of a ruling class, to which reference was made in the opening paragraph of this chapter. Superb in execution and refinement of detail as well as in conception, they were

[1] Dryburgh, No. 37. [2] See above, pp. 18, 40. [3] Ella S. Armitage (1912), 384.

on a grand scale, commensurate with the power and prestige of the nobles who erected them. Feudal residences of princely quality, they are typical of the most imposing European castle of enceinte of the second half of the thirteenth century.

The residential requirements of castle-building have not hitherto been considered. Normally the domestic household was accommodated in timber buildings within the courtyard; the military establishment, such as it was, would live in the towers which it was its duty to defend with appropriate ardour in time of need. From the first the royal and extra-important castles had a stalwart tower wherein were apartments for the lord and his domestic household suitable to the dignity of their rank. The conventional position for these early donjons, as Bothwell, Kildrummy and Inverlochy so clearly demonstrate, was in the rear of the enclosure, withdrawn from the entrance as far as prudence or tradition demanded and the nature of the site allowed. The Edwardian innovation of the gatehouse however tended to shift forward the centre of gravity of the defensive system. The weight of masonry was then obviously destined to be concentrated at one point in the front of the castle, no longer at the rear, a more aggressive conception than that inherent in the donjon where the strength is held in reserve.

Compare for example the plans of Bothwell and Kildrummy with Doune. In Bothwell the weight of masonry is greatest at the spectacular donjon in a corner remote from the gatehouse which, although itself of no inconsiderable size and strength, did not usurp the preeminence of the donjon either as a residence or a stronghold. At Kildrummy there is weight and power fore and aft, but its forward gatehouse, of Edwardian antecedents and double-towered like Bothwell's, is of another and later building period. As we understand it, Kildrummy is a transitional work, expressing in emphatic architectural terms the old and the new notions of strength reserved and strength aggressive.

Now turn to Doune (pl. 13; fig. 9), erected before 1400 for the Regent Albany, the Governor of Scotland in the minority of James I.[1] The rearward donjon has disappeared and so has the orthodox twin-towered gatehouse. The functions of both are combined in a powerful frontal mass behind which the curtain seems to trail, an unprotected appendage to confine lesser buildings whose loss to an enemy would not gravely inconvenience the occupants of the fore-work.

[1] W. M. Mackenzie (1927), 145.

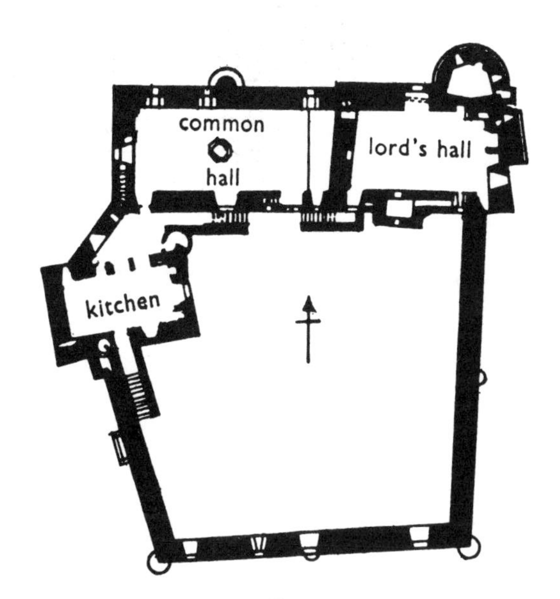

first floor

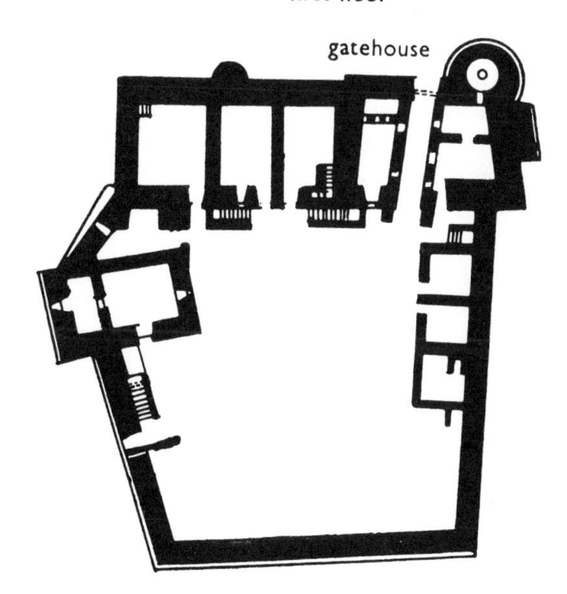

ground floor

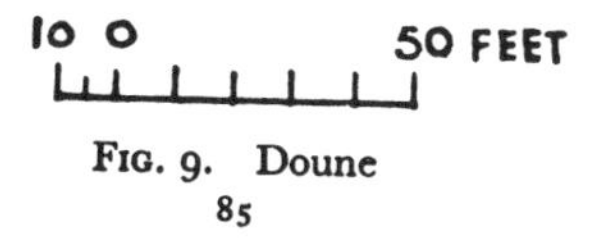

FIG. 9. Doune

Doune was conceived as a genuine courtyard castle. The free-standing curtains are misleading through lack of the intended buildings for which provision was made in them, most conspicuously in the fine windows of the south curtain where in all probability the chapel would have been.[1] The courtyard ranges were never built, save one, the entrance frontage, comprising a closely-knit group of three buildings providentially complete and in good repair: two massive tower-houses linked by a long hall. One tower is the gate-house and ducal residence, the other principally kitchen accommodation. The hall between them was the common hall of the household, an exceedingly large chamber with a high timber roof and an open hearth in the middle of the floor.

The Regent and his intimates were handsomely provided for in the entrance tower. The accommodation here is also very grand, with good auxiliary services of mural chambers and stairs to upper apartments. The hall occupies the first floor of this tower. At one end it has a fine double-arched fireplace of two bays separated by a stone partition wall which makes in fact two fireplaces side by side. The arches are segmental and moulded, and they rise from bulky twin wall-shafts with moulded capitals and bases of typical fourteenth-century profile recalling those which support the lintel of the probably contemporary (1374) fireplace of the early tower-house of Craigmillar. Before the opposite wall there is a screens passage with a (restored) timber screen and a gallery above it.

The kitchen tower in the middle of the west curtain is somewhat detached from the common hall, there being an entrance and service hall between them. This is separately entered by an outside stair in the courtyard. Another outside stair, against the west curtain (which would have been internal had the west range been built), admits directly into the kitchen. Two large open and arched service hatches pierce the thick wall between the kitchen and this vestibule. The needs of separate access to the common hall and kitchens and to the apartments above the kitchens, and of service to the common hall from the kitchens, was thus very cleverly managed by uncomplicated and imaginative planning as a glance at the plan will show.

Reference has been made elsewhere to the fundamental importance of plan, too often ignored or merely described where elevations and their embellishment receive the greater critical attention. But

[1] Cf. Bothwell for example.

an unselfconscious or commonplace elevation can rise from plans of great significance which taken as a whole reveal the notions which underlie and influence, doubtless unconsciously, the architect's or master mason's approach to the job, the angle from which he saw the solutions to the problems of site, purpose and appearance. Doune presents a striking example of a building whose particular interest derives wholly from its plan.

In its disregard of the curtain, the defensive wall-head and the projecting corner tower, Doune was a notable departure from the accepted formula for castle-building. The implications of the underlying theory are consistently realised throughout. The entrance passage to the courtyard penetrates the basement of the lord's tower. It is flanked by guardrooms and vulnerable to slits in the side walls. Its portcullis was operated in a window embrasure in the lord's tower. The lord's tower, or entrance tower as we have called it, thus controlled the entrance passage, and there was no other entrance to the castle save a small postern in the west curtain. The lord's tower has no access to the basement. Its only door is to the screens passage in the first-floor hall. This is reached by an external courtyard stair itself contained by walling, with a gate at the bottom and a barred door at the top. There was no communication between the lord's hall and the common hall which it immediately adjoins (the present through doorway is a modern insertion). On the other hand, the common hall block as well as having courtyard stairs to its first-floor level has also internal mural stairs from the basement storage vaults to the first-floor hall.

This conception of a castle, comprehending the entrance and a complete baronial residence capable of independent defence, is radically different from what has gone before. The form was anticipated at Dirleton and Caerlaverock where the frontal massing of the composite donjon and the unique importance of the twin-towered gatehouse respectively achieved precisely the same result. But these castles owe their forms to the limitations imposed upon them by the sites they occupy and to which they were necessarily adjusted.

Properly to understand the radical change in conception which Doune exemplifies more than a purely architectural interpretation is necessary. The growing importance of the gatehouse, regarded purely as a manifestation of inevitable architectural development, is not by itself sufficient to account for the rejection of the donjon, the reduction in importance of the curtain with its wall-head defences, and the establishment of a combined gatehouse and lordly residence capable of independent defence and furthermore cut off from adjacent buildings. Such an interpretation was first inferred by Simpson and stated thus[1]

> But in the later middle ages the attack and defence of fortified places had become a high art, for which the tumultuary feudal levies, ill equipped and untrained, were little fitted. Field warfare also had grown into a specialized science, and campaigns were now pushed forward ruthlessly until one or other side was broken.[2] *Der totale Krieg* had superseded the chivalric contests, with all their polite conventions, that adorn the picturesque pages of Froissart. For warfare of this new type the feudal levies, bound only to serve for short periods at a time, were no longer suitable. More and more, therefore, particularly in France during the social break-down that accompanied the Hundred Years War, the great barons in their chronic private quarrels came to rely on professional soldiers whom they maintained in their pay. For these mercenaries quarters had to be available; and this meant, for the first time, standing garrisons in each castle. Whereas in former days the castle, in time of peace, would contain only the lord's *familia* or household, it must now afford accommodation for a compact body of mercenary troops. The presence of these rough adventurers would always be inconvenient and not seldom dangerous, for they did not owe the tenurial loyalty or natural allegiance of vassals, and were at all times liable to be seduced by their employer's enemies.[3] Hence, for reasons both of privacy and safety, the great French lords of the fourteenth and fifteenth centuries took care to provide their castles with self-contained residences for their families and their personal retinue. And it was plain common sense that this self-contained residence of the lord should include the main entrance of the castle, which the lord could thus retain under the control of his own trusted servants.

But the *tour de force* of the keep-gatehouse had its practical disadvantages:

> The interpolation of the drawbridge and portcullis machinery, not to speak of other defensive tackle, into the midst of the principal residential appartments, was decidedly awkward. At Harlech and Caernarvon the portcullis was operated from the chapel! . . . The manifest failure of the keep-gatehouse plan to combine the requirements of residence and defence coupled with the fact that this type of structure emerged so near the end of English castle building, gives the type a limited chronological range—say from 1270-1370.

[1] W. D. Simpson (1946), 151-2.

[2] Contrast the French campaigns of Henry V with those of Edward III and the Black Prince.

[3] For the unstable allegiance of such indentured retainers see K. B. McFarlane (1944), 70-2.

This explains in social and economic terms the phenomenon of the Doune gatehouse and its parallels. But these compelling reasons were evidently not insistent enough to withstand practical disadvantages. The keep-gatehouse was in fact not entirely due to social causes nor to the use of mercenaries, who were in any case well-known long before this architectural innovation. Mercenaries were employed even before the Conquest. For that event Duke William recruited many, whom he thereafter maintained in England. His son Robert complained of being always but his father's mercenary and desired the means to give proper pay to his own followers. William Rufus was "a wonderful merchant and paymaster of Knights", by whom he was mourned because he had provided full employment and high wages. In 1102 mercenaries had an established status and were jealous of their professional reputation. In that year the castle and town of Bridgnorth was surrendered to Henry I by the Captains and Burgesses to whom their defence had been entrusted, but not before they had overcome the resistance of the mercenaries who had been engaged to assist them in the defence. Released by the victorious Henry with honour they did not hesitate to expose "the trickery of their associates, lest what had happened to them should bring other mercenaries into discredit".[1] In Scotland William the Lion in 1212 appealed to England for mercenaries to suppress rebellion.[2] In the Welsh war of 1277 the feudal levies were found wanting, but in the succeeding campaigns of 1282-3 the Edwardian host was more efficient because "a higher proportion was under contract to fight for pay".[3]

It is doubtful also if the Scottish nobility had the ready money to employ mercenaries to the extent necessary to cause a radical change in castle design. . "In a country [Scotland] where money was scarce, it was not only more honourable, it was actually easier, to maintain its members by enfeoffments of land than to raise the cash needed to pay the wages of professional hired soldiers."[4] This reference is to Scotland of the late twelfth century. Late fourteenth- and fifteenth-century conditions were hardly more propitious: the raising of forces was by calling up friends and kinsmen by summons to arms and penalty. "Moreover, because of the deterioration of fifteenth century coinage and the lack of any general banking system, people had difficulty in depositing and exchanging money and in collecting debts."[5]

[1] J. O. Prestwich (1954). [2] S. Painter (1949), 264. [3] G. W. S. Barrow (1956*b*), 363. [4] G. W. S. Barrow (1956*a*), 7. [5] Annie I. Dunlop (1950), 390.

The swagger and finery of the tower-house lords to which reference is made below[1] was not a squandering of surplus wealth: "In view of the hazards to which financial investments were exposed, it is not surprising that men were disposed to sink their capital in jewels and personal adornments, which were easily carried and could be turned to many purposes besides providing an outlet for the mediaeval love of splendour and pageantry."[2] The explanation of the keep-gatehouse surely is that in the late Middle Ages a change in the social structure of warfare, when barons engaged military vassals more than before, coincided with and doubtless influenced an inevitable stage in the architectural evolution of the castle to produce a distinctive architectural result.

The frontal mass of Caerlaverock (*c.* 1290) constitutes a keep-gatehouse, the earliest in Scotland. Erected upon a rock outcrop in a waste-land of marsh it is as likely to be the result of local conditions as of preconceived notions. The composite donjon of Dirleton by its frontal massing has some claim to be included in the category also, but it too is determined by a rocky site and does not contain the entrance. A fifteenth-century frontal building at Sanquhar resembles Doune; but it is Tantallon (East Lothian), first mentioned in 1373 and probably erected about 1350, which is the closest and most unequivocal analogy.

Tantallon consists of a lofty crenellated curtain of dressed ashlar 50 feet high, 12 feet thick, which extends across the neck of a sea promontory from cliff to cliff, a late mediaeval version of a prehistoric promontory fort. Before it, cutting off the promontory, is a deep and wide rock-cut ditch. Two towers terminate the curtain, one at each end: one is fully rounded, the other D-shaped in plan. A great rectangular keep-gatehouse straddles the curtain at its centre. Forty-two feet square, 80 feet high, and with four storeys of living accommodation over the portcullis chamber this is the very epitome of the type. No less strikingly does the vast expanse of wall exemplify all that the descriptive term "curtain" implies. If ever there was a curtain of stone, this is it. Red in colour, the fabric seems to hang upon an expanse of green, and behind it the vast expanse of a marine sky sets off the composition. In its colour, simplicity, directness, and grand scale undiminished by secondary detail, this is one of the most impressive sights in Scotland (pl. 12).

It fittingly brings this survey to a close, for the keep-gatehouse

[1] See below, pp. 129-30. [2] Annie I. Dunlop (1950), 391.

was the last and final manifestation of the tower in the development of the mediaeval castle, while the cannon-battered curtain wall on either side of it testifies to the destructive power of artillery which, employed at Crécy in 1346 and frequent in the last quarter of the fourteenth century, brought to an end the superiority of the defence. A failure in its context, the keep-gatehouse in its short life coincides with the end of the true mediaeval castle and the environment which caused it. In England in the last quarter of the fourteenth century the castle-idea expired, but in Scotland, an impoverished land, civil strife succeeded national warfare after the Wars of Independence, and the castle-idea survived. It did so in the like of a tower-house, albeit with ever-increasing concessions to comfort and convenience. The curtain shrinks to the barmkin or enclosure wall of domestic proportions, or vanishes to leave the tower in splendid isolation, "stark and upright like a warder", a gaunt reminder of unsettled times on an unkindly soil. It was to develop into one of the most remarkable manifestations in Europe of a national architecture, which will be described in chapters 3 and 5 below.

HALL-HOUSES

It is appropriate to introduce at this point an account of a small but important group of defensible dwellings whose analogy is the fortified manor-house of England. They are independent buildings, small and compact. They are not towers, and they are unconnected with curtain-walls. To distinguish them from strongholds which are characterised by one or other or both of these basic components, and particularly to distinguish them from tower-houses, which are also independent and free-standing, we might conveniently call them hall-houses.

The earliest of the few which can be identified (perhaps few were of stone) is incorporated, much ruined, in Skipness Castle, in the account of which it has been briefly mentioned. Some further words are necessary. It escaped recognition by MacGibbon and Ross in their description of that castle, which overlooked other important matters also.[1] But Graham and Collingwood made good this untypical lack of perspicacity in an imaginative and illuminating paper published in 1923,[2] a highly original work which should have exercised a greater influence upon the study of Scottish castles than it

[1] D. MacGibbon and T. Ross (1889), III.63-75.
[2] A. Graham and R. G. Collingwood (1923), 266-87.

has done. The first castle was an oblong of two storeys over an unvaulted and apparently unlit ground-floor storage. The first floor was the hall, lit by romanesque windows one in each side. They have splayed jambs and large rounded rear-arches with chamfered arrises. The building is now a shell lacking one of its long sides, having been absorbed in later ranges built against it to make it the corner block of a thirteenth-century courtyard castle. A sixteenth-century tower-house, surviving complete in an adjacent corner, is built upon one of the gables of the hall and so preserves the gable windows of its first and second floors as well as crenellations of an outer wall which, if later than the hall, is not much later. The existing long wall of the hall, now the northern "curtain" of the courtyard, contains one of those rounded windows at one end. In all likelihood another matched it in the demolished wall opposite. This window excels those in the gables, being a twin-light opening with good mouldings. It is tempting and reasonable to suppose that it indicates the high-table end of the hall, on the analogy of the traditional oriels still to be seen distinguishing this superior part in complete mediaeval halls elsewhere, e.g. Henry VIII's hall in Hampton Court, the halls of Oxford and Cambridge, the Lion chamber of Linlithgow, and so forth. And indeed the traditional pre-eminence of the windows at the high-table and fireplace end of a mediaeval hall is perpetuated even in tower-houses of later date, as we shall see.

The typical and orthodox mediaeval hall, with its arrangement of screens passage, common hall and solar, is best represented in Scotland in a castle or palace complex of buildings. At Linlithgow Palace (pl. 14), Edinburgh Castle (restored), Stirling and Doune the great halls are still among the most imposing structures. That of Linlithgow is of great height, has a towering stone barrel-vaulted bay over a long fireplace of three openings, a splendid clerestory range of windows, a lofty side window at the high table dais, stone benches down the long sides, and a massive stone screen pierced with service hatches over which was a stone barrel-vaulted musicians' gallery and behind which was a spacious kitchen with two large fireplaces. Dating from the first half of the fifteenth century, it remains to-day, although roofless, one of the most spectacular achievements of mediaeval domestic architecture in the country.

In the ruined halls of Bothwell, Dirleton and Kildrummy, at Stirling and in the foundations of an orieled hall at Falkland, there is much to indicate their importance in Scotland, no less than elsewhere, at least in the greater mediaeval establishments. But isolated halls are rare, and timber halls entirely absent.[1] Documentary references to halls are frequent enough in state papers, the Accounts of the Lord High Treasurer, the Exchequer Rolls and so forth, but no architectural inferences can usefully be drawn from them. Thus for 1263 reference is to be found to a new hall with wooden walls having been built in Caithness for the accommodation of Alexander III on the occasion of his visit in that year.[2] Field investigation might yield results, as it has done with conspicuous success at the site of the last refuge in Scotland of Edward Baliol, an oblong hall-house or fortified manor of the simplest kind, to-day only a grass-grown ruin on the small island of Hestan in Auchencairn Bay in Galloway.[3]

The Lanercost Chronicle relates that he retreated over the Border after the battle of Halidon Hill in 1333, "because he had no castle or town or refuge in Scotland where he could safely dwell". It was probably soon after this that his manor was erected or, if existing, was taken for his use. In 1342 it is referred to as a *pelum*, implying a palisade about it, in a writ of Edward III permitting Bristol merchants to ship wine, food and salt for its garrison.[4] In 1347 the fortress (*forcelet*), as the chronicle then refers to it, was occupied by him, his men-at-arms, and archers to keep guard. Charters are granted from it in 1348 and 1352. But the island of "Estholm", "which belongs to Edward de Balliol, King of Scots", was situated in a place of the utmost peril (*in loco periculoso valde*) amongst enemy Scots[5], and its history ceases with the failure of the Baliol cause.

The ruin is architecturally insignificant and of interest only in connection with this history. There is no other indication of substantial structures on the island, no satisfactory modern explanation of it, and nothing about it inconsistent with the documentary record. It consists of the lowest part, but 4 feet high, of an oblong building 37 feet by 15 feet in rubble walling 3 feet thick. There is a doorway in the centre of one long side and probably another off-centre in the opposite side. Significant are the rounded external corners, an early

[1] Nor has Scottish mediaeval archaeology, in the restricted sense of excavation, yielded evidence of any. It may well be that excavation of mediaeval sites according to the exacting standards which prehistoric and Roman archaeologists impose upon themselves will produce evidence of timber halls and other buildings.

[2] Chamberlains' Accounts I.22, 23.

[3] C. A. R. Radford (1957), 33-7; R. C. Reid (1957), 38-63.

[4] RS No. 1635.

[5] RS No. 1713.

indication, as is a single detached corbel of early type which lies detached in the garden of the island's only house nearby. This without reasonable doubt is the undercroft of a raised hall, the principal part of Baliol's residence.

A little-known ruin in Ayrshire is of early date and considerable importance. Craigie Castle (Ayrshire) had a rib-vaulted hall of three bays over an unvaulted basement. Hitherto unnoticed is the walled-up battlementing of an earlier hall incorporated in it. The first hall had a crenellated parapet of early type rising flush with the main wall-face. There was a generous paved wall-walk behind, and a round-arched doorway in the centre of one long wall at ground level. In the opposite wall a late mediaeval fireplace with decorated jambs, of later fifteenth-century date, has been built across another round-arched opening. In mounded debris and vegetation the plan is difficult to determine with confidence but appears to have been originally a simple rectangle, not large enough to be that of an open enclosure but about right for an early hall-house. It stands upon a mound, perhaps a motte hill, surrounded by a ditch of which a well-defined stretch still exists.

It seems that we have here a hall-house of late twelfth- or thirteenth-century date with a wide crenellated parapet enclosing a saddle-back roof. At a later date, probably fifteenth century according to the detailing, the crenellations were built over by new work, and an entirely new hall was fashioned upon the walls of its predecessor. It was ashlar, stone-vaulted in three bays, with ribs springing from sculptured corbels set into the original wall-walk, which was undisturbed and made a secure and convenient base for the new vault to be erected upon it. The evidence of this adjustment is fully revealed in the broken walls which show it clearly in section. On one long side of the old hall the new vault rests upon the parapet walk and rises from it. On the other it rises from the walk flush with its outer face but overlaps the inner face of the old hall, being applied to it like a skin some 18 inches thick. The wall-ribs of the vaulting serve to enclose the rear-arches of high stepped window embrasures rising from the level of the springing to rectangular windows, one in each bay.

Little can be said about the elevations and detailing of these buildings; of Hestan nothing whatever; Craigie was embattled; and Skipness had plain unbuttressed walls on a spreading base and rounded first-floor windows. Doubtless it was embattled also, but the general appearance to the modern eye would be of barn-like simplicity.

Its neighbour on the other side of Kilbrannan Sound, in Arran, shares this unsophisticated air. The original Lochranza castle is now involved in the sixteenth-century additions which give the structure its late appearance but, there is more work of a late thirteenth- to mid-fourteenth-century date in Lochranza than at first appears, however: a blocked original entrance passage with a heavily ribbed barrel-vault with meurtrière, long arrow-slits with wide lintelled embrasures steadily converging to the slits in the outer wall-face, and narrow windows also with widely splayed jambs and wide internal openings, this time semi-circular. A considerable amount of its ground and first floors remains to show that originally its stair went straight through the wall at right angles to the entrance passage, turned the corner and continued without interruption through the side wall to the wall-head, passing over the arches of the only ground-floor and first-floor windows in this side. From one corner of the oblong castle a square tower projects, one face in line with the entrance façade. It contains small chambers furnished with long arrow-slits, one in each wall, similar to that which protects the original entrance from an embrasure in the first flight of steps. This tower seems to have been erected primarily for defence, to judge by the smallness of its chambers and the number of its loops, and it is an early example of the added jamb or wing which marked the first stage in the evolution of the tower-house. Two further examples of the hall-house, one in the north, the other in the south, are more rewarding from an architectural point of view.

Morton Castle (Dumfriesshire) and Rait Castle (Nairnshire) lack their roofs and floors but are otherwise complete to the wall-heads. They have much important worked detail to assist dating and they are altogether outstanding examples of this type of building. They bear a strong resemblance to each other in general conception, particularly as it is expressed in that matter of fundamental importance, the plan. Each consists of a long hall over an unvaulted undercroft. Entrance to the hall is through a fine arched doorway at one end of the first floor. This admitted to a screens passage. At the far end of the hall is a fireplace and a projecting round tower.

Morton is laid across the point of a high promontory jutting into Morton Loch. It has relied in its defensive scheme, such as it was, upon a strong gate-house projecting from one end of its landward elevation. This was the show-façade and had no defence. Fine arched, mullioned and transomed windows lit the hall on the first floor along this side only. The gatehouse was a double-towered structure, now ruined. Each tower in it had a basement and four floors and each was D-shaped. Placed back to back they contained the entrance passage between them, well equipped with outer door, portcullis and inner door. The rounded ends of the towers faced outwards and sideways, one over the steep slope of the promontory, the other along the façade of the hall to confront a round corner tower projecting from its far end. Thus the hall was well defended on the vulnerable landward side by flanking towers, yet there are no defensive arrow-slits, neither in the towers nor in the long elevation between them.

The entrance passage extended backwards beyond the gable of the main hall block and led round its rear corner to an outside stair which gave access to the elevated doorway of the screens passage on the hall's first floor. However vulnerable the house was by reason of its large windows freely disposed on the approachable landward side, the entrances at least were carefully considered in equipment and siting. It is clear, however, that not bombardment but only the onward rush of men has been considered in the defensive scheme: not the walls but only their doors have been affected by considerations of security. And, nonetheless, the doorway to the hall has suffered no loss of art. It is a fine thing, a pointed arch with multiple mouldings dying into the jambs, the best piece of detailing in the building, obviously worked with an eye to contrast and effect, and with a proper regard to its importance. The undercroft is lit by a series of squarish windows with chamfered edges. Placed high in the wall along the landward side of the undercroft, with long stepped cills and doorlike embrasures entered through shouldered "Caernarvon" arches the interior aspect of this cellerage window range is quite impressive and proclaims a late thirteenth-century date. Hooded fireplaces with pronounced jambs bearing moulded capitals, benched window embrasures with segmental sconsion arches, and other minor details such as corbels confirm this.

The same expression of an idea, the same fulfilment of a particular and specific need, not only in detail but in the larger aspects of planning and composition, rhythm and proportion, is to be found in Rait Castle, whose plan differs significantly from Morton only in the lack of a gatehouse, and in the basement of Bishop's Palace,

ate 13
oune, Perthshire, *ante* 1400
ove
e gatehouse, exterior
ght
e gatehouse from the
urtyard side

Linlithgow Palace
West Lothian:
interior of great
hall or Lion Char
c. 1434

Plate 14

Rait, Nairnshire:
'a hall-house', late
thirteenth or early
fourteenth century

Kirkwall, now much altered, which is an oblong with one corner tower of good mediaeval bulk. The bishop's hall and *camera* were on the first floor. In the chamber below a series of eight arrow-slits proclaims a mid-thirteenth-century date, if not an earlier one, for it exploits in their jambs the decorative possibilities of polychrome masonry as it is handled in the adjacent St Magnus' Cathedral and nowhere else.[1] Alternate red and white courses of sandstone occur in the earliest work in the Cathedral (*c.* 1140) and more systematically and self-consciously in the lower courses of the west front and in an inserted doorway in the south transept gable (*c.* 1220). The rarity of sandstone in Orkney and the recurrence of a highly individual treatment of it in undoubtedly early arrow-slits makes it almost certain that the Bishop's Palace dates from the early thirteenth century. We may with especial regard behold in its lower chamber an authentic remnant of the hall in which the great King Hakon died after his defeat at Largs in 1263.

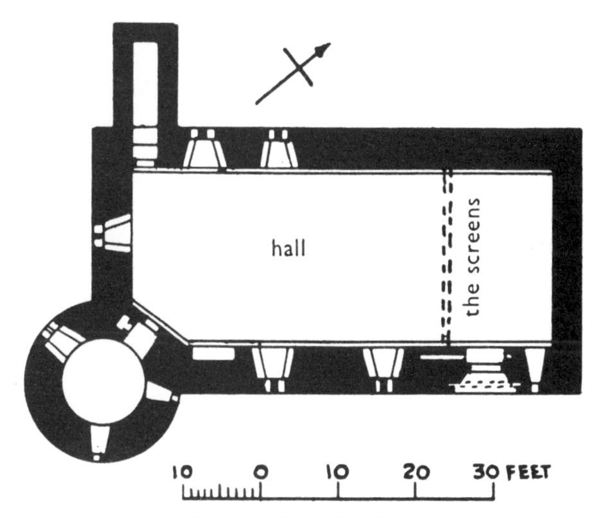

FIG. 10. Rait, first floor

Rait (pl. 14; fig. 10) is an oblong hall over an unvaulted undercroft. A round tower rising from a spreading base projects from one corner. The elevated entrance led into a screens passage separated from the hall by a timber screen, now vanished, as at Morton. Off this a small lancet window permitted the porter to observe the approach. The doorway is arched in receding orders of broad splays beneath a label

[1] See below, p. 184.

mould. A portcullis and draw-bar secured it. As at Morton baronial pride and caution are here combined. The doorway is greatly overdrawn, of immoderate size in relation to the modest hall it serves and to the elevation in which it is placed. Evidently the hall-house borrows from the castle when it can. At the far end of the hall is a hooded fireplace with sconces, one on either side. This late thirteenth-century feature is ubiquitous in Edward's castles of North Wales, but uncommon in Scotland, although present at the hooded fireplace of Tulliallan, another of this group, which is especially distinguished by a splendid undercroft, rib-vaulted from central piers, an achievement without parallel in Scottish secular architecture.

Two twin-light arched windows with pierced spandrels and ribbed soffits to their arched embrasures lit the dais end at Rait and did duty for the traditional oriel. In conjunction with the fireplace and adjacent entrance to the projecting tower, which afforded private withdrawing-room or solar accommodation, they make a tidy unit of planning which is closely paralleled at Morton. The tower is covered with a saucer dome of concentric rings of masonry. From the rear elevation a narrow garderobe tower projects as at Tulliallan and Roy. The undercroft, like that of Morton, is lit by squarish windows with chamfered edges high up in the wall. This style occurs at Lochindorb in the late thirteenth or early fourteenth century, and of this date they are presumptive evidence elsewhere. Rait carried a long pitched roof coming down to the wall-head of the hall along the sides, but the gables of the roof were set back behind an overhanging parapet at each end. Against the east gable there seems to have been an attached outbuilding, probably of timber and clay, communicating with the screens passage. As in neither the Morton undercroft nor in that at Rait was there a fireplace, the ancillary buildings attached to both were of no great substance nor architectural importance, and in all probability consisted of kitchen and storage.

The earliest lords of Rait of whom contemporary record exists took their designation from the manor of Rait, and although nothing certain is known of their origins they are reputed to have been Comyns.[1] The manor is first on record in an estate list of 1238.[2] References to Sir Gervaise de Rait and his younger brother Sir

[1] W. D. Simpson (1937), 109.
[2] RegEpMor 34.

Andrew are frequent in the last decade of the thirteenth century.[1] Both were well connected in the king's business, and in 1304 Sir Andrew was employed in a survey of the royal lands in Scotland. Unless the manor were a timber building, of which no evidence is visible in the neighbourhood (not even by a motte hill upon which it would presumably have been raised), this defensible hall-house must be the eponymous manor of the Raits, and of the late thirteenth or early fourteenth century, a likely enough conclusion, architectural evidence concurring with historical probability.

By comparison with Lochindorb the windows of the gatehouse of Dunstanburgh castle (*c.* 1313) and the general characteristics and probabilities deriving from the worked detailing and the fundamentally early type of plan, these two interesting and valuable structures can reasonably be dated to the late thirteenth century or first quarter of the fourteenth century, say 1290 to 1320. Their close correspondence and common difference from contemporary work put them in a class by themselves. They share, with the others with which they form a group, a marked departure from the curtain-wall mentality and no less from the tower-idea then currently emerging into the favour it never subsequently lost. The expression of a native partiality for vertical building, first heard in the late thirteenth century at Drum and echoed soon after by Hallforest and others described below, was nothing more than the hall-house up-ended.

[1] See W. D. Simpson (1937) for these references.

3

Tower-Houses

FOURTEENTH CENTURY

THE great curtain-wall castles of the thirteenth and early fourteenth century were royal or baronial. With the exception of the western seaboard and the historical Berwick-Roxburgh-Jedburgh groups they were not placed with demonstrable strategic intent, not at any rate in the strictly military sense. Only for the administration and control of the great feudal lordships may strategic siting be inferred.

The advance of Edward I round the north-west corner of Wales is commemorated by the chain of castles he planted to consolidate his successes; in Glamorgan the distribution of early Norman castles suggests that the dominant motive behind their erection was the control of the river valleys[1]; but in the south-west of Scotland, where mottes are widespread and numerous, their very number weakens the strategic explanation of their distribution and suggests with equal plausibility that it is due to expediency or geographical accident.

The co-existence of castles conveniently grouped according to strategic theory is frequently explained in terms such as "a chain of castles", "commanding a pass" or "controlling a frontier". Of no very precise meaning, these phrases overemphasise the military function. Unmindful of the particular history of each castle in the group, whose varying fortunes in ownership, possession, activity and decline discount the probability of concerted action, they tend to confuse modern and mediaeval geography as well as military technique and underestimate the domestic functions which considerably influenced design and situation. Not until the great Cromwellian fortifications of the mid-seventeenth century and their Hanover-

[1] B. H. St J. O'Neil and H. J. Randall (1949), 2.

ian successors of the eighteenth century come to be considered, can situation, plan and elevation be explained on strategic and tactical grounds.

The exaggeration, as well as being misleading, is harmful to the less factual but none the less important aesthetic consideration. If castles are pre-eminently regarded as the result of progressive developments in military science they will receive less than a just appreciation, for they are noble works of architecture at their best, bold and expressive, conceived and executed by architects and masons employed on other works, parish churches, abbeys, cathedrals and the like with unquestioned claims to aesthetic merit. Bothwell, Dirleton, Caerlaverock, Kildrummy and Doune, and the lesser works of Dunstaffnage, Inverlochy and Tioram are immensely satisfying. One feels that security was not the only consideration in the master mason's mind when the walls of Dunstaffnage and Tioram were precariously erected upon their rocky sites and followed the uneven surface in a rise and fall; nor that mangonels and trébuchets alone were envisaged when the lofty red curtain of Tantallon was hung across the horizon, later to receive a barbican of banded green and white stones. The bulky round corner towers of the squat and square enclosure of Inverlochy provide architectural punctuation marks just where they are needed, securing the long flat stretches of curtain wall visually as well as defensively, and the castle loses nothing in effect by being low-lying by the riverside and overwhelmed by Ben Nevis. "The towers seem to activate the passive and stolid stretches of wall, as in the knightly effigies on their tombs the crossed legs and hands on swords preserve a tense alertness even in the stillness of death"; in these fine words Brieger sums it up, and reminds us that the artistic tension which underlies mediaeval art is not wanting in castles.[1] By such means the castle impressed the beholder with a proper respect for feudal power and became the material expression of the pride and pomp of a ruling class. To what extent it did, and when, and to what extent aesthetic, symbolic and practical considerations interacted, conflicted, harmonised and were resolved, are matters which become increasingly prominent in the study of the Scottish castles of the late Middle Ages.

The great Norman keeps of the north, all English, none Scottish, occur along the debatable Border land but not north of it. Clustered most numerously at either end of it around Carlisle, Berwick and

[1] P. Brieger (1957), 259.

Newcastle, they do indeed comprise a body of strongholds suggestively situated. In Aberdeenshire the early castles of Mar, Kindrochit and Kildrummy have a seeming strategic significance in relation to natural routes as Simpson asserts.[1] He postulates no mediaeval Vauban or Brialmont in Mar, however, nor a contemporary erection of these strongholds, and justifies "strategy" on geographical considerations alone. This more cautious hypothesis still leaves room for doubt, as it implies a modern technique of warfare relying much on transport and communication and a concurrent state of readiness and effectiveness in all the members of the group which is not sustained by their known history.

Mediaeval campaigns were not long-term projects. The terms of feudal service prevented this. In Scotland as late as 1496 letters were despatched to sheriffs throughout the country ordering a muster of the king's lieges on 6 April "to remain with the King forty days thereafter"—the extreme period of feudal service[2]—and the food and equipment of those called to arms were provided by themselves during the short period of continuous service required of them.[3] Froissart (born *c.* 1337) writes in his Chronicles (published *c.* 1500) of Scottish hardihood on campaign. He describes how the Scots are inured to war and ride without halting twenty-four "leagues" night and day, how they bring no carriages, on account of the mountains, and carry no provisions but oatmeal.[4] The timely delivery of supplies and ammunition from afar was less essential then. They did not have to travel far to ensure success of action, however desirable it was for them to be able to do so. Even the mechanised arm of the mediaeval field force—most unadaptable it might be thought—could carry on without recourse to its base and construct heavy engines with local material and forced labour with less inconvenience than might at first thought be considered inevitable. The resourcefulness of the field army of Edward I when engaged in the successful attack on Bothwell in the late summer of 1301 is testified by entries in the Wardrobe Accounts: a timber bridge was built across the Clyde after the wood of Glasgow had been plundered; a corduroy road was laid up to the castle for the passage of *le Berefrey*, a wheeled tower which was constructed in Glasgow and transported in prefabricated parts in thirty wagons in two days; plumbers, carpenters and others bought and used lead, wax, wheels, cables and

[1] W. D. Simpson (1944), 132. [2] ALHT I.cxlv. [3] ALHT I.xxiii.
[4] Quoted by P. Hume Brown (1891), 8-9; W. C. Dickinson (1952), I.204.

other material punctiliously recorded.[1] Save in exceptional circumstances, with motive, means and opportunity agreeing, the strategic siting and planting of castles is a doubtful explanation of their existence.

The castle was at its greatest use in peace. It was an instrument of local power, planted to enforce authority and government. Its rise and decline reflect not only the changing military and political situation but the shifting social background of the feudal system. Imposing strongholds such as Bothwell, Kildrummy, Dirleton and Caerlaverock were paramount in their neighbourhood. From its resources of men and material the lord derived income and goods and he could discharge his feudal obligations of providing fighting men from the manpower it contained. Such castles constituted secure bases from which power was exercised and within which it was protected and maintained. That authority was widespread, even national, and the area of a castle's jurisdiction was correspondingly extensive. With the king in residence it was the ultimate source of authority, for the king not only ruled but governed, and where he was there was government, and the castles were an essential part of it. Forces opposed to the castles reviewed in the foregoing pages were likely to be large, and the structures took the form appropriate to their function, danger and ownership. Thus they were, in the thirteenth century, large, spacious and defendable high-walled enclosures capable of accommodating a numerous household of inmates, men-at-arms and visitors. The Scottish tower-houses of the later Middle Ages are not invested with this feudal spirit. They are very different things, had different causes and served different ends.

MacGibbon and Ross appeal to the Norman keep as the inspiration of the tower-house and to the experience of Scots nobles in England during the Wars of Independence as the reason for its introduction into Scotland in the fourteenth century. They instance this as an example of the influence of the Norman Conquest upon Scotland.[2] The long arm of influence is here extended too far. No Norman keeps in the grand manner of the White Tower, Rochester, and Dover were erected north of Norham on the Tweed, but Castle Sween, our closest approach to a Norman keep, Cubbie Roo's Castle of the mid-twelfth century, and Dunnideer and Yester of the

[1] *Roqero de Barneby clerico assignato ad vadia operariorum operancium circa ingenium dictum "le Berefrey" quod rex fieri fecit pro obsidione castri de Botheville.* J. Bain (1888), IV.451.
[2] D. MacGibbon and T. Ross (1889), III.17.

mid-thirteenth century provide us with first-class examples of the tower stronghold.

At Yester (East Lothian) we have substantial evidence of "what must have been a large rectangular stone donjon or tower-house of a type which it has been usual to think is not found earlier than the fourteenth century—but here at Yester must be assigned to before the year 1267".[1] The early stonework is a celebrated underground hall, crossed by a high pointed barrel-vault strengthened by chamfered transverse stone ribs of thirteenth-century aspect, as are the doorways leading to a long passage extending outwards on each side away from the hall at right angles to it. This submerged hall is the undercroft of a tower reduced in height to make way for a later reconstruction of the castle lay-out. Originally it was partially dug into the mound of a motte castle. After the reduction of the upper works the undercroft was covered over and now mysteriously survives to provoke conjectures of magic and wizardry.

In decline during the thirteenth century, when the curtain wall prevailed, the tower was revived in Scotland during the second War of Independence, when the country's exhaustion in and after that struggle, and a changing social background—the disruption of the feudal system prevalent throughout Europe—combined to bring the curtain-wall castle to an end. The economic, social and military forces at work in the fourteenth century which caused a reversion to the tower imposed a rigid standardisation on the form it took which lasted a full hundred years, and the tower idea was never again abandoned in Scotland as long as castellated architecture was required by lairds and nobles in no matter how diluted a form. For about three hundred years, from *c.* 1330 to *c.* 1600, it was the universal standard type. Although there were notable exceptions and variations—Tantallon, Doune, Hermitage and Crookston—the basic tower idea predominated for those three hundred years in no uncertain manner. Concurrently with the decline of the military importance of the mediaeval castle of the European and Byzantine tradition, the tower-house flourished as it never did anywhere else before or since.

The early examples are few in number. They are square or oblong vessels without projecting parts, containing usually three cells placed one upon another within the rectangle: a stone barrel-vaulted basement, a high vault above it, and frequently (but not

[1] W. D. Simpson "Yester Castle", TELAS v(1952), 52-8.

always) a third vault above that. The entrance is at ground-, first-, or second-floor level, by an outside timber stair or ladder, or at two levels. Otherwise the only apertures in the basement are narrow slits, not for defence but for ventilation, set high, and few in number. The basement was for storage. It might communicate with the first floor only by ladder and trap door. Each floor was one chamber. The high vault runs through two storeys in height. It was divided into two chambers, one upon the other, by a timber floor slung across it, whose main beams rested upon heavy stone corbels projecting from the side walls of the tower or upon a scarcement in them.

Cawdor Castle (Nairnshire) has a basement vault and a high vault above it which is divided into three floors. The episcopal tower-house of the Bishops of Moray at Spynie, erected between 1461 and 1482, had no less than six storeys, of which the fifth is covered by a stone vault 60 feet above the hall on the first floor. Tower-house accommodation was served by a wheel stair in the thickness of the main walling, usually in a corner, a most economical use of space. It rises like a vertical corridor to one chamber after another. Somewhere in its upward course it may be stopped at a floor level and transferred to another corner, thence to continue upwards, perhaps to be interrupted in like manner again. Secondary stairs may begin in upper floors, a trick much elaborated in later works, which, whether by accident or design, would effectively disconcert an onrush of intruders, not only by interrupting their progress but also by forcing them into the open in crossing a chamber publicly from one stairway to another.

The lower chamber of the high vault, the first floor of the tower, was the hall. The upper chamber of the high vault was the solar of the hall beneath. This is the traditional mediaeval hall up-ended, with the solar placed above the hall instead of at one end of it. The analogy can be carried further: the fireplace of the hall tends to be in a gable wall and to be flanked by two good windows, one in each of the side walls. They may well be the only windows in the hall. With wide embrasures and stone window seats they provided a little elbow room and pleasant sitting place with some welcome privacy at the superior end of a common hall. They are analogous to the oriel windows of the traditional plan. At the other end of the chamber the older lay-out is again recalled with the entry into the hall by a screens passage, not directly to the main floor space. Surviving timber screens being a rarity, the existence of this passage is apt to be overlooked. Despite the absence of the timber screen itself the sense of the cross passage at the end of the hall is imparted at Borthwick and Dirleton by handsome enriched buffet cupboards or aumbries in the middle of the end wall of the chamber where the screens passage was, and by the arrangement of the doorways which admitted to the passage from outside the hall. The arrangements are there, only the screen is lacking. A precious if late survival at Craigievar (*c.* 1620) shows how simple and effective the screen could be, while at Falkland the wide and lofty screens passage of the chapel, carrying a heavily screened gallery above, presents the feature in another setting. The Lion Chamber at Linlithgow (*c.* 1430) had a massive stone screen. The stumps remain, with the buffet and service hatches opening off the spacious kitchens. This must have been one of the most splendid halls in Scotland with its high clere-story passage down one side and an open timber roof over the main floor space. A stone barrel-vault covered the fireplace and high table dais.

The main walling of the fourteenth-century tower-house is of a great thickness scarcely diminished in the upper levels because of the need to provide abutment for the thrust of the high vault. The basement vault, with considerable solidness of masonry in its haunches, and being of no great height, afforded a very stable base for the weight of masonry above it. The distinctive spreading base of the thirteenth century is conspicuously absent, replaced by a plinth of modest splay. The upper vault was capped by a low-pitched saddle-back roof of stone slabs. This squatted behind a parapet wall and encircling wall-walk. Access to the wall-head was gained from the top of the wheel stair emerging into the open as a little turret or cap-house. This was the war-head of the castle. From it the only vigorous show of defiance could be made. Yet only Threave and Hermitage have evidence of defensive hourds, which seem to have been a permanent erection at the former.

Stone parapet walls overhanging the wall faces at first do so upon single stone corbels of modest projections as at Drum and Lochleven. At Hallforest, a structure of very primitive simplicity which is contemporary with them, the parapet rises flush with the wall faces as it does in the earlier battlements of Rothesay, Craigie and Skipness. From such small beginnings the corbel course and the parapet wall which it bore developed into one of the most distinctive features. By the early fifteenth century it was boldly over-sailing upon close-set heavy corbels of two or three members with machicolations between (pls. 8, 11, 16). This is the standard fifteenth-century pattern, well demonstrated upon the towers of Bothwell and Caerlaverock. The corbels of the fine south-east tower of the former are linked by small arches, a rare occurrence in mediaeval Scotland of a late fourteenth-century continental fashion sufficiently unusual to call for comment. In England, too, it is rare, and its occurrence upon the tall and slender tower of the brick castle of Caister, begun by Sir John Fastolf in 1423, has occasioned Rhenish analogies.[1] The wall-head projects indifferently upon a continuous corbel-course at Tantallon where machicolated parapets do not occur, while at Doune the parapets do not overhang at all and the only machicolation is isolated over a postern. By the early sixteenth century the functional antecedents were forgotten. Rows of corbels appear in a staggered setting of solid and void alternately, the lower projecting beneath a void, supporting nothing. This mannerism is even employed alternately with continuous corbelling, particularly beneath oversailing corner roundels. A combination of single and continuous corbelling is worked upon the same corbel table by a regular advance and recession of the continuous corbelling. This feature, first encountered in the royal tower of Holyroodhouse (*c.* 1500), is much exploited in Aberdeenshire in the late sixteenth and early seventeenth century. Thus a once functional feature degenerated to become a purely decorative device and as such it assumed a new importance in the mason's repertory. It was much employed in late sixteenth- and early seventeenth-century tower-houses as a decorative cresting above the main walls, which continued to be, without much concession to embellishment, the old plain surfaces of the early fourteenth century.

In the early prominence of the wall-head of an exceptionally severe and utilitarian fortification lay the germ of that proliferation of ornament in the upper works of late tower-houses which is their most distinctive characteristic. Here the tension between the necessities of security and the requirements of decoration were resolved. Never secure enough to reject defensive preparations altogether, the late mediaeval masons and their clients loaded the parapet with exuberant detail, concentrating upon the superstructure what might otherwise have been distributed over the whole. They left the main walling expansive, plain, unadorned and unweakened by enlarge-

[1] H. D. Barnes and W. D. Simpson (1952*a*), 44.

ment of windows, and they thus set off perfectly by contrast the richness above. The shift of emphasis in defence from the wall-head to ground level by the increase in use of heavy fire-arms from the early sixteenth century made possible this freedom to indulge in elevated inessentials, and they were all the more natural to the wall-head because it was here that the most detailed and arresting features had for so long been accepted. Thus the tension produced by the opposite pulls of defence and amenity, innovation and custom, was resolved at the wall-head by a solution which replaced it by another, the aesthetic tension, by the contrast of simplicity and elaboration.

The early towers relied mainly for their security upon their own thick walls, and perhaps an outer defence of ramparts and ditches such as are still to be seen in most impressive scale surrounding the ruined tower of Torthorwald (*c.* 1340) near Dumfries, a lofty structure of two vaults, and less conspicuously at Cessford (Roxburghshire) of the early fifteenth century. The late fourteenth- or early fifteenth-century Crookston (Renfrewshire) is wholly surrounded by an oval-shaped perimeter defence of wide bank and ditch. This is taken to be the defensive earthwork of a late twelfth-century castle of Robert Croc, an attribution which is speculative but doubtless correct.

If not within ramparts and ditches such as these the tower-house was attached to a stone barmkin wall. This is the shrunken descendant of the curtain, erected now to afford accommodation for cattle and provisions against the raider and not for a garrison against siege. The stone-vaulted basements are without firing loops to confront the outer world, and above them larger windows are but sparingly provided. This compromising insistence upon passive defence is a most striking and telling characteristic of the fourteenth-century tower-house, revealing a harassed and apprehensive attitude of mind and a lack of material resources to recover from it by more ambitious works. It recalls the broch of earlier times, with which other peculiarly Scottish architectural phenomenon some instructive comparisons can indeed be made. The fourteenth-century tower-house has no martial aspect but rather a stern and sullen one. It is a closed-up, inward-looking building.

A simple rectangular tower achieving height but not extent, having no defensive features but its own massive construction and an overhanging parapet, and with the minimum of rooms placed one upon another, is an inevitable result of conditions and requirements of impoverishment, the breakdown of the great areas of lordly jurisdiction, the need for security and the necessity for obtaining it cheaply. Albeit they were built by lords as well as lairds, such strongholds are not fortresses of lordly status but defensible manors of local gentry, constructed to withstand the foray, the sudden raid, but not the formal siege. They conformed to a wider policy, moreover, which was the royal discouragement of castle-building and the deliberate spoiling of castles in existence to deny them to the English during the uncertain days of the Wars of Independence. To these demands of security, economy and uncertain future a plain rectangular tower with exceedingly thick walls constructed all of stone was the obvious answer. It was also the reduction of the courtyard castle to a family dwelling and little more.

The resemblance to the Norman keep can be misleading. It was not consciously derived. In plan and elevation they differ fundamentally. Features characteristic of the Norman keep are absent from it. There are no round windows, no angle-shafts, no relieving of the expansive wall surfaces by the recession and projection of pilaster buttresses which only the altogether exceptional Castle Sween has, no central division of the interior by cross-wall and arcade, and no sculptural enrichment over door and window. Its austerity is uncompromising. The walls are plain and relieved only by the minimum number of windows of the smallest practicable size and "decorated" at the most with chamfered surrounds. But the masonry is frequently ashlar, most excellently dressed and laid in courses with exceedingly fine joints. This instantly imparts a quality to the towers thus constructed which rejects any opinions which their severity might produce that they are of no account. This redeeming characteristic affords the greatest pleasure to those who respond to good building. It is the explanation of so much main walling surviving to the present day with the roof long gone and interiors totally collapsed.

Simple in conception and with elevations and internal arrangements which could scarcely be more straightforward, they have every appearance of being of an early type. But the absence of enrichment and minor details which assist in placing a building renders dating by typology alone a hazardous exercise. Were it not for the fortunate concurrence of documentary records and the substantially surviving remains of three examples described below, Hallforest, Drum and Lochleven, the simplicity of conception and severity of execution which characterises them might justly be regarded as being indicative of low rank and insignificant purpose. Their history and high quality masonwork disprove this.

The crux of the matter is the lack of detail by which, normally, a historical building can be dated, irrespective of documentary evidence. When buildings are as non-committal as these early towers, it is wise to regard them as likely occurrences throughout a long period. Such caution is justified, for the simple early type did in fact occur throughout the fifteenth and sixteenth centuries, and was not uncommon in the early seventeenth century also. "Bruce's Castle" (Stirlingshire), for example, has a notably primitive air but nothing else of the early fourteenth century save a legend which can be disregarded or received with caution, for where legends are most expected the less can reliance be placed upon them. Likewise Covington Castle (Lanarkshire), which resembles "Bruce's Castle", is probably a fifteenth-century structure. The non-committal simplicity of the old castle of Wick of early date is characteristic of ruined Braal, also in Caithness. There, however, it accompanies a greater provision of mural chambers and larger windows with stone-benched embrasures. Braal was surrounded by a wet ditch and had no vaults, but its walls are uncommonly thick for a small unvaulted tower. This suggests an early date. The thirteenth century, therefore, is feasible for this simple building which has a traditional thirteenth-century association with Harald Earl of Caithness.

Equally severe, but twice vaulted and 60 feet high, is the ruin of the great oblong tower of Hallforest (Aberdeenshire), capital messuage of the old royal forest of Kintore which was granted in 1309 by Robert the Bruce to Sir Robert Keith, Great Marischal of Scotland. It was no less than six floors in height, including the garret. The walls are 7 feet thick. Two lofty barrel-vaults comprise the bulk of the tower; and each was sub-divided by a timber floor to provide a cellar with kitchen above it in the lower, and a hall with solar above it in the upper. Above this was another chamber, probably the lord's bedroom, with a garret over it entered from the wall-walk. Windows are small and few. In the ground-floor cellar they are merely slits at the outer end of long converging jambs. In the kitchen they are but a little larger. In the hall there are two of more reasonable size with wider splayed jambs to increase interior lighting. All these windows, save two slits, are in the south side. Within the tower there are no stairs nor evidence of stairs. Presumably communication was by timber stair and hatchway in the floor. An eighteenth-century description refers to entry by ladder to the second storey. Domestic arrangements could hardly be simpler than this nor more indicative of a hard and fearful existence. Whether erected by king or marischal is uncertain—the existence of a royal motte-castle at Kintore in 1246 suggests the latter—Hallforest cannot be precisely dated, but to the late thirteenth century or early fourteenth century it must surely belong.

A close parallel to Hallforest, and a superior building, is the tower of Drum near Aberdeen (pl. 15). It is very well-preserved and attached to a fine seventeenth-century mansion. This is still occupied by Irvines, descendants of the William de Irwin, armour-bearer and clerk-register of King Robert who bestowed the lands of Drum upon him by royal charter (still surviving in the house) in February 1323-4. The new house abuts on but does not surround the old castle, and all things considered its survival is as agreeable as one could wish for. It is a blunt and bulky tower, a simple rectangle with rounded corners and no projections save an overhanging latrine on the wall-walk. It measures 53 feet by 40 feet.

The walls rise sheer with a slight convergence towards the battlemented top, 70 feet above the ground. In the barrel-vaulted basement the walls are 12 feet thick without external openings save two extremely narrow slits with high stepped cills for ventilation. Two stone vaults above the basement were each divided into two storeys by timber floors. The entrance to the tower was by an outside timber stair or ladder to the first floor. This was the hall. Above it, beneath the arch of the vault, was the solar. The basement beneath was entered only by a straight stair descending from the hall within the thickness of a gable wall. Wholly within the thickness of one corner a wheel stair rises from first floor to battlements. Windows are few, small and featureless, but a good arched fireplace with moulded jambs bearing a stop chamfer indicates a late thirteenth-century date. The battlements are of very primitive type with high merlons stepping up to oversailing corners. These are rounded, as are the corners of the main block below them. Early battlements like this are very rare in tower-houses. This is the crenellation of an extended curtain of early date adopted in a tower. The parapet walk rises and falls in a series of water-sheds constructed of stone slabs placed one upon another to cast rainwater into the valleys between. As progress round the walk is consequently difficult, tiresome and dangerous, the inner face of the battlements is niched to provide foothold for those upon the wall-head. This is unique.

The third tower-house with a documentary history of the first half of the fourteenth century is Lochleven Castle (Fife). It was attacked by John de Strivilin (Stirling) for Edward Baliol in 1335 and defended against him by Alan de Vipont. It is a small tower of the simplest kind, 23 feet square inside walls 8 feet thick. It stands complete to its parapet. This projects slightly upon single corbels without machicolations. There are three roundels at the corners of the parapet most likely to need them for defence. There are five floors. The basement and first floor are barrel-vaulted, communication from one to the other being by hatchway in the crown of the lower vault. Thus even if the (probable) ground-level entrance to the basement were forced and admittance to the interior of the tower gained thereby, subsequent progress within would still be hazardous and detectable. The main entrance to the tower was directly into the hall at second-floor level through a doorway protected not only by altitude but strong draw-bars too. From here a wheel stair contained in the thickness of a corner descends to the first-floor common hall. This, consequently, could not be entered directly, but only by stairs up from the basement and down from the second floor. Direct access to a basement was doubtless welcome for the admittance of stores and provisions. Weakened security was compensated for by the strength of the basement's masonry, the stone vault, and the difficulties of communication.

Similar arrangements are to be found at Crichton. There the massive late fourteenth-century rectangular tower, the nucleus of a quadrangular development of later date, has an outside entrance to a barrel-vaulted basement and above it an elevated entrance directly to the first-floor hall. There is in this case no communication between basement and hall above. A polygonal curtain wall with a parapet walk merges into the north face of the Lochleven tower. To one corner of it a round tower was added, probably in the sixteenth century.

Some doubt attends the association of this tower and curtain with the history of the site: rebuilding upon older work is suspected. But there is no evidence of this, and to the plans of all floors it is difficult to deny an early fourteenth-century date. The unusually elevated entrance, the scarcity of stairs and windows and the total lack of mural chambers all proclaim an early work. Doubt is irrationally

Drum, Aberdeenshire,
late thirteenth century

Affleck, Angus,
later fifteenth century

Plate 16

above
Dundas, West Lothian:
the battlements, 1424

left
Muness, Unst, Shetland.
The most northerly castle
in Britain: roundel with
false machiocolation, 1598

provoked by the accomplished masonwork and state of completeness. Good material readily available and an island site, even now difficult to reach, provide sufficient explanation.

In such practical exercises in circulation and access can one follow the architect's mind as he seeks to solve the problems of security and convenience. This is evident in small towers as well as upon extensive ramparts. In plan can be read the purpose and fears of castle-builders. From methods of communication and isolation can the direction and development of expected assault be inferred. The placing of doorways, whether they open outwards or inwards, against which side they are barred, and so on, indicate purpose, use and movement. The tactical internal arrangements of Lochleven, if they can be so expressed, are unsophisticated when compared with those of the great gatehouse of Tonbridge (*c.* 1300) in Kent, which are extraordinarily revealing, or with those of Dirleton for example, but they are eloquent demonstrations of an attitude of mind for all that. The importance of the towers described is indicated by their history and status. None was insignificant. All are superior works. They are thus invaluable indicators of contemporary style.

The defensive features of these tower-houses being adequate, uncomplicated and suitable to the purse in hard times, the first changes in the form of the structure attempted to achieve more ample accommodation without reducing strength. This was partly accomplished in the second half of the century by the addition of a small wing or jamb to the tower and by the subtraction of small mural chambers from the thickness of its massive walls. Whenever there is this attempt to win more accommodation, however small, by encroachment into the main walls or by extension outside them, there we have later work. In the enlargement of window embrasures, in the provision of mural apartments (often opening off the embrasures), and in the progressive multiplication of them and of wheel stairs we follow subsequent development. But the tower remained otherwise unaltered, and the basic conception of its being a vertical range of rooms was unaffected. This is fundamental. It reveals the attitude to the job. One built vertically. There was no thought of spreading, of walking from one room to another. One went upstairs or down; no other route was possible.

So ingrained was this conception that the opportunities provided by the additional jamb were at first not fully realised. Small, tight and adhering closely to the parent block, it was not integrated with its floor levels, but divided into small chambers, one upon another, just as the main block was but with less headroom, so that there were more floors in the jamb than in the tower and no through passages. The transference of the old newel or wheel stair to the new jamb was no advantage as long as the stair was spiral, for the same stair within the thickness of the main wall used no space otherwise required, if the wall was thick enough to contain it without encroachment into the floor space. And in these early massive towers it was. Nor, in the conditions and methods of attack then obtaining, did it create a serious weakness in the fabric. An ordinary wheel stair in a square or rectangular projecting jamb is a waste of the possibilities the jamb provided. It should be something special—the spacious and sweeping curves of Fyvie, Falkland, Elcho and Noltland in the late sixteenth century, or the new style of straight flights and landings which the rectangular shape logically demanded and received at this date elsewhere, at Killochan for example, and which became extremely popular in the seventeenth century at Craigievar, Leslie, the Earl's Palace at Kirkwall, etc.

For almost the first three-quarters of the century improvements seem rarely to have been contemplated. The early works of Hallforest, Drum and Lochleven were followed by a few others like them, notably Threave and Dundonald. But the new-style high tower with a jamb took the first step beyond the restrictive oblong in 1367, in the royal castle of David II—David's Tower in Edinburgh Castle whose massive ruins are engulfed by the sixteenth-century Half-Moon Battery.[1] The Exchequer Rolls bear witness to its erection between that date and 1379, by which time it was complete save for its drawbridge and the paving of its entrance which were not completed until 1383. The work was done by an unnamed mason who in the Rolls of 1375 is the first recorded Master of Works ("*magister operis*") in Scottish history.[2] The jamb is small, its walls extremely thick. It contains no stair but the short straight flight through the wall from the ground-level entrance to a corridor through the jamb. The accommodation turnpike was situated at the end of this corridor.

Begun in the suburbs of the capital before David's Tower was finished, the first Craigmillar Castle (1374) is in every sense a close parallel, an oblong tower with small jamb with thick walls (pl. 18;

[1] The first mention of David's Tower in the Rolls is of a payment for repairs to William of Gupplyd *ad fabricam nove turris de Edynburgh* in 1367 (ER II.cix).

[2] ER II.475.

fig. 11). It is of outstanding importance. Hill Burton said of it: "there is perhaps no other instance in Scotland of a family mansion so systematically built on the principles of fortification in the fifteenth and sixteenth centuries".[1] He would have added, had he realised the fact, that the very date of the tower is of even greater significance, and that the later curtain which surrounds it is probably the earliest artillery fortification in Scotland. The historical interest of the

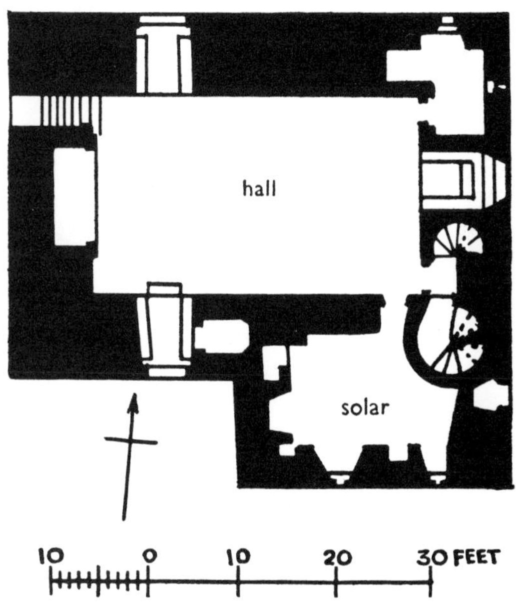

FIG. 11. Craigmillar, first floor

castle is enhanced by the size, condition and completeness of its survival. But before embarking upon a more detailed discussion of Craigmillar, it is advisable at this point to revert to Threave and consider its early gun-ports.

Threave (pl. 17) is a structure of the first order. It was erected between 1369 and 1390 by Archibald the Grim, third Earl of Douglas, one of the most distinguished warriors and noblemen of his age, a benefactor of Sweetheart Abbey and Holyrood Abbey, and founder of the Collegiate Churches of Bothwell and Lincluden, which are of conspicuous architectural merit. A building erected by such a Lord of Galloway as this, as a residence and stronghold in the troublesome district he determined to rule (and in the manner of doing so earned

[1] R. W. Billings (1852), vol. 1, under "Craigmillar".

his soubriquet) and for which he codified the Border Laws, could be no mere fortified manor house. It is a long rectangle 61 feet by 40 feet and 70 feet high to the highest surviving part of the battlements which rise flush with the wall-face. All its five floors are contained within the rectangle whose walls are 8 feet thick. Worked into these walls are but three small mural chambers, one on the entresol floor to a slit window, one in the first floor to a garderobe and one in the second floor also to a garderobe. All three are dog-legged in the thickness of the south-west angle. There is no other small accommodation. A high stone barrel-vault was divided by a timber floor. The lower chamber thus formed was basement cellarage. It contains a rock-cut well shaft originally lined with oak. The pointed-arch entrance to the tower is on the east wall of this chamber, a few feet above ground level. There are no windows but two narrow slits, high up, with long stepped cills. Between them is another penetrating straight through the wall from an accessible hollowed stone basin or sink. The north-west corner of the basement has been converted into a prison by the insertion of later walling. Above the basement was the kitchen, beneath the arch of the vault. Access from ground to first floor was by timber stair. Further progress upwards is by a wheel stair, beginning in the north-west corner of this floor, opposite the wall containing the ground-floor entrance and rising straight to the parapet. To reach it one has to cross the full width of the first-floor chamber. There is no other stairway or access to the upper floors and wall-walk save this. To win a little elbow-room it encroaches somewhat into the floor space of the rooms it serves by a thickening of wall which cuts across each corner. The masonry which thus thickens the corners is not carried down to the ground or, to put it another way, does not rise from the ground, but is supported by continuous corbelling dying away into the corner of the entresol. This is a purely structural expedient. It is one of some interest. It is the first instance of corbelling employed in this way in an interior. Were it an external feature in the re-entrant angle of the two jambs or wings of an L-plan house, we should have the most distinctive feature of that most distinctive type of later Scottish tower-house. Overhanging roundels containing stairs or small rooms have been attributed to French influence from the Loire in the sixteenth century. This attribution is doubtful.[1] While it is not suggested that Threave is the inspiration of this popular feature of

[1] See below, p. 195.

later times, its modest appearance here about 1370 is noteworthy.

Opening off the hall on the second floor is a small doorway directly over the entrance to the basement. Beneath this upper doorway were two corbels which bore beams of a timber structure connecting the hall and an upper chamber in the gatehouse of the curtain. The gatehouse is directly in front of the entrance, rises considerably higher than the parapet of the curtain, and has chases or housings for the raised drawbridge. The hall has a good fireplace with a label-moulding and a joggled lintel, and three twin-light mullioned windows with splayed ingoes and window benches in high round-arched embrasures. The floor above was divided by a cross wall into two bedrooms, each with a fireplace.

The uppermost storey of Threave has been dedicated to defence and probably housed the men-at-arms. The walls all round have a regular range of windows more liberally provided than in any of the apartments below. Round the outside of the north, south and west walls, at the same level as the windows and of the same height, are three rows of small square holes or recesses. At the same level, a narrow mural passage runs round all four sides and pierces the jambs of the windows. This is unique and of the utmost interest. Explanations vary and none is dogmatic save that of MacGibbon and Ross who, without questioning its purpose of carrying the timbers of an overhanging hoarding, matter-of-factly state that "It is one of the best preserved instances of this kind of defence in Scotland".[1] They surely err in believing the wall passage to be for access to the penetrating beams. The holes do not penetrate and the passage is a mere 16 inches by 20 inches. Yet the explanation must be functional, and what is more feasible than a permanent overhanging timber gallery, very adequately served by the series of quick-access doorways or windows?

Threave is perhaps the subtlest of these great quadrangular towers. Art plays no part in its hard and unrelenting mass. There are no minor works, no small-scale effects, no romantic charm. But it has character, perhaps not unlike that of its builder, the Earl Archibald, nicknamed "The Grim" "because of his terrible countenance in warfare", who died in it on Christmas Eve 1400. Its towering eminence is emphasised by its isolated island setting in flat country, out of sight of building, and by the contrast of an encircling curtain wall of indifferent height closely set about it. Beyond this

[1] D. MacGibbon and T. Ross (1887), I.164.

rampart a ditch, once filled with water drawn from the River Dee, skirts the wall of the tower.

The curtain is not high as mediaeval curtains go and it has a most unmediaeval external face with a long sloping splay from base to parapet. Along the inner face deep splayed embrasures, waist-high above ground, converge towards narrow vertical firing slits. The height of these embrasures above ground and the modest height of the opening itself are more suitable for crouching or recumbent gunners than for kneeling or standing archers or crossbow-men. In discussing the Westgate Canterbury key-hole gun-ports of 1380, the earliest gun-ports in England, O'Neil remarks that "the size of the round hole and the level of the bed of their embrasure above floor level [show] that they were for use with the new weapon".[1] Round corner towers recall earlier mediaeval works, but the key-hole and dumb-bell gun-ports with which they are well provided in ground and upper chambers suggest a date no later than the middle or the second half of the fifteenth century.

It has been suggested that this outer defence was erected in 1513 after Sir John Dunbar fell at Flodden and his successor the fifth Lord Maxwell had been directed to repair the castle then described as "falty, ruinous and fallin down in divers partis".[2] But these gun-ports are reliable indicators of a date between about 1460, when the type is securely placed at royal Ravenscraig (Fife) and about 1500, when it appears contemporaneously with its successor the horizontal wide-mouthed port in the basement of the royal tower of Falkland.

It is probable that key-hole ports antedate 1460, if their presence in the curtain and curtain towers of Craigmillar is original, for this work is dated 1427 by a recorded but now vanished inscription upon it.[3] Unfortunately the date 1427, which would make the Craigmillar key-holes the earliest gun-ports in Scotland, cannot be accepted without reservation, as the masonry suggests they are insertions.[4] Consequently the Ravenscraig defences of 1460, by the irreproachable evidence of the Exchequer Rolls between March 1460 and June 1463[5] are unquestionably the earliest authenticated appearance of those interesting features. The parallels are purely archaeological

[1] B. H. St J. O'Neil (1954), 45, and (1960), 8. [2] W. D. Simpson (1948), 2, 4.
[3] A. Nisbet (1816), I.305.
[4] The present writer believes them to be original. The apertures are formed by large boulder-like blocks difficult to hew, and the walling is poor quality rubble. The junction is inevitably ragged. This suggests insertion, but the interiors show no disturbance and the rybats bond into the curtain.
[5] ER VII.

but the inference legitimately drawn from them is supported by contemporary events and is as feasible as those enlisted in support of post-Flodden anxieties.

In 1454 the Douglases, pre-eminent among the baronial faction, were known to be fortifying the northern castles of Lochindorb and Darnaway, and Strathaven, Douglas, Abercorn and Threave in the south.[1] Threave was the last to hold out against the king. In 1455 it fell after a protracted artillery siege in which leading roles were played by James II in person and that notable bombard "Mons Meg". The tower bears no witness to bombardment and nothing about it suggests the preparations the Black Douglas was previously known to be making. The curtain wall on the other hand affords ample evidence of damage in two round towers cast down and the gatehouse sadly wrecked. An "artillery house" was repaired in 1458. Such misfortunes could have occurred at any subsequent date in this sombre tower's eventful history, even as late as 1640, when it was garrisoned for King Charles and battered by Covenanters and after a resistance of thirteen weeks fell and was slighted. Yet the explicit instructions of the local war committee regarding the slighting, to the "Lord of Balmaghie", whose task it was to be, make no mention of the outworks but only the tower. It is an hypothesis as reasonable as any other that this curtain represents the measures the Douglas took to strengthen his position in the prevailing atmosphere of royal suspicion in 1454. The archaeology of the gun-ports agrees with this. If the conclusion is correct then the curtain wall of Threave is, with the possible exception of Craigmillar, the earliest artillery fortification in Scotland. And if Craigmillar is earlier, Threave is a better and a more accomplished work.

The L-plan tower-house of about 1374 which is the nucleus of Craigmillar Castle continued in use as the principal building of an expanding complex of houses built around and against it in the fifteenth and sixteenth centuries. It survives to-day, substantially complete, when these additions are much ruined shells. The tower has two stone vaults. The first-floor hall has a fine hooded fireplace whose lintel is supported at each end upon boldly-modelled twin shafts with moulded capitals and bases of late fourteenth-century quasi-ecclesiastical type not unlike those which enhance the fireplace in the lord's hall at Doune. They anticipate the most characteristic internal feature of note in the next century. The fireplace occupies

[1] Annie I. Dunlop (1950), 156.

the traditional place discussed above, i.e. in the gable opposite the end of the hall which contains the entrance, and it is flanked by two large side windows with stone benches in their embrasures. There are no other windows, save a large one, similar to them, in the opposite gable. The tower has survived almost without alteration save that the original wheel stair in the jamb was superseded in the sixteenth century by a more ample turnpike built between the tower and an additional range of that date.

Convenience achieved at the cost of some security, evidently no longer a matter of over-riding anxiety, is well illustrated here. The original entrance was skilfully contrived in the re-entrant angle formed by the projection of the jamb on the south side of the main block. Along this side the tower straddles irregularities in the rocky outcrop upon which it is situated and which falls abruptly from its walls. Thus placed, the entrance was held in reserve and amply protected by the hazards of a circuitous approach, the cover of two walls, and a natural pitfall before it, as well as by ingenuities within, notably an internal window and timber deck covering the vestibule. Such intruders as might have passed the outside hazards successfully and were halted by the closed doors at the bottom of the stair were vulnerable still. The original stair remained in use, but the new stair permitted easy access from new apartments to old after the main walling of the tower had been breached where necessary on each floor.

Precisely the same adjustment was effected at Castle Campbell (Clackmannanshire)[1] where an additional late sixteenth-century range was erected against an earlier tower-house. This also continued to function very effectively and received a fine ribbed barrel-vault in its top storey, similar to one in the basement of the sixteenth-century range. It is appropriate to mention here that Castle Campbell also received a later curtain, which is the closest parallel to that of 1427 at Craigmillar in walling, corbelling, machicolations and slenderness of its round corner tower.

Ribbed vaults are uncommon in tower-houses, and where they occur they are of later date. They have no central pier but spring from corbels in the side walls. In this respect Dundonald Castle (Ayrshire) is exceptional for the fourteenth century, which enhances the merit and interest that this castle otherwise possesses. It was a royal castle, a favourite residence of Robert II, who founded it after

[1] S. H. Cruden (1953).

his accession in 1350 and "of a schort seknes" died in it in 1390. He reconstructed an older keep-gatehouse of the Criccieth model,[1] which had two half-round towers projecting beyond the frontal mass of the gate-house to flank a long entrance passage through its centre at ground level. This structure, probably that Dundonald known to have been recovered from the English with another in Carrick by Bruce and Angus Lord of the Isles, a loyal follower, was partly demolished in action or in accordance with Bruce's "scorched-earth" policy. Little can be said about the keep-gatehouse, for when Robert II reconstructed it he built upon its masonry, used much of the old stone, and radically altered the whole conception. He turned the old gatehouse into the new model tower-house by building along the original front wall and across the stumps of the round towers,[2] closed up the central entrance between them, ignored the side walls which flanked the passage inside (probably demolished them, for nothing remains), and turned his accommodation the other way round in proper tower-house style by erecting two superimposed lofty pointed barrel-vaults on the long axis of the building.

So, as a powerful Douglas earl built himself a tower-house, a king at the same time, with the substantial ruins of a keep-gatehouse to inspire him to do otherwise, did likewise nevertheless. He built himself a tower-house, upon a defensible site which had too much to commend it to be ignored, as a compact residence, with a small elevated entrance admitting directly into private apartments instead of a thoroughfare into an open yard. The main entrance to the yard, being closed, was transferred to the enclosure wall in repetition of a process occurring elsewhere in consequence of the failure of the keep-gatehouse to combine effectively the functions of residence and stronghold.[3] The lower vault was divided into two storeys in the usual way by a timber floor; the upper vault, some 25 feet high to the apex of its pointed arch, was the great hall, taking the full height of the vault. This hall is unusually grand. The vault was enriched with ribs. They spring from heavily moulded corbels in the side walls and mark the vault into two wide bays, with a third, a segmental smaller unribbed vault, at one end. Linking the corbels are wall ribs, kept low to avoid the overhang of the vault. The ribs are primarily decorative, as they are in a small adjoining chamber.

[1] For Criccieth see B. H. St J. O'Neil (1944), 1-51.

[2] The thirteenth-century curtain towers of Dirleton were also overbuilt by a hall in the fifteenth century.

[3] See above, p. 88.

Structurally the vault had no need of them. Aesthetically it had, for a barrel-vault is a dull affair. This practice is observed in collegiate churches of the fifteenth century[1] during the barrel-vaulted revival period in ecclesiastical architecture, but it is uncommon to find it in castellated work.

The fact that it is decorative adds to its interest just because it is a decorative and not a structural feature. It is a testimony of taste. For the hall of Dundonald to be under the arch of the barrel-vault would in itself be a sufficiently interesting although not important departure from custom, for the aesthetic value of a vault was not generally recognised. Much is seen to-day that was never meant to be seen and was probably unsuspected by the occupants. The splendid high vaults with the hooded fireplace dominating one end of them rightly arouses the admiration of the visitor, e.g. in Craigmillar. But the tell-tale row of corbels, the scarcement, or the row of deep square holes in the side walls half-way up indicate, unhappily, the presence of a flat timber ceiling originally there. There are exceptions—Borthwick of 1430 is notable—but usually the solar above the hall enjoyed the arch of the vault, and this was of secondary importance to the hall below, which did not.

The rejection of the vault as an aesthetic feature is due to the underlying preoccupation with massive security against fire as well as human misadventures. When in the late fifteenth and sixteenth centuries there was no longer need to adhere strictly to the restrictions on technique imposed by economic necessity and when it became possible again to build with an eye to effect as well as function, gothic ribbed vaults re-occur, albeit they never became characteristic features of tower-houses. They are to be found in Auchindoun (Banffshire), a late fifteenth-century L-plan tower attributed to Thomas Cochrane Earl of Mar, in Balbegno (Kincardineshire) with painted plaster severies of 1569, and in the associated castles Towie Barclay and Delgaty (Aberdeenshire) of the 1570's. But to those who dwelt in the structural barrel-vaults which are characteristic of the fourteenth and fifteenth century the essentially cellular nature of the structure would be no more suspected than is the steel-frame by office-workers and flat-dwellers to-day.

The barrel-vaulted main vessel is not characteristic of the Norman keep whose interiors were spanned by massive timber beams bearing

[1] e.g. Seton (East Lothian) where decorative ribs are applied over the chancel end of a barrel-vaulted choir to distinguish this part. S. H. Cruden (1956), 420.

upon end corbels and centre piers. These could quite easily have been used in Scotland had the tower-house builders been so minded. On the other hand the contrast of the tower-houses with the great enclosure castles they succeeded is even more remarkable. Had Archibald the Grim or Robert II lived sixty years earlier than they did they would assuredly not have built for themselves a tower and nothing but a tower to live in, nor would the Douglases at Hermitage have converted the familiar English-style hall-house of the Dacres into a tower-house as they did about the same time. A tower they all would certainly have had, to proclaim their feudal pride and power, and as a "mark of jurisdiction",[1] but there would be more of consequence besides. Buildings such as those described, and such as Dunottar, most probably the "castle or fortalice" erected by Sir William Keith Great Marischal of Scotland at the end of the fourteenth century, set a standard of judgment of the secular architecture of the fourteenth century which is the more valuable in that it derives from the best work.

Other types of castle are remarkably scarce for this period. In fact, only two stone castles, with the excavated evidence of another (there is no evidence of timber buildings) comprise another type of fortified dwelling, and they are but variations of the standard pattern. They possess the tendency to height, combined with an unorthodox expansion in floor plan. These exceptional works are Hermitage (Roxburghshire)[2] and Crookston (Renfrewshire).[3]

The original manor-house of the Dacres at Hermitage, erected between 1358 and 1365 in the English style with a typical parallel at Danby in the North Riding of Yorkshire, had two blocks flanking a small open court. This was converted or absorbed into a large tower-house in the current Scottish manner towards the end of the century. By about 1400 projecting square towers were added to the corners of this mass to give the building the striking appearance it retains to this day (pl. 17). The towers are exceedingly close together and linked by an overhanging parapet which without interruption continues across the deep recess between them. The elevations of each side are not unlike the west elevation of Borthwick of thirty years

[1] *Jus Feudale*, as quoted by W. M. Mackenzie (1927), 180: "Besides the power of the sword a baron is wont to have the right of instituting markets and also of (possessing) a turreted tower, that these may be marks of jurisdiction."

[2] W. D. Simpson (1957); RCAMS XIV (1956), 75-85.

[3] W. D. Simpson (1953*b*), 1-14; G. P. H. Watson (1949).

later, and indeed Borthwick and Hermitage are to be numbered among the most imposing late mediaeval castles in the British Isles. The elevations of Hermitage adventitiously anticipate Borthwick, but the plan resembles that of Crookston with its central block and four corner towers.

There is no planning in Crookston's central block. The chambers lie one upon the other in characteristic tower-house style. The basement is a stone barrel-vault amply reinforced by broad transverse arches reminiscent of the mid-thirteenth-century undercroft of Yester. The square tower at each corner gives Crookston a unique place in the history of Scottish castellated architecture. They are in no way comparable to the projecting towers of the Earl's Palace at Birsay in Orkney, or Barnes in East Lothian, for there they are wide-spread and mark the angles of long and narrow courtyard ranges. At Crookston they are close-set and rise high and compact with the tower-house they contain. For all their towering eminence and the great thickness of their walling there is more of the manor than the castle in this work. The central block is innocent of defensive loops, and what is more surprising so are the towers. Had aggressive measures of defence been seriously considered towers would surely have been more earnestly exploited. Thirteenth-century notions of enfilading fire were altogether less casual. At Dirleton, for example, an arrow-slit covers a projecting wall no more than about 6 feet distant. The wall faces of Crookston could have been effectively protected and the ground between the towers rendered untenable by fire from loops alone, but such defensive apparatus as the castle relied upon in time of need must have been upon the wall-head, now unfortunately gone.

Four substantial corner towers about a block which is itself towerlike in dimensions are paralleled among buildings surviving in height only at Hermitage, where they are partly absorbed in later additions. Excavated ruins of the royal castle of Kindrochit at Braemar (Aberdeenshire)[1] afford a closer parallel. Kindrochit is an early authenticated example of a fortified manor. It was a favourite hunting-lodge of Robert II between 1371 and 1388, the mediaeval Balmoral in fact. In 1390 Sir Malcolm Drummond, husband of the Countess of Mar, received royal licence to erect a tower at Kindrochit, which he proceeded to do, thrusting his great new tower-house, fifth largest plain oblong tower in Scotland, into

[1] W. D. Simpson (1949), 42-4.

the walls of an older building doubtless partly demolished before or at the commencement of the new work. The older building, inferentially that of Robert II, contained a great hall over a basement. At all four corners there were square towers, but nothing of this work exists in sufficient height to permit more than a record of its unusual plan.

Mr Geoffrey Webb, in referring to the ambiguous quasi-military architecture of the later thirteenth and fourteenth centuries in England observes that Wardour Castle is one of the most remarkable surviving examples.[1] Not only are his general observations relevant to Crookston, but Wardour is a particularly apt illustration. Its elevation bears a strong resemblance to Crookston in its square corner towers and comparatively short extent of tower-house elevation between them. And furthermore its wall-head has corbelled angle roundels. Bishop Burnell's palace of Acton Burnell is a late thirteenth-century example of the same notion, dignity and strength without aggression.[2]

One important tower recalls the Norman keep. The recollection is suitable, for it stands upon a motte hill. This is the castle of Duffus (Moray) which figures in the mid-twelfth century. David I resided in it in 1151 when visiting the work in progress at Kinloss Abbey which he founded. The motte hill, ditch and extensive outer bailey of this twelfth-century castle survive to-day. Upon the motte hill is the stone castle which recalls a keep. It is a rectangular stone tower. The walls rise from a double splayed ashlar plinth. The door and window openings have unusually broad chamfered surrounds. A series of ground-floor windows is closely paralleled at nearby Rait Castle of the late thirteenth or early fourteenth century. There are no vaults. There were three floors of timber with a 36-foot span and a row of central piers, all now vanished. The entrance is in the middle of the long wall overlooking the twelfth-century ditch and the bailey which is separated from the mount by the ditch. Off the short entrance passage a straight mural stair ascends to the first floor, as at Kinnaird, and as it does to the second floor and wall-head of Carrick. The wall on this side is thickened to contain this stair. The thickening does not extend the whole length of the wall to conform to the unbroken rectangular outline of the typical fourteenth-century tower-house, but returns to meet the wall face of the tower some 10 feet or so from either end. It is a

[1] G. Webb (1956), 158. [2] C. A. R. Radford (1956).

lengthy but moderate projection, made to take the stair and a small guardroom on the side of the entrance passage opposite the foot of the stair. From the guardroom a mural passage in the true thickness of the wall continues to its end. On the first floor it turns the corner and proceeds along the length of the adjacent wall which advances forward again in another large buttress-like projection.

The stair, not being in the true thickness of the wall, has some analogy to the outside stair rising up the exterior face of a Norman keep. The projection which contains it is accordingly analogous to the fore-building of a keep. The massive timber floor beams with their centre row of supporting piers dividing the room into two aisles is quite in the Norman keep tradition and unparalleled in Scottish tower-house architecture, mid-supports, as has been observed in connection with vaulted chambers in tower-houses, being almost wholly lacking. In the great donjon of Bothwell there is a central pier of late thirteenth-century date, and in the hall-house of Tulliallan two vaulted subcrofts have central piers. There are no other instances.

Duffus is difficult to date. Because of the likeness of the windows in its ground floor to the basement windows of Rait in the same neighbourhood, the late thirteenth or early fourteenth century is indicated. This is quite consistent with the structure, its situation upon a motte hill, and the history of the site. But a grant by Edward I in 1305 to his loyal supporter, Sir Reginald le Cheyne, who possessed Duffus since the end of the thirteenth century, of two hundred oak trees from the royal forests of Darnaway and Longmorn "to build his manor of Dufhous" suggests a castle of wood in the early fourteenth century. This is no more than a suggestion. It does not rule out the existing structure as being of this date. Timber manor and stone castle could well exist together, and it is not improbable that the damage Sir Reginald had suffered in the Moray rebellion against the English, and for which he was being compensated, was the burning of a manor and not the timber superstructure of a motte-castle. This is conjecture, however. Interesting speculation though it may be, the date of Duffus cannot exactly be determined; but in the fourteenth century it must be, and in the early years it should be.

Equally problematical is the date of the ruined fragment of the tower-house of Dunnideer (Aberdeenshire)[1] which is closely sur-

[1] W. D. Simpson (1935), 460-71.

rounded by the rampart of an Early Iron Age "vitrified fort", and somewhat more distantly by an earlier rampart and ditch of unknown but probably prehistoric date. The antiquity of the site, a prominent hill likely to attract attention, is thus archaeologically verified. The castle has been a simple rectangular tower, apparently unvaulted (which is indicative of early date), and has two narrow slit-windows in the basement. One gable standing high has a breached and broken lancet window. The masonry is of that rubble brought to frequent level courses by pinnings which is found at Lochindorb, Moulin, Coull, Balvenie and other thirteenth- and early fourteenth-century works to such an extent as to be considered a datable feature. If this ruin is indeed that of the "Castle of Dunidor" of 1260, referred to in the Chartulary of Lindores Abbey, it is of uncommon interest as the earliest authenticated tower-house in Scotland, after Cubbie Roo's of the mid-twelfth century. And as with the Orcadian castle there is nothing about the ruin of Dunnideer which is inconsistent with this date and no rival candidate on the site or near it.

FIFTEENTH CENTURY

The successive reigns of the first five Jameses (1406-1542) comprise for MacGibbon and Ross a single architectural period distinguished by castles erected on a courtyard plan, i.e. by an arrangement of buildings about an open court. Notable examples cited are the castles of Doune, Edinburgh and Stirling, and the palaces of Linlithgow and Falkland.[1] Literally, this is true enough. These edifices distinguish the period. But they do not characterise it. Nor do they anticipate another. They are exceptional. Dynastically convenient, the classification is architecturally misleading. Doune, in existence before 1400, comes at the beginning of this long period. It is the last of the old and obsolete castles of enceinte, not the first of a new courtyard type. The royal works reached their courtyard form not by design but by long and fortuitous development, particularly active in the sixteenth century. Even were the classification architecturally justified by castles erected according to an original courtyard conception, the examples cited leave the whole of the fifteenth century unaccounted for.

"Palatial" castles comprise another type alleged to characterise the fifteenth century.[2] Castles built palace-wise there were, but the

[1] D. MacGibbon and T. Ross (1887) I.222ff; (1889) III.22ff.
[2] W. M. Mackenzie (1927), 135ff.

outstanding examples of Rait, Morton and Tulliallan belong not to the fifteenth century but to the thirteenth and fourteenth centuries. To this number of earlier "palatial" castles, or hall-houses as we prefer to call them to point the contrast with the tower-houses, may be added Skipness, Craigie, Hestan and Kindrochit, their distant relations Hermitage and Crookston, and the more problematical oblong tower of Carrick which successfully combines the elements of both hall and tower, but which, having been drastically altered at an early date and comprehensively preserved at a late one, carries a reservation upon the fourteenth-century date one is inclined to attribute to its origin by the window arches and mouldings.

While the hall-house continued into the fifteenth century and beyond, e.g. Huntly (*c.* 1452) which was rebuilt on the same lines a hundred years later, the tower-house prevailed in no uncertain manner through the fifteenth century. There was neither "a radical change in the architectural conception of a castle" nor a "cardinal departure in castle-building".[1] That thesis depends much upon a misdating of the important earlier examples of recognised hall-houses and an oversight in the interpretation of Craigie. As is described above, this extremely interesting ruin has a low crenellated wall-head, unquestionably of a hall and not a tower, immured in a late fifteenth-century rib-vaulted hall erected upon it.

By the closing years of the fifteenth century, when the contemporary and similar royal towers of Holyroodhouse and Falkland were begun by James IV,[2] the simple tower-house as a progressive architectural form had run its logical course. With Borthwick (1430) and Elphinstone and Comlongon of a few years later, the century may justly be termed that of the classic tower-house. This classic quality is the fifteenth-century condition and the justification for distinguishing that century from the preceding. The late sixteenth-century and early seventeenth-century condition follows illogical treatment and is that of the tower-house in its romantic form.

Many existing tower-houses were added to during the fifteenth century and continuing in use became the nucleus of a more expansive establishment ranged round a courtyard. Craigmillar, Castle Campbell and Crichton (fig. 12) are first-rate examples; but such works do not permit classification because the extensions are of expediency and are not indicative of a real change in architectural thought. The "courtyard plan" classification is inadmissible until

[1] W. M. Mackenzie (1927), 149, 142. [2] But see p. 149.

Plate 17

above Threave, Kirkcudbrightshire, late fourteenth century

below Hermitage, Roxburghshire, fourteenth to sixteenth centuries

Plate 19 Carrick, Loch Goil, Argyll, late-fourteenth century

Elphinstone, East Lothian, *c.* 1440

Plate 20

Borthwick, Midlothian, 1430

there are buildings erected according to its principles from the outset. To be valid it must be preconceived, not adventitious.

Ample documentary evidence relating to surviving buildings and the existence of several exceptionally notable works add to the interest of the period. We see a reliable and comprehensive picture of its achievements, can date typical buildings with precision and can appreciate the development of the tower-house to its logical con-

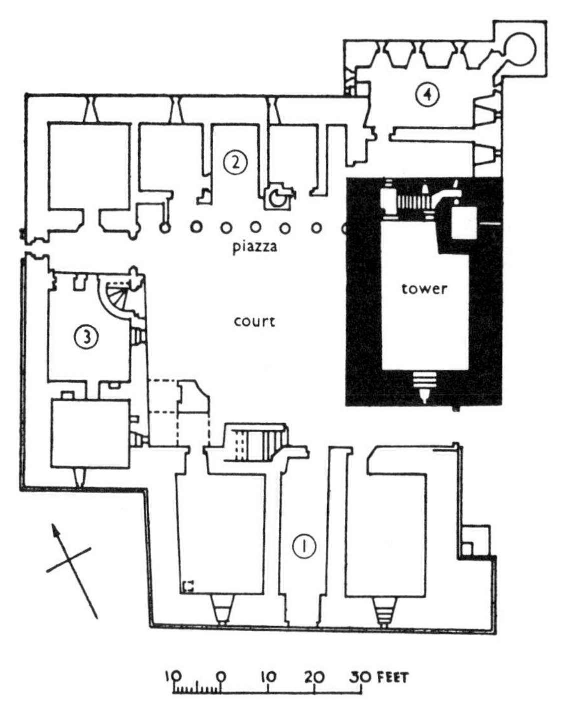

FIG. 12. Crichton, tower-house ground floor and later ranges added in the order 1, 2, 3, 4

clusion. Architectural details assist in the close dating suggested by charter evidence and licences to crenellate. They appear mainly in minor interior effects. Externally, window and door mouldings faithfully adhere to the simple chamfer, although a trefoiled window or moulded surround for a plaque or combination of plaques bearing arms over a doorway contribute notes of interest to the continuing austerity of the elevations. Boldly oversailing machicolated parapets and open rounds overhanging all corners are commonplace.

The interiors proclaim growing desires for decorative details and ampler means of gratifying them. The ostentation of dress, customs and behaviour which was characteristic of the age was none the less evident for Scotland's being "at the end of the earth and far distant from the Roman Court".[1] "The Scottish nobles of the fourteenth to the sixteenth century were probably the most turbulent, rapacious and ignorant in Europe."[2] From the great baronial households came men like William, sixth Earl of Douglas, who was executed in 1440 at the age of 18. He was convoyed with a thousand and sometimes two thousand horsemen, amongst whom he maintained a great company of thieves and murderers to impress upon the lieges a true sense of his power.[3] His kinsman and namesake, murdered by James II in Stirling Castle in 1452, was in Rome in 1450 with a great and honourable retinue and bore himself nobly everywhere in clothing, expenditure and all his actions, "wherefore he was commended by the Sovereign Pontiff above all pilgrims".[4] Kindred spirits from Scottish tower-houses comprised that corps d'élite, the Scots Guards, the Compagnie or Guarde Écossaise which wore the Scottish colours, "were more gorgeously clad than the rest" and were a credit to Charles VII as the senior company of his Life Guards after their reconstitution in 1445.

These mid-fifteenth-century demonstrations of baronial display—the siege of Threave is another example—are reflected in church and castellated architecture. To Borthwick (Midlothian), a romanesque church with an apsidal end, an aisle was erected in typical fifteenth-century barrel-vaulted form by Lord Borthwick whose painted effigy in full knightly accoutrements it still contains. In the adjacent tower-house and in nearby Elphinstone Tower (East Lothian) ambitious planning is successfully attempted for the first time and in most new tower-houses a heightened interest and expenditure in design and decoration is apparent. According to the weight of the purse a new effort is made to make the most of the limited possibilities for display and artistry afforded by an architecture still dominated by the tower idea. Features capable of independent treatment receive attention they have lacked for 150 years. The revival of this long-suppressed mediaeval partiality is expressed in fireplaces, aumbries, buffets, panel surrounds and so forth, which were supported, flanked, embellished and promoted from the merely utilitarian by borrowings from contemporary eccle-

[1] From a petition for an indulgence for Glasgow Cathedral 11 January 1449, quoted by Annie I. Dunlop (1950), 363, with references.
[2] J. Buchan (1928), 65.
[3] Lindsay of Pitscottie, 1.25.
[4] Annie I. Dunlop (1950), 364, with references.

siastical architecture. Clustered shafts support fireplace lintels, and buttresses flank aumbries with miniature vaulting beneath crocketted ogee arches. Heraldry, popular in contemporary ecclesiastical work on vault bosses and buttresses, is exploited over entrance doorways and on fireplace lintels. Blazoned in heraldic colour, these notes of interest were complementary to the sculptured decoration and painting of the wall and vault surfaces also indulged in at this time. Craigmillar has a stone shield carved on the wall beside the fireplace, but only at Dundonald is heraldry really conspicuous in the secular architecture of the fourteenth century, with a series of five heater shields on the outside face of the west elevation. Liberal painting of the ribbed vault of the great hall is likely.[1]

Concurrently with these improvements in incidental details goes a real improvement of the internal arrangements. Although strictly confined to the limitations of the prescription to build vertically, the builder becomes architect and plans his accommodation with much imagination and skill. Mural chambers, passages and wheel stairs within the main walling are multiplied, windows tend to be larger, more numerous and to have wider embrasures. An oratory is fashioned in a window embrasure at Borthwick, following Doune, and at Affleck later in the century another is richly worked as a small corner chamber hard against the fireplace in the hall. It opens through an unusually large arched opening. This was never closed, unless perhaps by curtains, and the oratory was separated from the hall only by a dwarf screen of wood, and perhaps hangings.

The epitome of this movement is Borthwick (pl. 20; fig. 13) a structure of surpassing interest and immense grandeur. It is beautifully constructed in large close-jointed ashlars and is one of the finest late mediaeval castles in Britain. By a happy concurrence of circumstances it is not only that but it is also securely dated, complete, unaltered, not added to (there has been no need) and, save for a brief period, continuously occupied to the present day. The licence "to construct a castle . . . and to erect and fortify the same" was granted to Sir William Borthwick, afterwards Lord Borthwick, by James I in 1430. The site chosen, commonly called the Mote of Lochorwart, was of ancient strength.

The building consists of a long rectangular tower with two wings

[1] The earliest collection of emblazoned Scottish coats of arms known to be extant is the *Armorial de Gelre*, a manuscript in the Bibliothèque Royale at Brussels. The 42 Scottish coats in the manuscript appear to have been emblazoned between the years 1370 and 1388, contemporary with Dundonald. Cf. A. H. Dunbar (1899), 165.

or jambs advancing boldly from either end of the same side. Each is exceptionally large and they dwarf the space between them even more than do the corner towers of Hermitage and Crookston. The basement cellars are barrel-vaulted. Their walls are 12 to 14 feet thick and without apertures save for one narrow slit in each chamber, high up, for light and ventilation, and a ground-floor doorway. The summit carries an oversailing machicolated parapet swelling out in open rounds over the corners. This cresting does not carry across the space between the wings, as it does at Hermitage, but logically follows the course of the walls beneath, doubling back with them to the main block. It is now absent along the long east side, which has neither wings nor other projections, having been damaged by Cromwellian artillery and thereafter rebuilt flush with the wall-face.

The castle stands within an enclosure wall which has wide-mouthed gun-ports which cannot be earlier than about 1500, a gatehouse with portcullis and drawbridge, corner towers and a ditch. The tower itself has no gun-ports or firing loops of any kind. Its whole defensive apparatus was on the wall-head. Security was further assured by an outer defence, which is embodied in the later loop-holed wall, the massive walls with minimal apertures, and the skilful placing of the outside entrances and internal stairs.

The main entrance is on the first floor, straight through the north gable-end of the main block. It is not covered by a projecting wing but only by a bretasche above it, and is reached from the gatehouse only by a circuitous approach round two sides of the tower. Access to this entrance was by a high bridge from the curtain as at Threave. The entrance passage has a guardroom opening off one side. The basement is entered separately at ground level and was thus more vulnerable, but the wheel stair at the doorway which affords communication between basement and first floor emerges through the centre of the first-floor guardroom; thus the intruder was trapped.

The hall occupies the whole of the first floor of the main block. It is covered by the high vault along its long axis. As the two projecting wings confront the outer gate, the main block containing the hall and principal apartments occupies the rear of the composition and is exposed to the least vulnerable part of the site, held in reserve as it were, just as the great hall of Kildrummy was withdrawn from the gatehouse. The long back wall of the hall has two windows. These are its only accessible windows. They have deep arched tunnel-like embrasures, unnecessarily high for the windows they contain but in scale with the overwhelming size of the vault. A large and handsome hooded fireplace, likewise in scale with its environment, occupies the end wall opposite the entrance and effectively dominates the scene, attracting and holding the attention from all angles. It is flanked by a window on either side. Each is high up and has a long stepped cill. The deep moulded lintel is supported upon massive clustered shafts with bell-bases and capitals enriched with foliage. A richly sculptured band of bulky leaf-and-branch

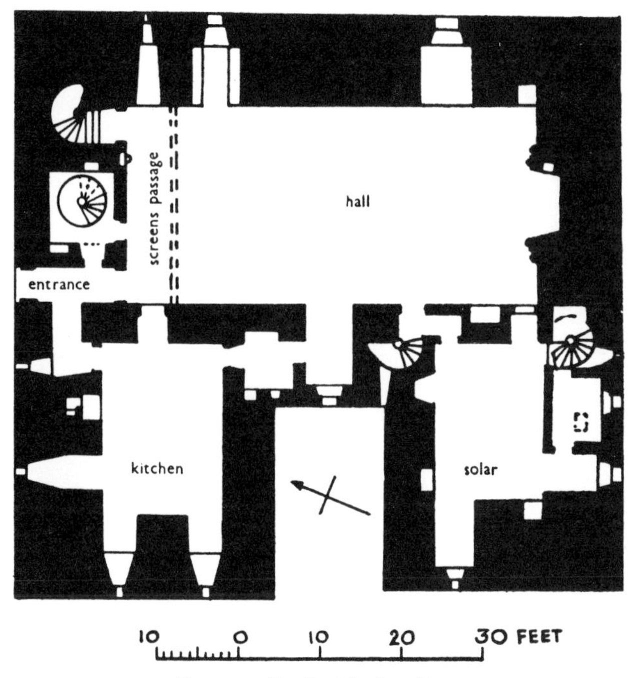

FIG. 13. Borthwick, first floor

foliage spreads along a projecting cornice course of the lintel. In the side wall close by the fireplace there is a buffet recess. It has moulded jambs and a cusped flat arch beneath an ogee containing-arch with foliaceous crockets.

Wall-cupboards or aumbries, for the safe-keeping of valuables or as buffets for the display or stacking of plate, pewter, pottery, treen and so on, are frequently to be found conveniently near fireplaces at the dais end of a hall where the high table was. In the near-contemporary Comlongon and Balvaird there are extremely handsome examples similarly enhanced by an architectural setting, that in Balvaird being a particularly close parallel. Aumbries occur elsewhere, in main walling, in window embrasures, and as buffets in the screens passage (pl. 21). A check or rebate on the outside indicates a closing wooden door. With their enrichment gilded and coloured, and little shields such as the Borthwick buffet has, emblazoned in heraldic tinctures, they must have presented bright and interesting notes of coloured sculpture and an attractive setting for the wares they contained.

The Borthwick vault was plastered and painted with allegorical scenes and motifs. The inscriptions "ye tempil of honour" and "ye tempil of religion" have now almost totally disappeared. Colour was all about one in a mediaeval household, and the mural cupboard, with the full fifteenth-century treatment of architectural embellishment, remains one of the most conspicuous features in a baronial hall whose purely decorative appurtenances, the arras, woodwork, painter plaster and so forth, have all entirely vanished with the wooden cupboards or buffets of which it is but a more durable example. The editor of the Accounts of the Lord High Treasurer draws attention to the importance and splendour of cupboards and to the frequent references in the Accounts of the "tursing" or carriage of the cupboard of plate in connection with the king's movements from one royal residence to another.[1] And it is appropriate to mention here that not only cupboards of plate but most other plenishings, including window frames and glass, travelled with their owners for use in different residences.

The great wings at Borthwick are integrated with the hall. They are *en suite* with it, that by the doorway being kitchens, that opening off the fireplace end being a private chamber or solar. The kitchen has an immense fireplace lit by no less than three narrow windows. To-day it enters directly into the hall, originally into a screens passage where the outer doorway also entered. In what was the screens passage a decorative stone niche and wash-hand basin imitates an ecclesiastical piscina, with its bowl corbelled from the wall-face. It is surmounted by an overhanging canopy with miniature ribbed vaulting on its underside and the front is sculptured in a series of decorated ogee arches with shields in their spandrels, doubtless once blazoned. This fine example of fifteenth-century design and craftsmanship echoes the splendour of the fireplace and buffet at the other end of the hall. It has a French ecclesiastical parallel in

[1] ALTH I.cci.

a contemporary piscina in the church of Semur-en-Auxois which is illustrated by Viollet-le-Duc.[1] Over the screens would be a trumpet gallery, lit by an existing window high up in the wall. The full arrangement of the mediaeval hall is here displayed unambiguously and all on the one level.

Adjoining the solar at the fireplace end of the hall is a garderobe chamber of unusual type, as advanced in its way as the rest of this remarkable structure is in other ways. The flue, instead of discharging into or upon the ground outside, had, because of the near proximity of a well, a system of movable containers. Those which were used in the garderobe chamber above were lowered and borne away through an aperture in the ceiling made for the purpose. Few sanitary appliances were made like this. The "grund-wa'-stane", or ground-wall-stone, which the treacherous Jock removed to introduce fire to Corgarff,[2] was the usual fitting in garderobe flues within the thickness of a wall and occurred as late as the seventeenth century at Castle Leod (Ross-shire). It blocked the chute at its exit and upon removal gave access for the cleaning of its pit. In the early fifteenth-century latrine tower in the south curtain of Bothwell the exit, rebated for the stone, is preserved. At Carrick there are two perfect pairs of garderobes with ground-level exits of unusual size and careful workmanship. Although the walling is rubble these are worked in dressed ashlar. They are of doorway dimensions, have pointed arches, and are checked for doors on the outside. Only the steeply sloping face of the chute which discharged over the threshold upon the rock outside dispels the impression of their being doorways. Balvaird, another superior work, had its garderobes so arranged that all the flues were gathered into one vent. The soil fell into a small chamber in the ground floor and to this there was access by the "ground-wall-stone".

Over the hall of Borthwick are three floors, each within a rounded barrel-vault. They do not run well with the upper levels of the wings. This was a special success reserved for the first-floor suite. But the whole building is a *tour de force*. An oratory with piscina and aumbry is contrived in a window embrasure on the second floor. Two rooms, one upon the other, have a long sloping end wall, which is a chimney flue climbing its long way to the vertical, two storeys above. Over the first floor the wings were designed as bedrooms

[1] E. Viollet-le-Duc (1879*b*), VII. 197.
[2] The Ballad of Edom O'Gordon, for which see F. J. Child (1898), III.423-38.

and as separate quarters for servants, with suitably disposed stairs, straight and spiral, in the thicknesses of the walls, an ingenious system, affording privacy as well as security. It requires, incidentally, much local knowledge, such as no intruder or stranger could have. Once committed to a wheel stair in Borthwick the wanderer is likely to be discharged far past his objective, whose correct access may for long remain an exhausting mystery.

This complication of stairs, both private and public, serves the separate needs of the three distinct blocks which comprise the castle and connects one with another. At Elphinstone (pl. 20; fig. 14) there are no additional wings for extra accommodation, either for stairs or for apartments. This tower-house is rectangular without projections of any kind. The principal apartments are one upon another, five storeys in all. They consist of a barrel-vaulted basement with a timber floor dividing it into two storeys, a vaulted hall (not divided) and two unvaulted storeys above that. All this is contained by the four walls 9 feet thick. Above this level there is an unprecedented borrowing of space from them. Stairs and mural chambers are extraordinarily numerous. Void prevails over solid. The thick-wall construction becomes hollow-wall or cellular, and the solid weight of masonry in the haunches of the vaults is burrowed into for entre-sol floors. Even the flue of the great fireplace in the hall contains a little chamber with a window overlooking the hall, opening off a private suite in the thickness of the north-west corner of the tower. This was served only by a private wheel stair from the hall, going no further. The window, being large, was no mere "spy-hole" but an observation post for the owner. A spy-hole of small size does, however, open into the fireplace itself from a wheel stair in the adjoining corner. Walls had ears in Elphinstone—and in Affleck and other tower-houses also, to such number that those little openings were colloquially called "luggies".[1] A series of five carved heraldic shields over the hall fireplace and a painted shield on the soffit of a mural closet date the tower to about 1440.

A tower-house may not have been designed to resist a formal siege nor to function as a *place d'armes*, but it had not a few canny measures of internal security such as these luggies. Interrupted stairs were more obstacles than aids to progress for the uninvited. Their entrances and exits were so placed that progress interrupted was resumed only after publicly crossing the common hall, as in

[1] From the vulgar "lug", an ear.

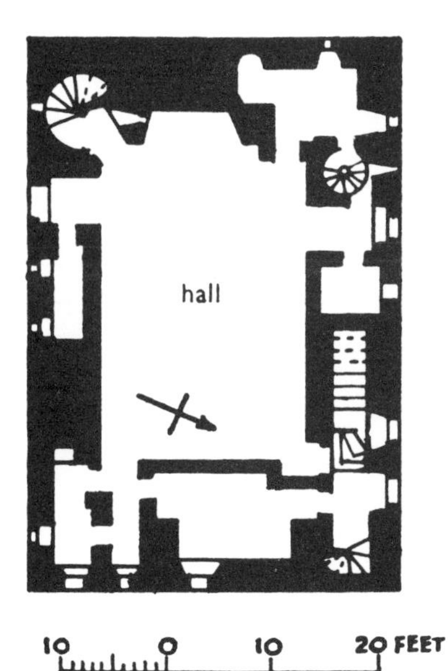

Fig. 14. Elphinstone, first floor plan, and section

Affleck for example, or more private rooms. Pit prisons, rare in England, were common conveniences. Usually worked into the haunches of the lower vault or in the thickness of a main wall they have but a slit window for air, sometimes not even that. They were commonly entered only by dropping, or being dropped, through a hatch in the floor of a mural chamber. The pit at Comlongon (Dumfriesshire) has two floors in the thickness of the main wall. There is a mural guardroom outside the upper prison, which has a small garderobe and a slit window. The lower chamber has no openings whatever save a hatch in its vaulted ceiling opening in the floor of the guardroom above.

Comlongon bears considerable resemblances to Elphinstone and is clearly of about the same date. It presents the same ineloquent exterior, reticent and massive, which characterises Elphinstone and all the towers of the fourteenth and fifteenth centuries, and which gives no hint of whether their internal arrangements are eventful or not. As in Borthwick and Elphinstone they are exceptionally so. The walls are honeycombed with mural chambers, closets and stairs, although not to the same extent. The conception of a tower consisting of distinct floors occupying all the plan area, one upon another, is maintained throughout at Comlongon, whereas at Borthwick and Elphinstone it breaks down in a three-dimensional warren unregardful of floor levels. There is a subdivided basement vault only; above it are three timbered floors. The first-floor hall has a fine fireplace with elevated flanking windows such as occur at Borthwick and Castle Campbell. Its lintel is supported by clustered shafts with sculptured bell-capitals and bases, and it has a cornice enriched with vine-leaf and stem foliage growing from the grasping mouth of a beast-head almost identically repeated on a sixteenth-century capital in the crossing of the collegiate church of Seton (East Lothian).[1] At the other end of the hall is a second large fireplace within a deep arched recess, entered directly from the corner turnpike which admits to the hall also. This recess was the kitchen, its fire the cooking fire. Now separated from the hall by a late wall, probably on the line of an original screen containing service hatches, this recess is really a built-in screens passage and kitchen combined. A similar arrangement occurs in the hall of Elphinstone, likewise at the end of the hall opposite the social end which enjoyed the common fireplace and large windows.

[1] S. H. Cruden (1956), pl. LV.

A related group of small oblong towers in the same locality of Ayrshire, the castles of Little Cumbrae, Law, Fairlie and Skelmorlie, which belong to the end of the fifteenth century or the commencement of the sixteenth century, demonstrate a similar kitchen arrangement. At Skelmorlie (*c.* 1502) the fireplace-kitchen was separated from the body of the hall not only by a partition wall but by a proper screens passage also. This was entered at one end by the principal wheel stair in one main wall and lit at the other by a window in the opposite wall. At Portincross, also on the Clyde coast of Ayrshire, a somewhat similar arrangement is to be found in a small jamb

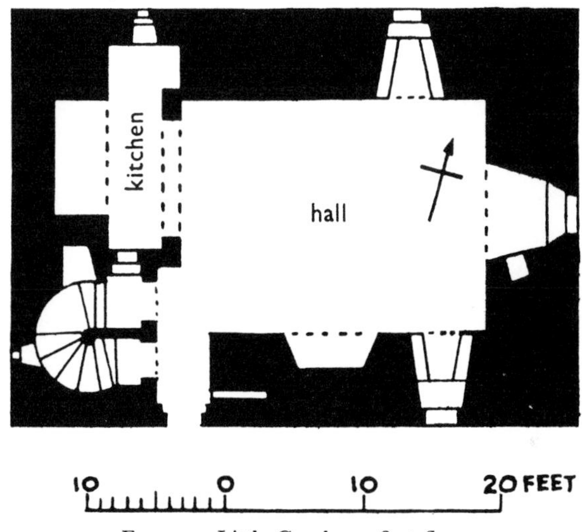

FIG. 15. Little Cumbrae, first floor

which projects from one end in line with one of the long walls of the tower. This in itself is unusual. Pre-Reformation jambs invariably project from one of the long sides, in line with a gable end. But the most surprising peculiarities of Portincross are the provision of two kitchens, one in the ground floor of the jamb, the other in the first floor, and the disposition of the stairs and doorways with which the kitchens must be considered. There are two entrances, one ground-floor, one first-floor; and two stairs, a straight stair beginning on the ground floor, a turnpike on the first. From the ground floor one could ascend to the battlements without disturbing the occupants of the hall. By the first-floor entrance and stair one must enter the hall, and ascend after crossing it by the wheel stair which succeeds the straight stair at this level.

On architectural evidence Portincross is earlier than the fifteenth-century towers discussed. By documentary evidence it is contemporary with Craigmillar (which also has a kitchen accommodated in its small tight-fitting jamb) if it is the place of signature of a charter of Robert II signed "apud Arnele" in 1372. As it was the capital messuage of the barony of Arnele there seems no reason to doubt this identification. It is of interest to observe at this early date a tower planned for domestic convenience unmindful of defensive considerations. Clearly the household was planned for servants and retainers on the ground floor with the lord's hall above. This is explained by its status and the frequent visits of royalty known to have been made to it.

These arrangements for the provision and isolation of kitchens, although less ambitious and imaginative than those of Borthwick, are a real advance in domestic amenity and indicate a purposeful attempt to provide separate kitchen accommodation when it was usual to prepare meals in the hall itself or in outbuildings, presumably of timber, which have vanished. While the examples of Elphinstone and Comlongon and of the group of related Ayrshire towers of somewhat later date in the century are about the best that could be contrived within the confines of an oblong, the earlier Portincross and Dunottar[1] solutions show what could be done by exceeding them. This suggests that the impulse which occasioned projecting wings was essentially domestic and not military. Yet the projecting square tower at Lochranza Castle (Arran) contains only small chambers, obviously defensive, with long arrow-slits of early type.

Beside the Comlongon fireplace is a wall aumbry, grooved for a shelf and flanked by the shafts with bell capitals and bases which so frequently support the heavy fireplace lintels of the period. From the capitals springs a semi-circular arch with dropped cusping and finials on either side of it. The arch is false, being wrought in two stones. They do not meet as they should, the cusping is sadly distorted, and the workmanship is much inferior to that of the Balvaird and Borthwick parallels although the design is not. Carved heraldic shields over the fireplace adorn the corbels which carry the joists of the floor above. The system of stairs is much simplified. The corner wheel opening off the main entrance passage on the ground floor rises without interruption to the battlements and admits to every floor including an entre-sol in the haunch of the vault, eventually emerging at the wall-head as a cap-house or watch-turret. Over-

[1] For Dunottar Castle see W. D. Simpson (1941), 93.

sailing open parapets upon a multiple corbel-course are crenellated along three sides but along the fourth side the parapet is roofed as a long gallery. This might not be an original finish, but it is not recent. It illustrates a late development of the wall-head, when its defensive antecedents were forgotten and it was absorbed into the roof space.

The description of these three outstanding monuments has been given in some detail because they represent the ultimate form of the classic tower-house. And they are securely dated to the second quarter of the fifteenth century. Certainly no more could be done within four walls than Elphinstone achieved, and Borthwick with its double jambs and first-floor planning is a revolutionary enterprise a hundred years ahead of its time. Smaller towers for smaller lairds show the new influences at work in minor detailing wrought with first-class skill at Dundas (West Lothian), Inverquharity and Affleck (Angus), Mearns (Renfrewshire) and Cardoness (Kirkcudbrightshire), especially notable among a host of contemporaries.

Dundas (pl. 16) is an L-plan structure of very early date to which was added, seemingly not long afterwards, yet another jamb. Such early efforts to increase accommodation without radical alteration to the basic tower idea have no military relevance. Although the Dundas jambs, by their projection from the corners of the main rectangular block, could provide a covering fire across three sides of it, they have no loops to do so. The entrance on the ground floor in the re-entrant angle is very adequately secured by a wrought iron yett before the door and by a draw-bar behind it, but the wheel stair opens vulnerably off the short entrance passage through the wall and is not withdrawn or secured against invasion. The hall fireplace has an arched opening. The arch is segmental, moulded, and springs not from the side piers but from their heavy capitals. These are tied into the wall in a manner reminiscent of the late thirteenth- and early fourteenth-century fireplaces in Conway, Beaumaris, Caernarvon, Harlech and Tulliallan.

Of existing tower-houses, Dundas has the earliest licence to crenellate. It is dated 1424 and refers specifically to this defensive feature as typical in the following terms: "... licence and special favour to build a tower or fortalice of Dundas in the manner of a castle with the kernels [*le kyrnelys*], etc. usual in a fortalice of this sort according to the manner of the Kingdom of Scotland".[1] Such

[1] RMS quoted and translated by W. M. Mackenzie (1927), 223.

references are few and afford only presumptive evidence of the date of a building. Architectural corroboration is needful (and usually forthcoming) but they are unequivocal in their general descriptions of contemporary fortifications. The Cawdor licence of 1454 for example permits the thane to erect and fortify his castle—an oblong tower which survives as the nucleus of an expansive establishment built around it in the sixteenth and seventeenth centuries—"with

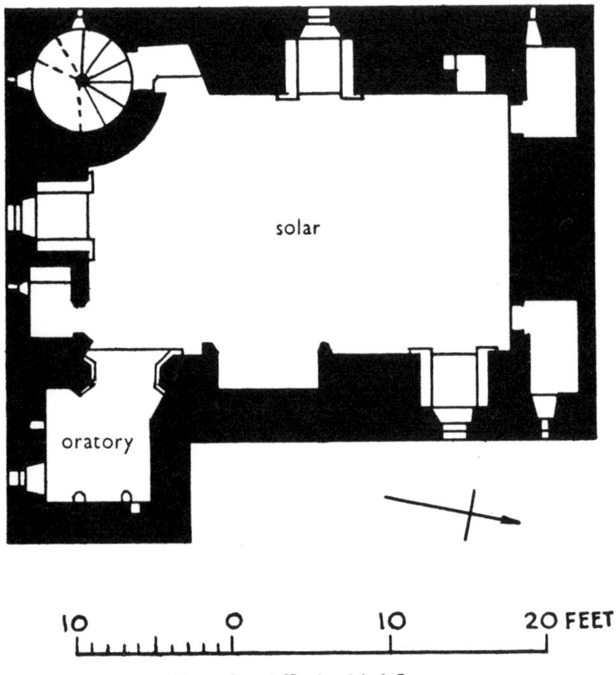

FIG. 16. Affleck, third floor

walls and ditches and equip the summit with turrets and means of defence, with warlike provisions and strengths" . . . provided that it be always open and ready for the King's use and his successors.[1]

Mearns Tower is valuable as a licence-dated smaller tower-house with an overhanging machicolated parapet on corbels of three members conformable to the date. Licence was granted by James II to Herbert Lord Maxwell in 1449 "to build a castle or fortalice on the Barony of Mearns in Renfrewshire, to surround and fortify it with walls and ditches, to strengthen by iron gates and to erect on the top of it all warlike apparatus necessary for its defence". Otherwise the

[1] *The Book of the Thanes of Cawdor*, ed. C. Innes (1859), 20.

tower had no warlike apparatus. There are no loops in the ground floor, only two extremely narrow slits for ventilation. The main entrance is at first-floor level, reached by ladder. No particular measures were taken to secure the straight stair rising from the basement to the first floor, from which a wheel stair, continuing the straight stair from the ground, rises to the parapet and serves the upper floors in passing.

This uncomplicated tower is typical of many, such as the first Burleigh (Kinross-shire), Benholm (Kincardineshire), Newark (Selkirkshire), which is called the "new Werk" in a charter of Archibald Earl of Douglas dated 1423, the first Falside (East Lothian), the first Dean Castle (Ayrshire) and so on. Affleck (pl. 15) is probably well into the second half of the century, as Cardoness is (pl. 21). Like it, it has considerable refinement in its detailing and its masonwork is first-class throughout. Even the ingoes of the window embrasures are lined with smooth ashlar although the main walling is rubble, originally rendered over with harl or plaster, as they all were, outside and in. Each of those towers has good worked detail, fireplaces with shafted jambs and moulded capitals and bases, etc, characteristic of later fifteenth-century work, and key-hole gun-ports, which we date to about 1460-1500.[1]

[1] See below, p. 216.

4

The Long Pause and the Court School

THE great tower-house achievements dramatically assert the turbulent fifteenth century and particularly the first half, to which they belong. Pre-eminent among all towers, Borthwick, Elphinstone and Comlongon were never to be surpassed in scale or strength. The immense size of Borthwick, its advanced planning, and the internal ingenuities of Elphinstone, were not repeated. But the innumerable smaller towers of later date bear ample witness to their influence and indicate an easing of domestic conditions and something like a return to prosperity which affords a revealing contrast to the political insecurity of that "obscure period of plotting and reshuffling". To contemporary patrons and masons the influence of these outstanding mid-fifteenth-century achievements lay paradoxically in their minor decorative effects which led to the revival of ornament in the domestic sphere. The times were favourable for this, for the fifteenth century was unusually rich in ecclesiastical new work, mostly in secular collegiate foundations. But the prescription for vertical building to which patron and mason clung tenaciously for so long precluded significant architectural advances. By the end of the fifteenth century supply satisfied demands. For the gentry who had need to consider defensive measures in their house-building there was an abundance of strong and adequate towers, well-constructed and resistant to accidental destruction by fire as well as deliberate damage by force. The baronial conflict, at its height in mid-century, petered out in the decline of the Douglas power, after whose fall in 1455 the barons rebelled not in their own name and interest but in the name and cause of good government and monarchy.

From 1480 or thereabouts until after the Scottish Reformation of 1560 few tower-houses of consequence were built. The impetus to building flagged. It died with the mediaeval chivalry of Scotland

Dirleton, East Lothian:
buffet in screens passage,
mid-fifteenth century

Plate 21

Cardoness, Kirkcudbrightshire,
later fifteenth century

Plate 22 Falkland Palace, Fife: Renaissance façade, 1538 × 1542

Plate 24

above

Falkland Palace, Fife: the gatehouse, *c.* 1500

left

Holyroodhouse, Edinburgh *c.* 1500

Plate 25 *(facing page)*

Stirling: the palace bloc[k]
James V column, *c.* 154[0]
(see pl. 27)

Plate 26 Stirling: the palace block, *c.* 1540
above corbels of wall-shafts (see pl. 23)
below the wall-head

at Flodden in 1513. Then all Scotland was in mourning. The lost generation could not build. Hertford invaded for Henry VIII in 1540, and the following years of the Reformation were not propitious. The continuation of the tower-house tradition was thus interrupted for some 80 years. But building did not cease altogether. In 1500 the lairds of Esselmont and Innerleith were granted licences to erect towers and make provision for defence with iron yetts, battlementing and so forth. Craig Castle (Aberdeenshire) was erected about 1548 with wide-mouthed gun ports low down. On Deeside Crathes was begun. Earlshall in Fife was built. The Estates legislated in 1535 in the following (modernised) terms:

> It is statute and ordained for saving of men their goods and gear upon the borders in time of war and of other troublous time, that every landed man dwelling in the inland or upon the borders having there a hundred pound land of new extent shall build a sufficient barmkin upon his heritage and lands in place most convenient of stone and lime, containing 3 score feet of the square, an ell thick and 6 ells high, for the resset and defence of him his tenants and their goods in troublous time; with a tower in the same for himself if he thinks it expedient. And that all other landed men of smaller rent and revenue build peels and great strengths as they please for saving of themselves men tenants and goods. And that all the said strengths barmkins and peels be built and completed within two years under the pain.

But by and large, in comparison with the great numbers of tower-houses of the fourteenth and fifteenth centuries and their proliferation after 1560, the blankness of the secular architectural record of the first half of the sixteenth century is one of the most remarkable in Scotland's building history. It is emphasised in contrast by the singular interest of the work which was done by the Court School at this time.

It is for the first time "palatial" in the regal sense of the term. Stirling, Holyroodhouse, Falkland and Linlithgow are all invested with a stylistic panache which was quite new and must have been a startling occurrence. Yet it came to nothing. The most critical moment in the history of Scottish domestic and castellated architecture, when the royal introduction of Renaissance ornament and façade-designing might have diverted its course along new channels to fresh experiments and new achievements, passed by without effecting any fundamental changes in the old tower-house tradition.

Now the tower-house is a non-committal classless building. Small lairds and great nobles alike erected them. The inherent architectural reticence which is characteristic of the elevations of towers both large and small discloses little or nothing of their ownership. It is impossible to connect different towers with different social categories, for all but the humble required the same sort of accommodation and it was forced into the restrictive pattern of an austere rectangular tower. The royal works were entirely different. Their most accomplished manifestations were occasioned by exceptional circumstances, and these fall into a short period between about 1530 and 1540. The Court School exclusively distinguishes the long pause of the first half of the sixteenth century, after which about 1560 the tower-house tradition of less exalted patronage resumes its triumphant course in an astonishing revival of old forms romantically presented.

The force behind the special sixteenth-century achievements of the Court School was the impact of the European Renaissance working through King James IV and James V. The first notable royal work to be touched with its influence is the Parliament Hall of Stirling Castle completed by James IV *c.* 1505. It is a large chamber of conventional mediaeval plan with screens passage and fireplace at the opposite end, flanked by two bay windows, mullioned and transomed, rising the full height of the building to arched soffits. On the outside the windows display a full treatment of Gothic buttresses and small effigies in niches framed by Gothic features in reduced scale. The general effect is Gothic, but the looped intersecting tracery in the bay windows betrays Renaissance influence.

The hall forms one side of a quadrangle of considerable interest. The Chapel Royal of 1594 occupies another. It contains a painted plaster frieze and is entered by a classical doorway with Roman Doric columns and entablature. The east side is flanked by the royal palace block of James V,[1] with Renaissance subject-matter worked into an architecture essentially Gothic in spirit although many of its details are not. Sculptured Renaissance statues, in full size and worked in the round, stand upon baluster wall-shafts of Renaissance type with low relief foliage all over (pls. 23, 25-7). The figures are derived from classical sources but have a wild exuberance alien to classical Renaissance tradition and are more akin to baroque or mediaeval native art than to classical. The battlemented parapet and the crow-stepped gable surmounted grandly by a lion sejant

[1] Begun by Andrew Aytoun for James IV in 1496 (ALHT I.cclxvi). Walter Merlion was paid "in erlis" (contract money) in the same year (ALHT I.277, 284, cclxv). Being completed about 1540 it assumed its present form in the programme of James V.

supporting a crown, the simple plan of the four ranges which form the palace about an open court (the "Lion's Den") and the fireplaces with heavy lintels supported by short columns with bulky sculptured capitals, are all quite mediaeval. But the detail is not. The winged faces and the panels of thin foliage on square columns are straight from the Renaissance repertory. Like the renowned "Stirling Heads", fifty-six large oaken portrait roundels which were set into the flat timber ceiling of the King's presence chamber, they could have been carved by the same hands which were at work outside. The parapet which oversails the wall-face is supported by a cornice inhabited by cheerful winged angel-faces, not Gothic at all but putti from France or Italy. They are to be found in the corbelling which supports the overhang of the embattled and embrasured parapet of Carberry Tower (Midlothian) of the same date, but they are otherwise totally absent from the vocabulary of ornament with which the later sixteenth-century Scots mason so vigorously expressed himself.

These energetic sculptures are obviously derivative. The source is less obvious. Posed and posturing within Gothic wall-arches with dropped cusping identical with that enclosing the sculptures over both ends of the east entrance passage at Linlithgow (*c.* 1434), they perversely suggest Blois and the work of François I. This is a likely enough derivation, for James V before his marriage to the daughter of François was at the French Court and thereafter introduced French carvers and masons to responsible posts in the Scottish Office of Works. But the source is not proved by probability alone. Contemporary effigies at Falkland were carved by Peter Flemisman who "hewed five gret stane imagis to be set upone the V buttrissis on the south syd of the new chapell" in 1538-9.[1] If the Stirling effigies are of French derivation they seem to be provincial interpretations by local sculptors, perhaps the work of Robert Robertson, "carvour", who received a grant under the Privy Seal making him "principal overseer and master of all works concerning his craft and others within the castle of Stirling" in 1541.[2]

In seeking enlightenment and explanation for this highly original and un-Scottish design we refer naturally to France, because of royal connections with the French court and the promise of Mary of Lorraine to send masons for the work. That French masons were

[1] AMW I.256.
[2] R. S. Mylne (1896), 53; AMW I.xxvi; RSS 31 August 1541.

employed in the Scottish Office of Works at this time has for long been known, and is further discussed below, but of their connection with Lorraine no indication has yet been found in Scottish or French records. The most striking resemblance to the architectural mannerisms of Stirling occurs in fact far from Lorraine, in Brittany, at the Château de Josselin, Morbihan (1490-1505). The flamboyant courtyard façade of that château is embellished with purely decorative long slender wall-shafts with low relief ornament. They rise from sculptured corbels low down to exceptionally large gargoyle-like grotesques of great projection.[1] The statues are without parallel in British sculpture. Derivation from German books of engravings is more than likely[2] (cf. Edzell Castle below).

In the attitudinising of the figures there is overmuch licence for the work to be a product of French hands. One is tempted to look elsewhere for sources of inspiration for this remarkable façade which has no parallel in Britain: to the Renaissance art of the Netherlands and Flanders, to the robust late gothic carvings of Jan van Mansdale on the Maison Échevinal, Malines, and to Spanish work of Emanuelino style, also historically probable. The heathenish fountain of St Wolfgang, a German work of 1515, bears reliefs with figures of frenzied prudishness most strongly resembling the Stirling effigies, and in subject-matter and detail of their apparel and minor effects the resemblances are as striking.[3]

The most uncompromising Renaissance work is the courtyard façade of the south range at Falkand (pl. 22), dated 1537-42. It is a Renaissance screen which hangs in front of an unaffected Gothic range a corridor's breadth behind, whose bold buttresses on the south façade with the "five grate stane imagis" confront the village street outside. This is window-dressing, a two-dimensional exercise in Renaissance design. The palace which was thus improved by James V in preparation for first one and then another French bride was first set out by James IV about 1500. It is a building of quite unusual interest, happily still inhabited. A tower-house with massive corner roundels rising from ground to oversailing crenellated parapets contains (as its close and contemporary parallel of Holyroodhouse does not) an arched entrance passage through the centre of its ground floor (pl. 24). From one side extends the aforesaid contemporary south courtyard range. These are the last of the true oblong tower-houses. The co-existence of a range alongside the Falkland

[1] Joan Evans (1948), pl. 165. [2] RCAMS, *Stirlingshire*, vol. 1. (1963), 221.
[3] F. Saxl (1938), 182-3.

gatehouse recalls the late mediaeval castles of Poitiers, Pierrefonds and Tattershall, where a great tower affords accommodation for the household of the Constable of the Castle, fitting to his rank and dignity, as it still does at Falkland.

The Falkland tower has been dated on good authority to 1537-42[1] on the evidence of building accounts. But about 1500 is more likely, on the analogy of Holyroodhouse which Walter Merlion completed in 1505[2] and by contrast with its own Renaissance courtyard façade of 1537-42 with which it surely cannot be contemporary.[3]

While buildings datable to the first half of the sixteenth century are excessively few and of no great consequence save for the royal works, there emerges in the decade following the Reformation a national architecture owing almost everything to its own national antecedents and little to foreign inspiration apart from a tendency to grandiosity and ostentation of elevation inspired if not borrowed from Elizabethan and Jacobean houses. This phase marks the culmination of the Scottish tower-house tradition.

[1] RCAMS XI (1933), 135-42. [2] ALHT III.85-6; V.lxxvi.

[3] The importance of the courtyard facade at Falkland cannot be overestimated. It is the earliest Renaissance building in Britain. No architecture is more securely placed. It is French, of the Loire, and it proclaims its date unequivocally in a series of decorative cyphers, badges and initials upon its Renaissance buttresses. Artistically and architecturally it is an embellishment, a show-facade, added to a late fifteenth or early sixteenth-century hall (now chapel). In the present writer's opinion, this hall is integral with the towered gatehouse, the hall for retainers the tower for the lord and his familiars, a typical medieval arrangement. The gatehouse is similar to the Great Tower of Holyroodhouse (pl. 24).

The date of the Great Tower is disputable, depending upon the identification of two recorded towers, one of which no longer exists. Two dates are available, *c.* 1500-1505, and 1529-1532. Mr J. G. Dunbar (Arch.J. 1963, 242-54), argues persuasively for the later date, with the Falkland gatehouse following, but we prefer the earlier because of Falkland's key-hole gun-ports and concurrence with the hall.

5
Post-Reformation Tower-Houses

SCOTTISH castellated architecture arranges itself uncommonly well into the convenient divisions of centuries and historical periods. A "post-Reformation" classification is entirely just. After the long lull of the first half of the sixteenth century there was a sudden resumption of building activity in the 1560's which was rapid, widespread and vigorous. The traditional style was revived and swiftly carried along new ways.

When Mary Queen of Scots returned from France in 1561 to rule a Protestant Scotland, she did so as a new phase of English architecture was inaugurated. Characterised by the "new style" ornament of continental, especially Low Country, derivation, this "Elizabethan" style runs parallel with the Scottish movement and like it flourished particularly in the 1570's and 1580's. But while the great English "prodigy-houses" erected in honour of Elizabeth were suitable to her courtly progresses, Scottish wealth and loyalty did not extend to such enthusiasms. The achievements at Longleat, Wollaton and Burghley were not attempted nor even imitated until the nineteenth century. However, they possess an ostentation which is characteristic of this last phase of the tower-house and might have inspired or encouraged it. Apart from this they had little influence upon Scottish masons and patrons. In both countries, however, the events which encouraged and maintained the impetus to build were mutual and connected. As a consequence of the dissolution of the monasteries and the re-distribution of church lands and property, the gentry could indulge in spirited architectural endeavours with a new freedom.

Funds hitherto dedicated to private and votive masses, to the building and endowment of collegiate churches and to the founding of chantry chapels in cathedral, parish and monastic churches were now available for castle- and house-building. This wealth and new wealth derived from the spoils of church afforded an entirely new source of income to the lay patron. With these economic encouragements came the end of the barons' wars and the impact of the Renaissance in art and architecture, most conspicuously evident in England. The prodigious building activity south of the Border, by gentry similarly inspired by Protestant security and Catholic wealth, afforded a secondary source of quasi-Renaissance decorative details derived mainly from German and Low Country late Renaissance buildings and art with which Scottish noblemen, merchants and artisans had for long been acquainted by travel, trade and personal contact with foreign artists.

From about 1570 the movement is in full swing. Between that date and about 1620 the number of dated first-class new towers is truly astonishing: Claypotts (1569-88), Gardyne (1568), Balbegno (1569), Irvine (1570), Menzies (1571-7), Megginch (1575), Brackie and Greenknowe (1581), Colliston (1583), Tolquhon (1584-9), Drochil (*c.* 1570-80), Muness (1598), Fyvie, Blairfindy and McLellan's (1582) and Glenbuchat, Hillslap, Elcho and Noltland—to name but a few from all over Scotland in the last quarter of the sixteenth century. In the early seventeenth century Amisfield, Craigston, Scalloway, the Earl's Palace at Kirkwall, Muchalls, Fraser, Craigievar and Crathes serve to represent the extent of a wide and fruitful field traversed in the volumes of MacGibbon and Ross. The impetus was sustained until the 1630's, when there is a noticeable falling-off in numbers, and the recurrence of religious strife, coming to a head with the Covenant of 1637, interrupted architectural progress once again.

When resumed after the Restoration it was in new form, embodying ideas no longer Scottish and reflecting a new way of life. A definition which deprives the tower-house of its long supremacy was voiced in a lawsuit in 1630: "This House", it was argued, "was not a Tower or Fortalice . . . and had neither Fosse nor Barmkin-wall about it, nor Battling, but was only an ordinary house."[1] The Earl of Strathmore, with his own castles of Huntly and Glamis in mind, could say in 1677 that "such houses truly are quite out of fashion, as feuds are . . . the country being generally more civilised than it was of ancient times." The tower-house or late mediaeval Scottish castle had finally played itself out.

[1] Durie's *Decisions*, p. 549, quoted by W. M. Mackenzie (1927), 74, 194.

Yet it persisted at Scotstarvit (Fife) where in 1627 an L-plan tower-house of the earliest austerity and accomplished masonwork was erected, Coxton (Moray) 1644 (pl. 36), King's College (Aberdeen) 1657, Leslie (Aberdeenshire) 1661, Clounie Crichton (Aberdeenshire) 1667 and Lethendy (Perthshire) 1678, without staleness or debasement. This need occasion no surprise, for in Scotland the mediaeval way of life was as long-lived, mediaeval craftsmanship as persistent, and mediaeval building is vertical building.

THE DEVELOPMENT OF PLAN

This period of building enterprise, from the Reformation to the Covenant, is a genuine continuation of the old traditional tower-house, both in plan and elevation. We have seen that early towers on the whole are small, uncomplicated, ineloquent and of modest internal arrangements, with little matter for study save the ingenuities of the masons who contrived to borrow space from their massive walls, despite the restrictions they imposed upon themselves by long and stubborn adherence to the tower form. A style of such long life, specialised plan and restricted space might well have expired during the long hiatus of the first half of the century, especially when social and economic conditions upon the resumption of activity were greatly different from those which obtained when the interruption began.

The only possible development of the basic and tenacious tower idea, without a drastic departure from it, was to increase the size of the towers or to combine two or three closely together, tall, narrow, compact. This is in fact what happened. The needful multiplication of towers is the simple explanation of the ubiquitous occurrence of two ingenious standard plans—the so-called Z- and L-plans—which are characteristic of no other country. As before, the desire for greater accommodation was the strongest compulsion to change. Strength remained important but the domestic influence prevailed in function and design. The military aspect of castle-building and the practice of the art of war received perfunctory consideration compared with current continental methods and theories. The implications of ordnance were imperfectly understood and indifferently employed, as we shall see, although in one of the earliest Z-plan towers, Claypotts (1569), ground-level defence all round by hand-guns or small cannon was evidently in the mind of the builder, for the two round towers at diagonally opposite corners of the main block provided an effective and unobscured field of fire along all walls. Such an unequivocal statement of defensive intent is rarely repeated. On the contrary, in the new plans defensive efficiency is too frequently vitiated or ignored for us to doubt that the cause of expansion was primarily the demand for more ample accommodation and privacy.

To gain these desirable improvements in amenity within a single tower, that tower had to enlarge its area upon the ground, as Craignethan does, or rise to excessive height above an average or moderate ground plan as Amisfield (pl. 30) and Elsieshiels do. These Dumfriesshire towers are the more successful compositions, which is to be expected of a Scottish partiality for vertical building. While extremely high towers such as these are therefore naturally not uncommon, the enlarged oblong plan is. Craignethan (Lanarkshire) is one of the few. It is almost square in plan and is divided down the middle by a cross-wall. Consequently chambers lie side by side within it. This is unusual. The elevations are quite orthodox however. But because the tower is squarish and low in relation to its length and breadth it looks wrong, neither high enough for a tower nor long and narrow enough for a hall. The attempt preserved the traditional compact security of the tower-house. It also had traditional inconveniences. It is not a successful solution to the problem of reconciling strength, amenity and good looks. Nor was the extended elevation a solution. The imposing south front of Fyvie, a veritable "show façade", 150 feet long, with a full-sized angle-turreted tower-house at each end and an immense gatehouse-tower projecting from the centre, perhaps the noblest of all Scottish baronial elevations, is quite exceptional. Only at the first Thirlestane (Berwickshire) was there anything like this exercise in length and height attempted elsewhere, in a large oblong block contained by a massive round tower at each corner with the long sides divided into bays from top to bottom by engaged half-round towers. The Fyvie lay-out is in fact a vernacular rendering of the Tantallon theme with its terminal and mid-towers; and while the arched mid-tower recalls Craigston, the spread of the elevation is decidedly French in conception, in which connection it is discussed below.[1]

Native conservatism in design regarded with disfavour such elongated solutions to the problems of additional accommodation. Customary structural method played its part in resisting horizontal expansion or spread. The chambers of tower-houses occupied all

[1] See below, pp. 191ff.

the floor of each storey or at most shared it with a side corridor running along one wall, an improvement in circulation and privacy which grew from the short mural passage serving two adjacent rooms as at Cardoness (Kirkcudbrightshire) where rooms were end to end in an oblong tower. From the small span and barrel-vault tradition these chambers were covered in one span, either by stone vault or timber beam. No tower-house is aisled, as we have had occasion to observe, and none has a central support. The only centrally supported floors in the whole range of the tower-house period are in unorthodox works, Tulliallan, an early fourteenth century hall-house, and Duffus of the same date.

By placing a suite of rooms upon a tower or combination of towers, as at Claypotts (1569-88), or by combining towers in one block, the partiality for height was satisfied and convenience was improved upstairs. The so-called L-plan was well suited to such adjustments and it occurs throughout the entire period under review and in the succeeding period also when castellated houses were thoroughly domestic. For example, Balbithan (Aberdeenshire) has the projecting jamb of its L-plan extended to such great length that all thought of its being just a helpful adjunct is absent. Although the house is obviously one of the tower-house family, with corner turrets, steep and straight gables and predominance of wall over window, it is the tower-house spread out. Relaxation and a freedom from the restrictions of the tower permit Balbithan's stair to be on straight flights against a panel of wall, and the additional jamb which contains the stair is in fact extended far beyond it. Balbithan is an important work, because it is late (of the second half of the seventeenth century), remains unaltered, and represents the ultimate extension of the L-plan.

The addition of towers to an unchanged original block is an unsophisticated procedure not uncommon in early work: in Saxon churches, or early Scottish churches, such as St Rule's (St Andrews), Leuchars and Dalmeny, all of the twelfth century, where nave, chancel and apse are added as separate units one to the other. The system of adding unit to unit, and the resultant compartmentation, is of the very essence of Scottish vernacular architecture. Scottish builders and their patrons liked it; it was repeated; and additional towers were multiplied. In the angle contained by the two wings yet another tower was erected in the re-entrant angle to make a "stepped" plan (fig. 19); at the corner of the main block diagonally opposite the jamb of the L another tower, sometimes round, sometimes square, made the so-called Z-plan. The main block retained its tower-like form. When, as at Castle Menzies (1571) and Elcho of about the same date, there was more than one room side by side on each main floor space, they too were added one to another *en suite*, not with free circulation about corridors or neutral spaces such as halls or vestibules admitting to the chambers separately and privately in the modern manner. The notable exception of Drochil and its few parallels, which were quite exceptionally advanced in this respect, are discussed below.

Thus in the second half of the sixteenth century there rose closely-knit crowded compositions of tall towers asserting their individuality with an outward show of importance which the interiors did not always have. The style prevailed throughout the post-Reformation period until the Restoration of 1660 introduced a new style of domestic building and saw the end of the aggressively fortified tower-house in Leslie Castle (Aberdeenshire) which was erected in 1661 on the "stepped" L-plan with a subsidiary re-entrant tower and gun-ports. Leslie wears the outward appearance of the standard type, but inside, the separateness of the towers has been resolved. The chambers throughout the first floor are integrated, and the promise of the first floor of Borthwick is at last fulfilled (fig. 19).

The earliest date of a Z-plan castle is about 1452, when Strathbogie or Huntly Castle was erected after the destruction of its predecessor on the site by the Earl of Moray in that year.[1] The existing ruin (*c.* 1551-4) rises from the foundations of this original plan. It consists of an oblong tower with an uncommonly large drum-tower projecting far beyond one corner (pl. 28; fig. 17). A smaller stair tower, a rebuilding of *c.* 1602, advances from the corner diagonally opposite. If it perpetuates an older tower as the drum tower does, and it is likely that it does, we have at Huntly the oldest identifiable Z-plan in Scotland and the only pre-Reformation example of the type.

There is no delay in the post-Reformation phase before the developed Z-plan appears. In 1561 the diminutive Terpersie (Aberdeenshire) was erected. The two round towers at diagonally opposite corners of the parent block retain something of the bold mediaeval tradition. Neither contains the stair which from ground to first floor is straight in the old manner within the thickness of a gable and thereafter spiral in a corbelled roundel overhanging a

[1] See W. D. Simpson (1954*c*), 6.

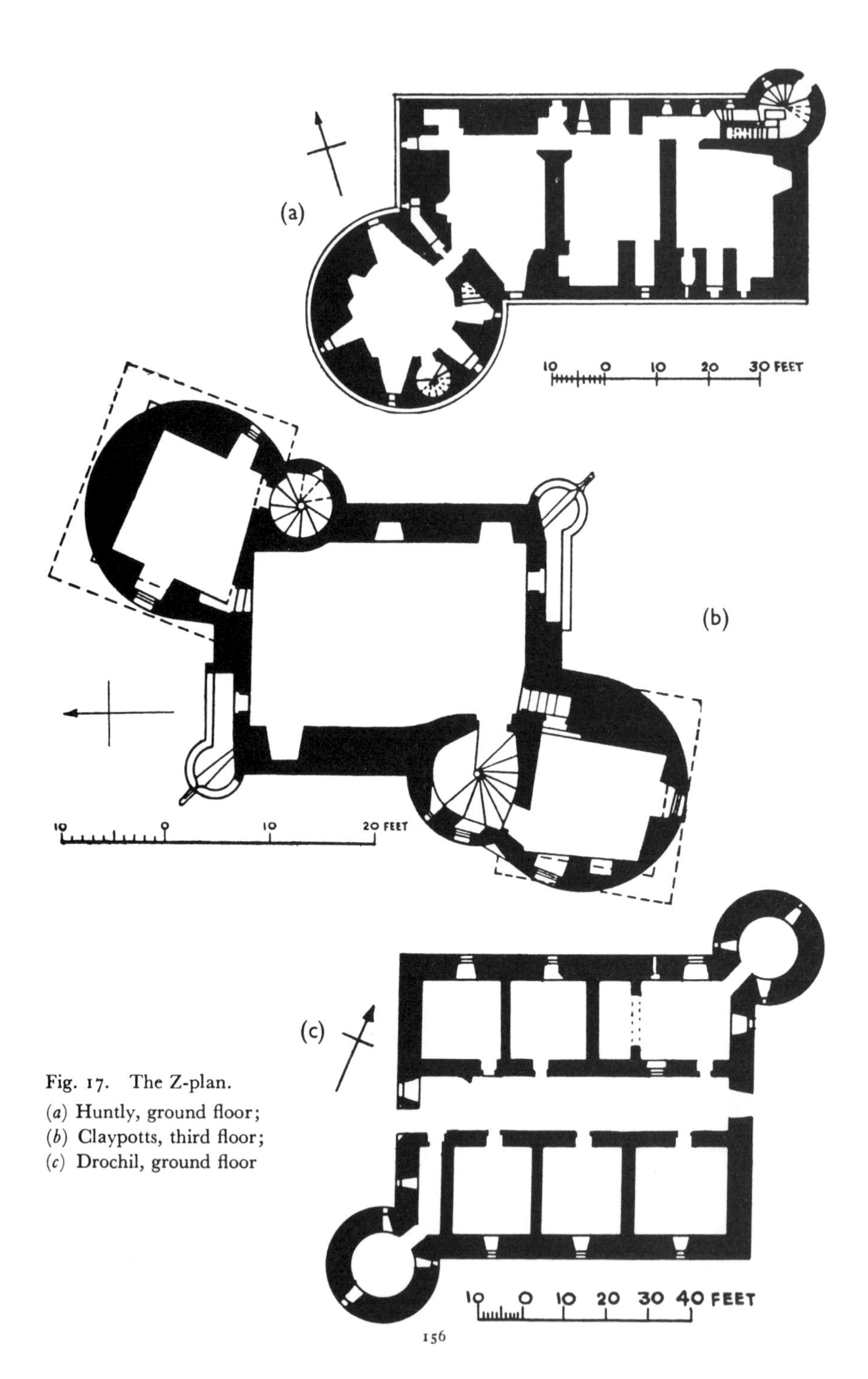

Fig. 17. The Z-plan.
(*a*) Huntly, ground floor;
(*b*) Claypotts, third floor;
(*c*) Drochil, ground floor

re-entrant angle. For defence, the castle was surrounded by a water moat. Musketry shot-holes in the towers cover all the walls of the main block.

Claypotts (1569) is another early example.[1] It is of considerable interest apart from its early date. Complete, roofed and unaltered, it has two corner round towers. Defence was from the ground floor of these two opposite towers. Wide-mouthed gun-ports cover all walls of the castle, not without some unconventional ingenuity. One port is in the kitchen fireplace, another points straight at a subsidiary round stair tower in the re-entrant angle a few feet away, which is perforce deeply channelled for the free passage of shot. The channel—or gash—in the facework suggests that the ports are later insertions and the channel an unfortunate necessity, but there is no other evidence in the masonry to uphold this and the channel must be accepted as original. These expedients, the all-round field of fire thus achieved, and the lack of stairs in the towers indicate that the towers of Claypotts were erected for defence. They thus mark a notable advance in tactical efficiency and enterprise over the simple rectangular tower-house or its improved version with the small stair jamb projecting from one corner. They also mark a movement of defence from the wall-head to the ground, and denote a change in defensive technique resulting from the use of fire-arms.[2]

The extra accommodation thus adventitiously acquired is not integrated with the rest of the floor plan, however, except on the first floor where one tower provides a small chamber entered directly from the hall. The same tower admits directly to one part of the basement of the main block. Otherwise the chambers of the towers are separate. They are also square, and the top floor chamber is similar to those below it. In the elevations there is a startling and illogical distinction between upper and lower parts; the upper room of each tower is square outside as well as inside (pl. 28; fig. 17). There is thus conveyed an instant and misleading impression that what is within them is different from the interiors of the lower floors which are within round towers. It is not so. The interiors, if not identical, are similar. The violent and unexpected contrast between the lower

[1] M. R. Apted (1957).

[2] Ordnance mounted upon mediaeval battlements was difficult to train and fire, and its concussion was injurious to them. This as much as scientific gunnery was responsible for the radical changes in ramparts which gunpowder effected. Dürer (1471-1528) altered round towers into bastions, and before him Alberti, in a treatise published in 1540, said that over-high walls were a disadvantage. As early as 1482 Martini realised that bombardment should be resisted by the plan rather than by the strength of ramparts.

and upper parts of the building is romantic and for appearances' sake. There is no thought of form following function. Such self-conscious theoretical rules are not to be inferred in Scottish tower-houses. In point of fact it is the upper part of Claypotts which is theoretically correct, with the square exteriors expressing square interiors, and the lower part which is wrong, with its round towers about rectangular interiors.

The sudden change from the circle to the square relies upon the structural trick of corbelling, by means of which an overhanging mass is supported, its weight conducted to the wall beyond which it projects and its mass pleasingly gathered in to it. Square upper chambers placed tangentially upon the round, so that the protruding corners emerged effortlessly upon their corbelling, became commonplace; or they overhung the circle all round, so that the walls of the square as well as the corners were corbelled out; or they were placed behind one face of the circular tower. The latter method occurs at Claypotts in one tower but not the other, at Drochil about ten years later, at Kilcoy and elsewhere, but being less pleasing it was less frequently employed. The other methods were immediately accepted into the masons' stock-in-trade and became ubiquitous in post-Reformation castles. Corbelling was exploited with undiminished enthusiasm in supporting the characteristic profusion of turrets, garrets, gables and so on which sprout all over the upperworks of the later tower-houses. Thus for the patron and the builder alike a picturesque grouping of parts and a romantic silhouette could be achieved by an agreeable structural method.

Of the 64 identified examples of the Z-plan 19 are to be found in the district between the Dee and the Spey, i.e. in the north-east knuckle of the mainland between Aberdeen and Elgin. Of these, 11 belong to the districts of Mar and the Garioch in Aberdeenshire. With Huntly and Terpersie, the earliest examples, in this area, it does seem that the type originated there.

Although accommodation generally was forced into the pre-determined basic rectangle, Z- and L-plans, there are variations of them which are of more than passing interest as attempts to improve stairs and to depart from the restrictive tower-like elevations. Rowallan (Ayrshire) with two ranges at right-angles dates from the 1560's. The side range has characteristic good proportion of length to height, solid to void, and is equipped with "dumb-bell" gun-ports along its basement. The fore-work is decidedly the "show-façade". Two imposing round towers project from the elevation to flank a long entrance passage which penetrates the range to a courtyard behind, as in a thirteenth-century keep-gatehouse. As at Tolquhon and Fyvie, the towers invest the building with a suitably martial air but served no warlike purpose. Barra Castle (Aberdeenshire) effectively combines two short ranges with bulky corner towers of mediaeval aspect rising from ground level and a mid-tower, all ranged about an open court whose fourth side is an enclosure wall.

The later tendency to length, which has been observed at its logical climax at Balbithan in thoroughly domestic context, occurs in more emphatically fortified buildings. In the well-defended Muness Castle (1598) on the island of Unst (Shetland), the most northerly castle in the British Isles, the stair is of the improved and spacious scale-and-platt type placed comfortably in the oblong main block. It rises from the doorway which is not tucked into a re-entrant angle of either of the opposite round towers of the familiar Z-plan. But the most remarkable variation or adjustment of the ubiquitous Z-plan is to be found at the other end of Scotland, however, in Drochil Castle (Peeblesshire) (fig. 17).

Drochil was erected for the Regent Morton who was executed in 1581. It is of the Z-plan but the main block is nearly square and so large that the projecting towers, which are round, seem small and distant, and the close-set contained effect which is so striking at Claypotts is thus diminished. But their smallness is only relative. They are in fact uncommonly large. The parent block, to which they are appendages rather than supports, is massive. The peculiarity of Drochil is that all its four floors and garret are divided down the middle by a central corridor extending the length of the building. The ground-floor corridor was barrel-vaulted in stone; the upper floors were timbered. Off the corridors opened the various rooms: barrel-vaulted cellars and kitchen on the ground floor; hall, solar and bedrooms off the upper corridors. The bedrooms are separate lodgings with doors only to the corridor. The round towers have circular chambers in the basement, square above, as at Claypotts; and, also as at Claypotts, the towers carry upper chambers which are square inside and out. The main wheel stair is at one end of the ground-floor corridor, beside the main entrance. From the first floor upwards subsidiary wheel stairs within corbelled roundels (the private as opposed to the public stairs) overhang the re-entrant angles of the towers and main block. Their corbelling and that of other secondary features about the building is enriched with surface decoration. This variation of the Z-plan at Drochil, the first attempt at modern domestic planning, like the revolutionary Falkland façade, had little influence on Scottish architectural history. Yet it is a historic work, perhaps by William Schaw, who was Master of Works to James VI from 1583 until his death in 1602.

French parallels quoted for this work, particularly of Du Cerceau's plan "*toute une masse*" such as Chenonceaux (ante 1521) and Martainville (1485) whose plan "is in all essentials that of Drochil", save that they have four corner towers, are entirely convincing.[1] Less so is an alleged correspondence with Tolquhon, and Boyne in Banffshire, which castles are assembled round a courtyard. While corridors have length and direction, courtyards have not. The idea is different.

A noble like the Regent Morton would command the best of architects. Their work should typify the most advanced of acceptable styles. At Edinburgh Castle he erected the Portcullis Gate whose round-arched entrance-way is embellished with a fine display of flat architectural motifs derived from the vocabulary of classical orders. But they are severely stylised and reveal no real knowledge, far less understanding, of the language they speak. Similar work signed by Morton at Aberdour Castle (Fife) is obviously by the same hands, with evidence of a central corridor, which enhances the interest of that ruin. The two upper floors of Spedlin's Tower (Dumfriesshire), which by the evidence of a dated armorial panel were added in 1605 to an almost square tower-house of early sixteenth-century date, have a central corridor. There are two roofs. Their inner slopes fell to a flat roof over the central corridor. At each angle of the wall-head a corbelled round turret with pepper-pot roof curtailed the length of the outer roof slope and its crow-stepped gable-end, as so often happened when turrets and gable ends competed. The fenestration of the upper floors is quite regular. Even the turret windows conform to the series of lights which runs symmetrically round all four walls. In this unusual agreement, the similarity of the corner roundels (they are, in fact, identical) and the remarkable double gables, each lop-sided but symmetrical about the centre-line, Spedlin's presents in its upper works a remarkable sense of style and balance.

Castle Lachlan (Argyll) has a corridor open to the sky. An oversailing timber gallery hung along one long side and returned

[1] W. D. Simpson (1952*b*), 77.

Plate 27
Stirling: the palace block, *c.* 1540

above pseudo-portrait of James V (detail of pl. 25)

right column figure (cf. pl. 23)

Plate 28 *above* Huntly, Aberdeenshire: the oriel windows, 1602

left
Claypotts, Angus, 1569-88

Plate 29

above Menzies, Perthshire, 1571-7

below Elcho, Perthshire, *c.* 1580

Plate 30 Amisfield, Dumfriesshire, 1600

round one end to provide access and communication to the upper floors—a unique system in private self-contained houses as far as one knows, but of common enough occurrence in the wynds, closes and vennels of the congested towns and cities. There is a close resemblance to the first Hermitage plan (late fourteenth century) in this narrow open court with tenements on either side, the door at one end of the court and the stair and enclosing wall at the other.

But evidently there was little demand on the patron's part to depart from the standard plans. These were in the main very much alike, differing principally in the size and shape of the stair, now

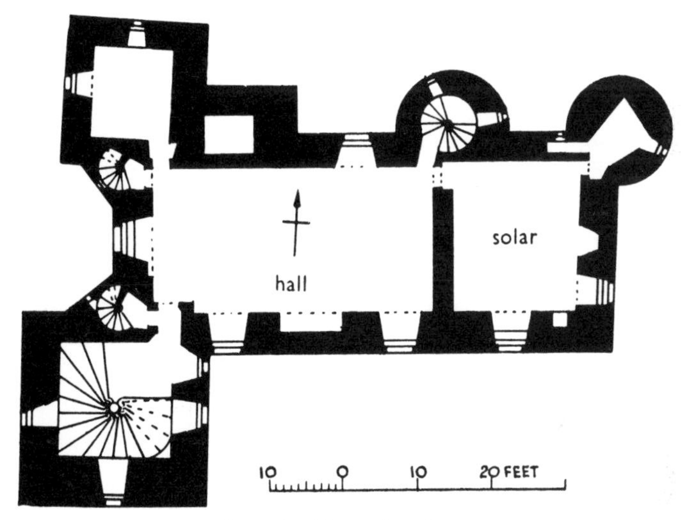

Fig. 18. Elcho, first floor

capable of straight flights and in the extent (but not the nature) of additional accommodation. Some buildings such as Elcho (Perthshire) about 1570-80, and MacLellan's Castle (Kirkcudbrightshire) 1582, while quite unconventional, retain in their haphazard placing and accretion of towers, however, the native propensity for adding unit to unit.

ELEVATIONS

Elevations no less than plans were subject to this partiality for stressing subsidiary parts. The small-scale relief to contrast the plainness of the main walling below was otherwise provided by corbelling and the broken silhouettes of crow-step gables. Within a year or two of the completion of Claypotts, Castle Menzies in Perthshire (pl. 29) was begun. Dated 1571 in its doorway panel and 1577 in a dormer pediment, it is one of the earliest of the mature Z-plan buildings. Its jambs are themselves substantial, no less commodious than many an isolated tower-house of the same period. The walls of the main block and jambs are pierced by windows unadorned save by a bull-nosed moulding round the opening. The plainness and predominance of blank walling forces attention upwards to the wall-head where the decorative ambitions of the Scottish masons found a free and fruitful field for expression, and where in its fulfilment there was strong contrast to the ground-level gun-ports reflecting the graver side of the times.

At the wall-head the eye is captivated and carried round the changing planes of the masses by a series of high and elaborate dormers and by short and sturdy roundels emerging from rather than overhanging some but not all corners. The continuous corbelling which supports them is of large section, in scale with the high-relief rolled mouldings which frame their small windows. Short dumpy roundels such as these, whose corbelling is deeply penetrated by the angle of the main walling below and which contain heavily framed small windows, are characteristic of late sixteenth-century work. The corners of Menzies which have no roundels have crow-steps rising from moulded skew-puts to roof-ridge or gable chimney. The dormers are crowned with pediments and the daylight openings are flanked with narrow ornamental wall shafts with a moulded cap, base and central collar. Along the south front the pediments are triangular and semi-circular alternately, and they are heavily but simply decorated with repetitive mouldings. The alternation of the round with the triangular pediment is a subtle thing, and so is the use of squared and rounded mouldings on the caps, bases and collars of the side shafts. The triangular pedimented windows have squared mouldings to the shafts; the semi-circular have rounded mouldings. The windows have heavily moulded lintels and dropped sills, and the pediments are surmounted and flanked by finials. The general effect is extremely rich in a barbaric sort of way.

Well-wrought detailing is characteristic of the best work of the period, e.g. at Carnasserie Castle (Argyll), the west front of St Andrews Castle, the Morton work at Aberdour, the Portcullis Gate in Edinburgh Castle, and Drochil. The emphasis on the upper part of a building is also typical. Ornament was rarely misapplied, as it was at Crathes, for example; although it is rich it is controlled as it were by the sturdy roundels which provide weightier points of interest. Such effects as we have at Menzies occurred similarly at Claypotts, which displayed a series of dormers with elaborate pediments flanked by side shafts, matching in interest and variety at the wall-head the changing forms of the corbelled upper chambers and crow-stepped gables. In the better works of this period the Scots architect and mason achieved an almost perfect balance of enrichment and austerity, solid and void contrast, vertical and horizontal emphasis. The eye, attracted upward by the richness above, unchallenged by distractions below, is led with increasing interest and gratification round the projections and recessions of the building.

It is in just this seemingly instinctive sense of balance, correct placing of features of special interest and right scale and projection of mouldings that the nineteenth-century "baronialist" was so often wrong. The baronial wing of Menzies, to the west of the original castle, illustrates this. An un-Scottish oriel window advances disconcertingly from the main wall, disturbs the scale and rhythm of the fenestration and strikes a prominent note where reticence is expected. The scale of the dormers and roundels is thin and mean compared with the adjacent originals. It is instructive to stand before the middle of the south front and compare *à coup-d'oeil* the two façades, particularly on a sunny day when the mouldings are expressive. The nineteenth-century mouldings are thin and lack vigour. Those of the sixteenth century speak out boldly.

The crowding of upper-works upon a very simple square is highly developed at Amisfield (1600), already noted as an outstanding example of compact tall building. All manner of new combinations of forms are exploited although none of the components are new. This is not just a matter of applied ornament, but also of volumes, their size and shape, and an arbitrary disposition regardless of floor levels. The plan and its outward expression are hardly related, so conspicuous is the secondary matter. Projecting parts, round and rectangular, of different sizes and lengths hang as much as they rise. They seem to be draped about the upper part of the square tower, descending with different lengths down the corners. One begins (or ends) at first-floor level and expands into a square overhanging chamber at the wall-head. At Claypotts the round towers are part of the basic upper-floor plan. At Amisfield the roundel is an appendage and the square chamber upon it rises through two storeys and has its own dormers, while, climbing upon its shoulders, yet another rises up upon corbels beyond the face of the part below. All this is assembled 70 feet above the ground, balanced upon a square of 30 feet externally containing single-room storeys only 21 feet square inside. The plan is almost entirely disguised by the multiplicity of turrets of various shapes and sizes piled up upon it, and one is filled with wonder that so much could have been erected upon so small a plan without looking cheap and overdressed, which it does not, for the scale is faultless.

The long soaring roundels of Amisfield, Fernieherst, Scalloway, Likleyhead, Castle Stewart, etc., corbelled out only a few feet above the ground, demonstrate the sixteenth-century Scottish masons' love of this contrivance. The thing is surely done for the sake of effect, for little else is gained, and some convenience and stability are lost in not building from the foundations. The mason is designing from the wall-head down, not planning. He is thinking of turrets descending from the wall-head, not rising from the ground. These corner roundels are not descendants of the earlier mediaeval tower rising from the ground; their affinities are with the swelling corner of the overhanging parapet wall of the earliest towers, Drum, Lochleven and Crookston. A further mediaeval echo is the Amisfield dormer. Pedimented, it rises its full daylight height above the wall-head from a corbelled bretasche with a machicolation over an unpretentious doorway. Thus is the defensive war-head domesticated (pl. 30).

In this wayward profusion and irrational importance of secondary features the romantic notions underlying the later tower-houses are most picturesquely and dramatically effected. Theoretically the correct elevation of any building should reveal or be a logical expression of the plan which is the beginning of design. This is not so with the later towers. Great liberty is taken with elevations. Each is a personal expression of patron or mason and so each is different in a greater or less degree.

The tower-house style is an accessible style, easy to comprehend. Its attractiveness owes much to an intimate homeliness. Without the more-than-human scale of more ambitious works it remains a thoroughly domestic architecture, but not the palatial domestic of the "stately home" which attempted an effect greater than the purpose demanded. It is not great art; it achieves no sublimity[1]; it forms no laws and conforms to none. Whimsical and capricious,

[1] Save at Craigievar and the courtyard side of Midmar, which are both exceptionally sensitive compositions.

its creators, mason-architects, depended upon personal inclination, were uncertain on occasion, and were prone to imitate. Whereas in classical styles the whole composition consists less of variety of form than in the subtleties in the use of basic forms, with detail subservient, never abused, strictly controlled and employed to enhance the greater qualities of mass and line, the architecture of the romantic tower-house on the other hand is instinctive and arbitrary, the work of skilled artisans. The nineteenth-century "baronial" mansions carry much recognisable detail suggesting the period poetically approved. It is clearly labelled "Gothic" and appropriate to houses called "Castles". But the old and unaffected qualities which inspired it—the sense of scale, proportion of part to part, part to the whole, contrast of solid and void, etc.—is lost. Authentic detailing was curiously misunderstood by the baronialists, and the subtle and elusive spirit of the traditional work they conscientiously imitated invariably escaped them, as one realises on first beholding such genuine masterpieces as Craigievar and Midmar. Subtly rounded angles, convergence of verticals, and mouldings softer than baronialists ever made or suspected, moderate the top-heavy concentration of arresting features.

The long persistence of a limited architectural vocabulary encouraged personal interpretations. Local groups have significant peculiarities of plan or decoration not evident outside the group, although these peculiarities are but variations of standard themes. Two groups in Aberdeenshire distinguish themselves particularly. In plan and in stone rib-vaulting Towie Barclay, Delgaty, Gight and Craig, of the third quarter of the sixteenth century,[1] are obviously related. At the close of the century and in the early years of the seventeenth another related group of the highest imaginative quality and technical ability is associated directly or by analogy with the Midmar masons, father and son, of the family of Bell.

Towie Barclay is distinguished by a fine rib-vaulted hall. The doorway in the re-entrant angle admits to a small rib-vaulted vestibule. From this a passage penetrates the wall on either side. At one end a wheel stair contained within the thickness of the wall rises to the hall on the first floor. The passage leading to the stair is dog-legged, and in the deflection is an embrasure serving a narrow vertical loop in the re-entrant angle of this L-planned building. The stair is unusually generous in comparison with the usual tower-house

[1] W. D. Simpson (1930), 48-96.

turnpike which tends to be cramped. It begins with a short straight flight from the passage end and continues spiral-wise to a short straight mural passage which admits to the hall. This is all skilfully contrived and a great improvement upon the older and less accommodating turnpike which pitches the breathless climber abruptly into chambers opening too suddenly off it. In the entrance vestibule the vault ribs rise from ornamental corbels to meet in a boldly sculptured boss.

The hall is one of the noblest and most imaginative of all the tower-house interiors and enlarges upon the mediaeval atmosphere to which the vestibule quickly introduces the incomer. It consists of a single high rib-vaulted chamber in two bays, with ridge and transverse ribs, diagonal ribs and wall ribs, sculptured corbels and heavy pendant bosses also sculptured. At the end of the chamber opposite the doorway a spacious fireplace, wide and deep, with decorated aumbries in its jambs, occupies most of the lower wall space. Three high windows set in deep round-arched embrasures rising the full height of the bay light the chamber more than adequately, and off one opens a small mural chamber with a window overlooking the entrance below.

But the most remarkable feature is a small oratory above the entrance to the hall, situated above the passage and reached by an ingenious mural stair which passes unseen over the doorway. The oratory seems to be borrowed from the thickness of the wall, and opens into the body of the hall. The passage leading to the hall doorway is the old screens passage, and the oratory is the traditional mediaeval music gallery revived in new form and purpose over it. An altar shelf projects from its east wall with an effigy corbel alongside it. The oratory, being entirely open and separated from the body of the hall only by its elevation and a traceried parapet wall, would be used not only by the laird and his family at their private orisons but doubtless also at more public services at which the tenantry attended mustered in the hall below. The recess is arched and rib-vaulted. The arch ribs, like those in the vestibule and vault of the hall, are of round fat section with fillets, quite lacking the best mediaeval scale and refinement but, nevertheless, conceived in the Gothic spirit of the symbols of the four Evangelists worked upon the corbels supporting them. Nowhere else does the Gothic spirit communicate itself so unambiguously as in Towie Barclay.

A few other tower-houses contain ribbed vaults, notably Mauchline Tower (Ayrshire) and Delgaty, another of the group, and Balbegno (1569), whose vault panels are plastered and painted with heraldry. At Craig, much modernised, there is evidence of another oratory similar to that in Towie Barclay, and for comparison one may refer to the Affleck oratory, likewise open to the hall but contained in a small chamber opening directly off it on the same level beside the fireplace. The provision in Towie Barclay of tall undefended and vulnerable windows incidentally makes nonsense of the keyhole-crosslet loop and the wide-mouthed gun-port as serious measures of defence.

As long as there was a bold oversailing parapet encircling the main mass, with a wall-walk behind it and a pitched roof, usually low, within this walk, there was a distinct finish to the elevation. The composition finished with the parapet. Dormers to light roof spaces are withdrawn behind the parapet and rarely seen or even suspected from the ground. But whenever the defensive needs of a parapet and wall-walk were subordinated to other considerations, when the demands and requirements of defence were of subordinate importance, greater attention was paid to design for its own sake, and for the sake of picturesqueness—an important factor, however unselfconscious, in romantic towers. Then the parapet was dispensed with and the roof was carried down to the outer edge of the wall-head. The dormer was brought forward, flush with the wall-face, and, being a small feature capable of independent treatment, it received it in good measure, for the Scots mason, as long as he worked in the Scottish idiom no matter how variously, was Gothic at heart, and like his mediaeval ancestors was quick to seize upon opportunities thus provided for embellishment and variety no matter how obscure they would be or how indifferently the results might be appreciated by the onlooker.

The lower parts of towers continued to be plain. There is no even spread of interest over a façade. All the emphasis is concentrated at the top and receives full value there, thrown into all the greater relief by the plainness of the main mass of building below. The deep-rooted preference for the upper part is to be found not only in the treatment of main massing but in the designing of the secondary features themselves. There is a tendency for them to grow upwards and ever upwards, gathering volume with astonishing rapidity, sometimes with bizarre results, more frequently with perfect balance. At its simplest expression we have the dormer enlarged to contain two or even three storeys, so that it becomes a young gable rising illogically from a side wall, as can be seen for example at Gladstone's Land in the Lawnmarket, Edinburgh, and in other "lands" of the lofty Old Town of the sixteenth century. At Glamis (pl. 31) a dormer window pierces the main wall and rises above the eaves level, but instead of being surmounted by a pediment blossoms out into a full-size roundel with its own windows and conical roof. The dormer thus carries a small chamber. Near it an oriel upon continuous corbelling rises to become part of a battlemented parapet.

The upper-works of Glamis are full of illogicalities like this and the structure is disguised by them. For example, the roof lines of its Z-plan are falsified with an open balustraded straight gable-end. In the middle of this a little open belfry or pavilion upon continuous corbelling emerges from the traceried or latticed balustrade. The correct, or at least the logical and "truthful", form of this roof is of course a pitched gable. Such "deception" is very rare in Scottish vernacular, but it occurs in similar fashion at Crathes, in the second Aberdeenshire group.

A remarkable richness of decoration and stylistic mannerisms in the handling of traditional forms characterise the group. Peculiarities of plan are not to be found in it. Its interest and significance reside in the personal element revealed in the mannerisms. Somewhat later in date than the Towie Barclay group, and not all of one period of building activity, they are characterised by features which are closely dated and which can directly or by analogy be attributed to the Bell family. The distinctive parts fall into the period between the last years of the sixteenth century and the first quarter of the seventeenth century. They mark the end and the apotheosis of the tower-house style. Later examples, already quoted, denote a stubborn persistence of the tower idea but not a continuation of the tradition as a developing architectural form with slow and unconscious change from generation to generation.

A knowledge of the environment which produced the earlier tower-house is a sufficient explanation of them and of the restricted form they took. A description of two or three is a description of the essentials of the type generally. Parallels and derivations, development and variations, need little further discussion than has been attempted in the foregoing pages. But this Aberdeenshire group, in the districts of Mar and the Garioch, presents a more personal

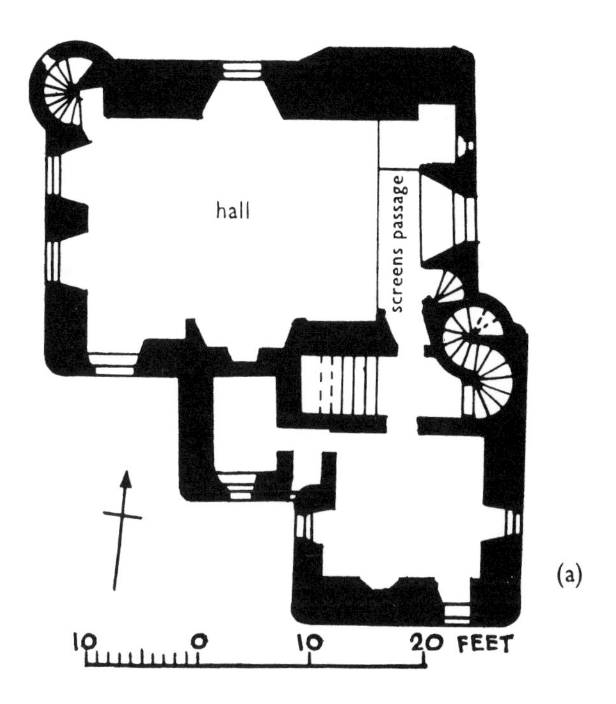

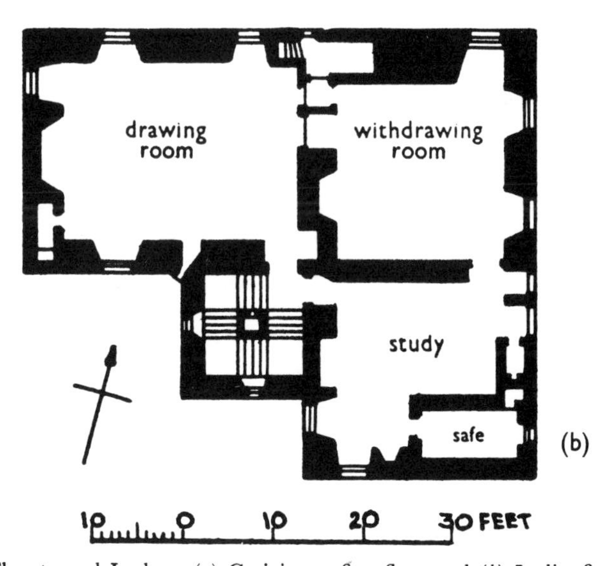

FIG. 19. The stepped L-plan. (*a*) Craigievar, first floor and (*b*) Leslie, first floor

and atypical complex of buildings deserving special mention, for the treatment of detail is arresting and individual.

The castles in the group are Crathes, Midmar, Fraser, Craigievar and Fyvie (figs. 19, 20). They are of great renown and compelling interest, and they are charged with rare beauty, so much so that critical analysis is stilled and description tends to dwell upon their undoubted poetic quality. Something might usefully be said about other qualities however.

Crathes (pl. 32) bears a panel dated 1553 upon its south wall and a pendant boss in the barrel-vault of its first-floor hall with the date 1554. This seems to commemorate the beginning of the building which, according to another panel, was finished in 1596. None other in the group can claim with any probability such an early beginning as this. But to infer from these dates a beginning and an end of building activity, as though work were in progress for some 40 years, is surely wrong. Ten years is long enough. It is not unlikely that the lower parts were begun and perhaps even completed by 1553 or 1554 and that the upper parts represent a late remodelling under the singular influence of the Bell family of masons, of whom George died in 1575, and I. Bell and David were at work in the early years of the seventeenth century.

Crathes is an L-plan tower-house. It contains a re-entrant stair tower of unusual size extending from the re-entrant angle to the gable-end of the principal wing, which is thus two wings wide. By this extension the stair tower is absorbed into the main block.[1] As this is correspondingly enlarged, the lesser wing is small in relation to it and projects with diminished effect. The plan of the whole is a square with a small oblong area subtracted from it. This produces a lumpish elevation and unsatisfactory oblique views. The span of the principal block being awkwardly large, twin roofs, side by side, are structurally necessary, as at Spedlin's Tower. But the two gables are not revealed at Crathes as they are at Spedlin's. Instead, in the important south elevation, they are united and disguised thereby, in the manner of Glamis, by a screen wall erected from chimney to chimney across the valley between them. With an embattled

[1] This happened also at Castle Leod (Ross-shire), an L-plan tower with corbelling and other details of considerable richness and variety strongly reminiscent of the towers of Mar and the Garioch which presumably inspired it. Great richness and sophistication were not confined to rich and populous districts. Castle Craig on the Black Isle, an oblong tower, has a quite useless corbelled parapet across one of its surviving gabies, which is heavily sculptured with cable-moulding and dog-tooth ornament.

cresting, elaborate corbelling and a series of long cannon-barrel gargoyles, also highly decorated, this screen wall is designed as a balcony joining the tall chimney stacks which would, if separate, bring the gables to lofty and imposing terminations. From the false balcony, in the centre of the expansive façade, a long engaged stair-turret, half-rectangular half-round, descends to the second-floor level where it succeeds the straight flights of the re-entrant stairway.

The result is unsuccessful by cancelling out the upward and separate movements of the gables just where vertical emphasis is needed to redeem the formless spread of the lower parts. From the sides, most noticeably the east, the screen wall is visible, thin and high, above the roof ridges. It is unrelated to them and the building, and obscures an emergent roundel with conical roof, invariably a distinctive and rarely, if ever, an obscure note in tower-house composition. A further uncertainty of handling deprives a wandering string-course of relationship with the elevation. It contains three heraldic panels and it links the short corner roundel with the long half-round turret in the centre of the façade.

The fault lies in the width of the principal jamb. That the stair tower was added to an original wing of usual dimension, or that an earlier has been enlarged are not impossible explanations. In either event the long mid-turret would have been an overhanging corner roundel. Yet if this were so the change in plan cannot have been long delayed, for the mouldings and technique are the same throughout. Early modification in building progress is evident in Castle Fraser, where a loop in the re-entrant angle is blocked by a re-entrant roundel descending to the ground. This was probably originally intended to corbel out at first-floor level or thereabouts thus clearing the loop beside the entrance, as at Midmar, where a long cone of multiple mouldings carries a stair turret which soars splendidly without a break to overtop the wall-head (pl. 36).

The richness of detail, light and shade, and changing profile, which especially distinguishes the post-Reformation castle is most marked in this Aberdeenshire group of the late sixteenth to early seventeenth century, particularly in features datable to the first quarter of the seventeenth century. The dual natures of the elevations have been remarked upon by previous writers. Billings observes of Castle Fraser that the upper parts "will be seen to be of very different character from the lower architectural department, which probably was the unadorned square tower of the fifteenth century".[1] But MacGibbon and Ross vigorously maintain that its Z-plan cannot be earlier than the mid-sixteenth century and that the upper parts are characteristic of Scottish works as a whole. As a general proposition this view is unquestionably sound. But without specific documentary or architectural evidence to support it and corroborate assumptions it is imprudent to dogmatise about building periods in particular cases. Much evidence is doubtless hidden behind the harling which correctly clothes the rubble fabric and sets off the exposed dressed masonry to its full and intended advantage.

Castle Fraser itself serves as a cautionary instance. Internal alterations subsequent to the statements of Billings and MacGibbon and Ross have proved the former nearer the mark, and recent stripping of the harling has revealed a significant change in the technique of forming quoins just where the ornamental upper parts begin; and attention has already been drawn to a blocked original loop. Fraser at least is a composite structure. To the square corner tower and main block an extension and diagonally opposite round tower were added, probably in the early seventeenth century, when a magnificent heraldic table was mounted high upon the wall-head overlooking the forecourt. It includes a panel modestly inscribed "*I. Bell. 1617. M.M.F.*" (? for Master Mason to Fraser). The dormer pediments are sculptured with cyphers and heraldic devices and dated 1618. The corbelling at the wall-head of the main block is a decorative band with false gun-barrel gargoyles. It steps up and down in characteristic Aberdeenshire fashion to meet the corbelling of corner roundels of moderate overhang. The style of corbelling, the use of a bold cable-moulding, and the profile of the roundels is matched among the sculptural felicities of Crathes, Midmar, Fyvie and Craigievar, and dated to the closing years of the sixteenth century and the first quarter of the seventeenth century.

Triplet pistol-holes in the basement and a pendant boss in a barrel-vault in the lower part of Fraser are both paralleled at Tolquhon (1584-9), where the pendant boss hangs from the courtyard entrance passage. A similar boss in a similar position is to be found in the Gate of Honour of Gonville and Caius, Cambridge (*c.* 1570); others, in barrel-vaults, occur in Crathes and Towie Barclay of the same period.

With George Bell master mason at Midmar "deceisit" in 1575 and that charming work strongly suggesting in its restraint an early

[1] R. W. Billings (1852).

appearance of the features which were highly developed in the others of known later date, it does seem that the local style originated here. It is also possible that this remarkable Aberdeenshire group is not all the work of one period, but of two, not necessarily long separated. The parts which especially distinguish them could be delayed completion or later remodelling of more conventional compositions, such as Glenbuchat and Tillycairn represent—but neither of these is by any means unimaginative.

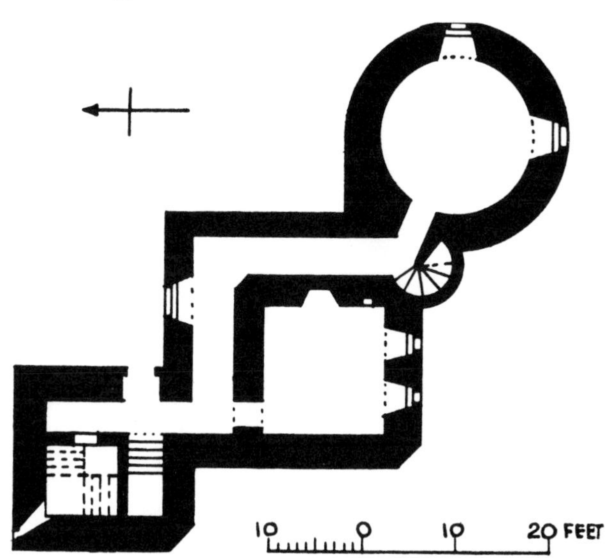

FIG. 20. Midmar, ground floor

The interest and special importance which these castles hold in Scottish architectural history are not thereby diminished. New building may well be content to imitate long-established style or even be archaic revival of it, but additions and alterations are likely to be up-to-date, part if not all of the reasons for such work on an old house being to achieve that condition. Consequently what is altered or added is likely to be a promising indicator of contemporary taste.

As a testimony of taste Craigievar ranks with any representative building in Britain. As a work of art it claims a Scottish place in the front rank of European architecture. Completed in 1626, it has remained unaltered and continuously inhabited. Its interior contains in perfect preservation moulded plaster ceilings and a great groined vault over the hall which preserves its relief plaster surface decoration of raised panels, heraldry, foliage, classical portrait medallions and elaborate pendants. The fireplace is surmounted by an immense armorial table, with achievement, supporters, and flanking debased caryatid figures familiar in innumerable Renaissance compositions at this time. They occur in pairs in a similar composition in Muchalls (Kincardineshire) in 1624 and Glamis in 1620, executed by the same hands which made the Craigievar plasterwork a year or so later. At one end of the hall the timber screen of the traditional screens passage is a rare and interesting survival of an essentially mediaeval feature (fig. 19).

Its elevations are outstanding. Despite the top-heavy burden of incident the whole achieves a slenderness by well-considered proportions, converging vertical lines and rounded corners. There is a sort of sublimity about the front elevations of Craigievar (pl. 33), a serene assurance not communicated by any other tower-house however pleasing. No infelicity of mass or exaggeration of detail suggest room for improvement. Quite perfect, lightly poised upon the ground, it is the apotheosis of its type.

It is somewhat remarkable that probably the very finest example of true Elizabethan design is to be found at Kirkwall in the Orkneys. Here, in the opening years of the seventeenth century, the tyrannical Earl Patrick Stewart built for himself a splendid mansion which is known to-day as the Earl's Palace to distinguish it from the Bishop's Palace which it immediately adjoins (pl. 34; fig. 21). Earl Patrick also erected the castle of Scalloway in Shetland, and considerations of style make it clear that Muness Castle and the completion of Noltland Castle, if not the whole, were the work of the same architect.

Of the earl's state and behaviour we have an arresting picture from the pen of a contemporary writer.

> This Patrick, Earl of Orkney, was long in favour with the King. He had a princely and royal revenue, and indeed behaved himself there with such sovereignty, and if I durst say the plain verity, rather tyrannically, by the shadow of Danish laws, different and more rigorous than the municipal or criminal laws of the rest of Scotland; whereby no man of rent or purse might enjoy his property in Orkney, without his special favour, and the same dear bought; whereby it followed that feigned and forged faults were so devised against many of them that they were compelled by imprisonment and small reward to resign their heritable titles unto him; and if he had an empty purse, and no rent, there was some crime devised against him whereby he was compelled to lose either half or whole thereof, if not life and all

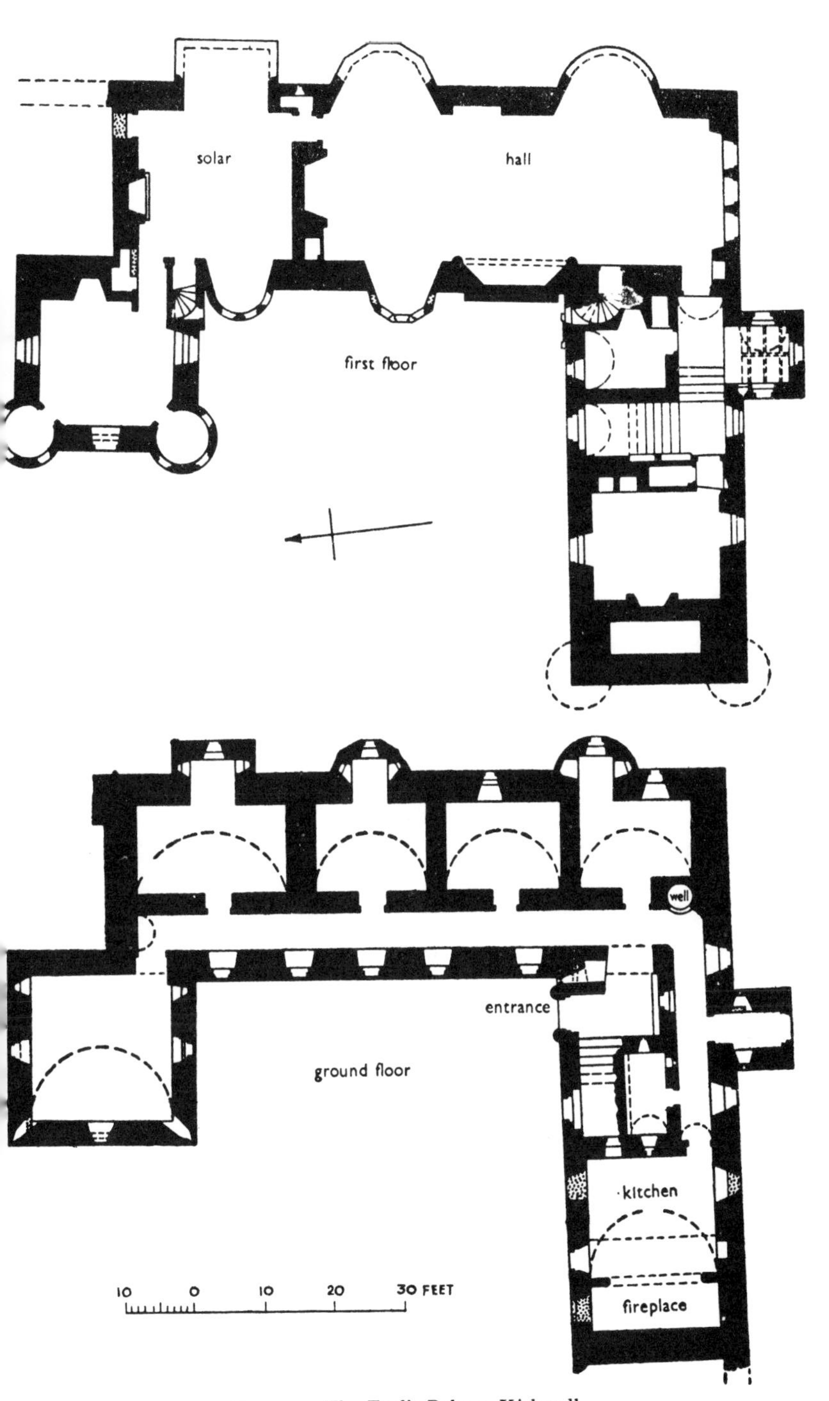

FIG. 21. The Earl's Palace, Kirkwall

> beside. And his pomp was so great there that he went never from his Castle to the Kirk, nor abroad otherwise, without the convoy of fifty musketeers and other gentlemen of convoy and guard; and similarly before dinner and supper there were three trumpeters that sounded still until the meat of the first service was set at table and similarly at the second service and consequently after the Grace. He had also his ships directed to the sea to intercept pirates and collect tribute of foreign fishers that came yearly to these seas; whereby he made such collection of great guns and other weapons for war as no house, palace or castle, yea in all Scotland, was furnished with the like.[1]

This true Renaissance patron created in his palace at Kirkwall a building which is unrivalled in Scotland for ability in planning and for the refinement of its design and detailing, its style and highly original plan, the imaginative use of oriels and bay windows, and the splendour of its hall. The palace was never finished. It represents only a part of a much larger scheme which the stern hand of justice prevented its author from completing. Earl Patrick intended to remodel the adjacent Bishop's Palace, which he did, and to incorporate it into his new establishment, which would have served to accommodate his convoy of fifty musketeers "and other gentlemen" without whom he never stirred abroad.

[1] T. Thomson (1825), 386-7.

Plate 31 Glamis, Angus, late sixteenth century; low wings modern

Plate 32

right
Crathes,
Aberdeenshire,
c. 1596

below
Craigievar,
Aberdeenshire,
c. 1626

Plate 33 Craigievar, Aberdeenshire, *c.* 1626

Plate 34 The Earl's Palace, Kirkwall, *c.* 1600

Plate 35 Scalloway, Shetland, *c.* 1600

Plate 36

right
Midmar, Aberdeenshire,
c. 1570

below
Coxton, Moray,
1644

6

Courtyards and Lodgings

To buildings arranged about an open court as appendages to an earlier tower-house the classification "courtyard castle" is inadmissible, for such an ensemble does not represent a type of structure or a change in architectural thought. It does not constitute the concrete embodiment of an idea, the fulfilment of a particular and specific need. It is merely, as the examples show, the inevitable response to a demand for greater accommodation which the still useful tower could not in itself provide. Added as and when required these additional ranges haphazardly supplement but do not supersede the tower-house. Craigmillar is a classic instance of this natural growth, achieving incidentally with its outer curtains of fifteenth- and sixteenth-century dates an accidental parallel to the concentric castle of the thirteenth century. Castle Campbell and Crichton (fig. 12) are notable among other examples of the courtyard lay-out formed fortuitously about a tower-house as nucleus. In both its importance is maintained, even when the additions were of outstanding architectural merit, as is the diamond-faceted or nail-head masonwork of the Italianate courtyard facade of Crichton of between 1581 and 1592 (pl. 40). Examples of a coherent preconceived courtyard plan are exceedingly rare in Scottish castellated architecture and are certainly too few to constitute a "type" or to justify the legitimate inferences of common and identifiable characteristics upon which such abstract terminology relies.[1]

Four castellated structures, all different, widely separated and of different dates, were conceived and executed on a genuine courtyard plan. They are Drumlanrig Castle (Dumfriesshire), George Heriot's Hospital (Edinburgh) now a school, Barnes Castle (East Lothian),

[1] Doune was conceived as a courtyard castle, but was not completed as such. Skipness is an earlier example in similar case.

and the Earl's Palace at Birsay (Orkney). Doune, which was conceived as a courtyard castle, was not completed as one, but as a curtain-wall castle of the older type.

Drumlanrig in its present form belongs to the last quarter of the seventeenth century. Of the "hall-house and palace" built by Sir James Douglas of Drumlanrig sometime between 1513 and 1578 nothing can be identified. The castle was razed to the ground in 1575 and afterwards rebuilt[1] by the first Duke of Queensberry who dedicated the last years of his life, and his fortune, to the undertaking. The result is an overwhelming mansion which, raised upon its balustraded terrace with open aspect of parkland and parterre, is more reminiscent of some great English "stately home" than of a typical reserved Scottish castle (pl. 38, and cf. fig. 22). Innocent of even the smallest hint of military influences, it would not be considered here were it not for the fact that it is "the last great gesture of the Scottish castle style".[2]

It consists of four ranges, 146 feet by 120 feet, about an open quadrangle 77 feet by 57 feet, which has an arched loggia along one side. In the corners of the quadrangle stair-towers encroach into the courtyard space as at Linlithgow and Heriot's. These are familiar notes in re-entrant angles, most commonly employed in L-plan castles. The corners of the enclosing ranges are square tower-houses. They are incorporated into the plan but preserve an individual importance by projecting beyond the façades between them, considerably in advance of the side elevations, less so at back and front. In this respect they afford instructive comparisons with those of Heriot's, which also project, and those of Linlithgow which do not, save above the wall-head, where they emerge in saddle-back roofs with gable-ends. The Drumlanrig towers proclaim their tower-house ancestry with small corner roundels which overhang slightly. Those of three elevations are carried by continuous corbelling of which the upper member is a heavy cable moulding fashionable in the late sixteenth century, as at Crichton for example, from which project gargoyles imitating cannon.

This is traditional enough. But the treatment of the turret features on the north elevation is not. They submit to a sterner discipline. They do not grow out of the body of the flanking towers but are perched upon a heavy moulded cornice of classical section which replaces the corbel course along the entire length of the façade

[1] L. Weaver (1913), 382-90. [2] J. Summerson (1953), 334.

but occurs nowhere on the other three elevations. It draws the elevation together, gives a horizontal emphasis at the wall-head, and firmly separates the main walling from the superstructure, to the latter's disadvantage. This is quite untraditional, indeed alien to the native style of eventful skyline and wayward growth above the structural wall-head. So is the balustrade which links the roundels —although it was popular in parts of early seventeenth-century tower-houses in Aberdeenshire, e.g. Craigievar, Midmar and Castle Fraser, as a cresting upon the summit of a re-entrant tower or one tower of a composite group. The cornice returns briefly round the outer sides of the towers, where it is succeeded by the traditional corbel course. This carries the roundels at the rear of the towers and continues along the lengths of the other three elevations. It returns round the length of the inner sides of the towers, however, to make the classical façade complete and unimpaired by the traditional wall-head finish.

The little roundels stubbornly persist as a native echo in an overwhelming classical theme. Behind the façade the round stair turrets in the corners of the quadrangle loom large and peer over the top to re-assert the Scottish partiality for independent masses and broken skyline, much to the discomfiture of the flat and careful façade in front of them. A giant Corinthian order of eight applied pilasters rises through the height of the ground and first floors to a straight entablature carrying a balustrade upon the aforesaid cornice enriched with consols. In the centre a square porch advances from the façade into the terrace. It is pierced by a doorway in each of its three sides at ground-floor level. The porch is surmounted by a semi-circular pediment, behind and apparently on top of which an octagon crowns the porch with a cupola designed as a ducal coronet. This square porch—a young tower—provides an abrupt interruption in the pilaster and entablature motif, projecting even further than the corner towers do, with a most emphatic and unclassical movement. The main walling of the façade is one bay longer than the pilastered frontispiece at either end and these bays rise one floor higher. The massive flanking towers rise one floor higher yet to a total of four floors, each marked by a single pedimented window but not by string courses.

In the swagger of this show-façade certain improprieties in the handling of the classical formula imply theoretical ignorance rather than Baroque indulgence. Heavy steep-sided almost equilateral triangular pediments, filled with carving, surmount the windows in the tradition of tower-house dormers. The pediments of the upper windows lie wholly in the entablature of the pilaster sequence while those at the ends of the elevation are lost in the balustrading above them. The pilasters do no work, nor do they convey an idea of doing so. The uninterrupted run of architrave, frieze and cornice is thus disturbed by the intrusion of motifs which would be more comfortably accommodated in the bays of the main walling below.

The loss in the relationship between the pilasters and the lintels they theoretically support occurs in the elevations of Kinross House (1684-95), where giant Corinthian pilasters are corner features only and the unsupported entablature between them is so excessively long that one is painfully conscious of the lack of intermediate support. Matters are arranged better in the quadrangle of Holyroodhouse, begun in 1671, where superimposed Doric, Ionic and Corinthian pilasters each extend the height of one floor only and are suitably spaced with restrained fenestration easily contained in the main wall surfaces. The elevations of Drumlanrig which are published in *Vitruvius Britannicus* are subjected to a more severe Palladian treatment. The pediments of the windows are less steep. They do not encroach into the cills of those above nor do they intrude into the architrave of the pilasters. The upper windows of the corner towers are not semicircular but segmental. They do not penetrate the balustrade. The small corner roundels are capped by ogee roofs and have small quatre-foil openings which are to be found likewise in the turrets of Heriot's School.

Stylistic mannerisms associate Holyroodhouse and Drumlanrig. In both the terminal corner towers step down to the centre of the frontage. In both the centre-piece is a great crown worked in stone, appropriate to the dignity of the builders, king and duke. Each has an arched loggia with massive square piers in the courtyard. The correspondence in these features and their dates introduces Sir William Bruce of Balcaskie as the designer of Drumlanrig, although the only name authentically associated with it is that of William Lukup, who is commemorated on his children's tombstone in the churchyard of Durisdeer nearby as Master of Work in Drumlanrig 1685. The stone bears an effigy of a mason clad in a long coat with reversed cuffs, an apron round his waist, flowing hair and a round feathered cap upon his head. In his right hand he clasps a mason's mell or mallet, in his left a chisel. Two Dutch masons known to have come to work on Drumlanrig from Kinross House in 1686 provide further presumptive evidence of Bruce's revolutionary influence upon Scottish post-Restoration architecture and his presence at Drumlanrig. Distinctive features in other buildings by him, the high rounded pediment in the French style in the original Hopetoun House, for example, are echoed in the Drumlanrig porch and windows.

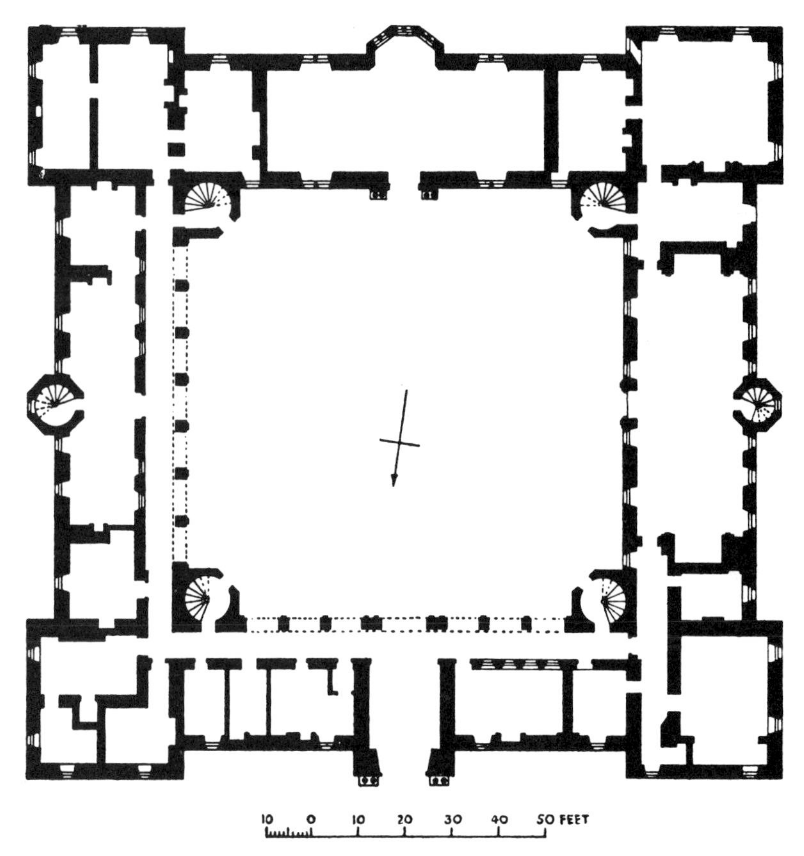

Fig. 22. George Heriot's School, ground floor

The ancestor of Drumlanrig is Heriot's Hospital (pl. 39). The plans are similar although the elevations of Heriot's are conceived in different terms altogether. While the courtyard and show-front of Drumlanrig are probably grafted on to an older and plainer structure—the contrast between these and the other three exterior fronts with their traditional corbelled wall-head is pronounced—the work of

Heriot's is homogeneous. It falls outside the scope of this survey, as Drumlanrig does, but like that ducal mansion it owes much to native tower-house style with turreted tower-houses at each corner of its four ranges. From every point of view, not least for its eclectic assemblage of motifs and the problems of their derivation from English Jacobean, Flemish and French work as well as a stubborn Scottishness in the general effect, Heriot's is one of the most remarkable and fascinating edifices in Scotland. Begun in 1627 by William Wallace, it was continued and completed by William Aitoun about 1650. Wallace was Principal Master Mason to the Crown from 1617 until his death in 1631. Much of the rich Renaissance-style carving of pediments, twisted chimneys, strap-work etc. which distinguishes notable town and country houses in this period is his or derived from his work: at Pinkie in Midlothian (1613); the King's Lodging in Edinburgh Castle (1615); Winton in East Lothian (1620), and the north range of Linlithgow (1620). By his radical departure from traditional design he prepared the way for Sir William Bruce and the classical school in Scotland.

Holyroodhouse as we know it to-day comes twenty years after this. It was begun in 1671, while Drumlanrig was still building, by Robert Mylne, the King's Principal Master Mason, working under the skilled supervision of Sir William Bruce, General Overseer and Superintendent of royal buildings. The classical façades of the Holyroodhouse quadrangle are the first Scottish experience of the grave new learning expressed in architecture. Holyroodhouse is a turning-point in Scottish architectural history, and in its complete rejection of the old manner, which neither Heriot's nor the earlier part of Drumlanrig effected, introduced the style which was to become fashionable in superior works, particularly after the Union of Parliaments in 1707.

The other two great courtyard schemes are earlier than the foregoing. They naturally have stronger affinities to defensive castles. Barnes Castle (East Lothian) comprises a large almost square enclosure with projecting square towers with enfilading gun-ports. There is one at each corner, one half-way along each of the two shorter sides, and two mural towers spaced equally along each of the longer sides. A small wing advances into the courtyard at each end of the residential block, which was placed along one of the shorter sides. In the re-entrant angles thus formed a small square tower contains a wheel stair, quite in the traditional manner. The building was begun and completed in plan, but not in height, by John Seton of Barnes, who died in 1594. We thus return from the post-Reformation ducal extravagances of the mansion of Drumlanrig and the entirely peaceful Heriot's Hospital to a period of more earnest castellated architecture when defensive considerations were not entirely overlooked. Their requirements were even more purposefully recognised in the Earl's Palace at Birsay in Orkney.

As we have observed, the Earl's Palace at Kirkwall, erected about 1600 by the despot Earl Patrick Stewart, a truly Renaissance figure of tyranny and taste, is the most accomplished Elizabethan building in Scotland. The Earl's Palace at Birsay is attributed to his father, Earl Robert, and from him it gets its name. A seventeenth-century drawing in the General Register House, Edinburgh, gives the plan with "uprights" alongside. Above the main entrance are the initials E R O for Robert Earl of Orkney, with the date 1574. Above the gateway the earl erected an equivocal inscription which was reassuring neither of his loyalty nor his latinity, "that inscription so much talkt of, and reputed treasonable by King James the 6th *Robertus Steuartus Filius Jacobi 5ti Rex Scotorum Hoc Aedificium Instruxit*".[1]

The Palace is, like Barnes, now the midden of a farm steading. Much stands high but is rapidly deteriorating. Much has gone or is buried in grass-covered debris. A large oblong court was surrounded on all sides by a narrow range of buildings with ground-floor chambers opening separately and directly off the courtyard, save on the north, where the range is of later date and stands outside the true courtyard area. Rectangular towers at three external corners retain a full mediaeval projection. The fourth tower was never built, its position being occupied by the north range whose gable runs in line with the west façade. The first floor of this front is distinguished by an imposing series of large windows continuing into the gable of the north range. Along the ground floor of the west range and the three towers double-splayed wide-mouthed gun-ports of the late sixteenth century have been contrived by remodelling older apertures. They occur in business-like number and position, and were clearly intended for use and no nonsense about it. This is the work of Robert. The original antedates him, probably by a considerable period, and might represent a bishop's palace before the earl's.

Upon the small tidal island known as the Brough of Birsay, not

[1] J. Brand (1703), 31.

a mile away, have been exposed the complete lower parts of the Christ Church, "the splendid minster" which Earl Thorfinn the Mighty erected about 1050,[1] and the lower parts of a twelfth-century bishop's palace which was raised round a small court against its north wall.[2] There is no masonry on the island later than about 1300. The ruins of the Christ Church survive in eleventh-century form save for two minor twelfth-century modifications—the slapping of a door through the north wall of the nave to serve the bishop's palace when it was added and the forming of a semi-circular altar niche in each of the west flanks of the chancel arch. As it is unlikely that the church would have survived unchanged throughout a long life it is probable that its continuing use was for special services only, such as pilgrimages, which are recorded for late pre-Reformation dates. Even as late as 1774 the building is shown in a drawing as almost complete.[3]

When the great new cathedral of St Magnus in Kirkwall was sufficiently advanced to be put to use about 1150 it replaced the minister on Birsay as the cathedral of the diocese. The episcopal palace would also be transferred to Kirkwall, where the ruins of the Bishop's Palace standing to the south of the cathedral probably occupy its site today. This building is a long hall-house with a large drum tower advancing prominently from one corner. It dates from the early thirteenth century and has polychrome masonry used decoratively in the jambs of slit windows or arrow loops which are now blocked up. Red and white freestone (a rare material in Orkney) is similarly employed in mid- twelfth- and early thirteenth-century work in the cathedral. The masonry which stands high at the Bishop's Palace is mostly of fifteenth-century to seventeenth-century date and represents various modifications and building periods upon the thirteenth-century foundations.

The palace on Birsay would also continue in use for some time after the transfer to Kirkwall, but the reduced importance of the settlement combined with the inconveniences attending its situation upon a tidal island caused a transfer at some unknown date in the Middle Ages to the mainland. A residence in the bishop's important holding at the north end of the Orkney mainland, some 16 miles from the new palace in Kirkwall, would be a necessity. The obvious place in the barony is the present hamlet of Birsay; the obvious site is that

[1] A. B. Taylor (1938), 189. [2] C. A. R. Radford (1959).
[3] G. Low (1774), pl. LI.

of the existing ruined Earl's Palace, from which the hamlet derives its name.

It seems likely that the bishop moved his seat early in the fourteenth century, if not before. The Earl's Palace, in its earliest work, probably represents the palace which succeeded the abandoned residence on the island. Two parts of a broken lintel stone, built into the wall of the seventeenth-century parish church and a nearby house afford feasible evidence of episcopal residence with an inscription "*Mons: bellus*" in Lombardic lettering. This would be appropriate over the doorway of a great house. An Orkney bishop, Adam Bothwell (1559-93), dated a letter "At Monsbellus in Orkney".[1]

Narrow ranges about an open court, separately entered from it, were known as lodgings. In earlier mediaeval plans they formed two opposite sides of a quadrangle linked across one end by the great hall range containing the kitchen and solar. The fourth side was frequently an enclosure wall only. This is very likely to have been the lay-out of Birsay in its first phase.

Remains of "lodgings" are exceedingly rare. The "gentlemen's chalmeris" in St Andrews Castle were doubtless lodgings about the courtyard. The "King's Lodgings" were ranged along the east side of what is now known as Crown Square in Edinburgh Castle on the site of the citadel at its highest point. But "Waterton's lodgings" at Dunnottar is a seventeenth-century reference to a free-standing house of sixteenth-century date in the centre of the plateau over which the castle has developed since the late fourteenth century. The use of the word in this general sense of dwelling is cautionary. However, at Dunnottar there is the finest of the few "lodgings" in the particular sense of an extended suite of private chambers opening separately and directly off a courtyard. They comprise the ground floor of the west range of a new "palace" built in the last quarter of the sixteenth century by George Keith fourth Earl Marshall when he removed his residence from the confinement of the old tower-house to occupy the open north-east corner of the plateau with an extended house of ample accommodation adequate for numerous guests and retainers.

The new residence, known as the "Palace", was quadrangular. The west range is the oldest part. The lodgings in its ground floor consist of a series of seven chambers side by side. Over them runs a

[1] H. Marwick (1951), 38. This letter is in the National Library of Scotland, Edinburgh.

long gallery, before them a wide cobbled path leading round the court to the hall and kitchens in the north range. Each lodging has, beside its doorway, a window to the court and a fireplace with good if subdued detailing. In the wall opposite the doorway there is a single window. The lodgings are separated by cross walls rising to the floor level of the long gallery which extended without interruption over all seven chambers. There was no communication between lodgings, nor from them to the hall above.

The evidence of "lodgings" in Scotland being scanty the survival of the range at Dunottar is all the more fortunate by preserving a first-rate example of an imported English idea. There is nothing quite like it in Scotland save in the thirteenth-century courtyard of Caerlaverock where, against the west curtain, a row of late lodgings opens its doors directly to the court. Each chamber here has a window opening to the court, and a fine fireplace with late fifteenth- or early sixteenth-century shafted jambs enriched with late Gothic foliage carving. These lodgings served the retinue of gentlemen who accompanied the nobles sharing my lord's hospitality in the keep-gatehouse until the extremely fine Renaissance building of 1634 against the east curtain superseded them. As part of the same adjustment the great rib-vaulted hall in the thirteenth-century gatehouse was to have been superseded by a hall laid across the length of the south or basal side of Caerlaverock's triangular plan.

The quadrangular lay-out at Dunottar fulfils the requirements of a courtyard "type" which, it has been maintained above, must be preconceived not adventitious in order to be valid. It is the expression of an idea, with this condition added, that it responds to particular and specific needs. The three ranges of the courtyard are interdependent—lodgings and gallery; great hall and kitchen; larder, brew-house and bakery. No demonstration could more forcibly illustrate the native propensity for vertical building than this "palace" and the singularity of its occurrence.

Its affinities lie in England, with the country houses of the Elizabethan gentry, e.g. Kirby Hall (1570-5), which affords instructive comparisons and many significant similarities. The extended plan is quite at variance with Scottish practice although the detailed treatment of its elevations is traditional. The usual process is thus reversed. Imported styles are normally expressed in incidental detail upon a stubbornly native plan and elevation.

7

Native and Foreign Influences

DECORATIVE oddities, peculiarities of plan and constructional features of local and not widespread occurrence afford interesting variations on the standard themes. The Gothic ribbed vaults and the distinctive plan of the Towie Barclay group for example suggest not only a local Aberdeenshire tradition but the work of the same masons' yard in the 1570's and '80's. The decorative splendour of the Midmar, Crathes and Craigievar group as clearly proclaims individuality and a common source of inspiration in Mar and the Garioch as the sixteenth century advances into the seventeenth. In the south, where elevational treatment is outclassed by the imaginative achievements of the north-east, arresting parallel variations from the conventional plans are to be found in the towers of Dryhope and Gamelscleugh in Selkirkshire; and in the kitchen arrangements of Little Cumbrae, Law, Fairlie and Skelmorlie Castles in Ayrshire, to which reference has already been made. The Earl's Palace at Kirkwall and the latest work of the adjacent Bishop's Palace are clearly related to the most northerly two castles in the British Isles, Scalloway (1600) and Muness (1598) in Shetland. They, in their turn, share significant similarities of arrangement with that other astonishing *tour de force* of the far north, the mighty edifice of Noltland Castle on the remote Orkney island of Westray. However, it is not in their general similarities alone that these groups distinguish themselves, but in the close correspondence of unusual features.

Uncommon features occurring in a group may occur sporadically elsewhere, and they may indicate nothing more significant than local popularity. Distinctive quatre-foil and encircled pistol-holes lavishly provided at the Earl's Palace in Kirkwall are conspicuous at Muness in Shetland, but they occur in the garden-house of the pleasance of Edzell in Angus at the same time, at the turn of the sixteenth century. As a connection between Noltland and Elcho in Perthshire is not unlikely on architectural grounds,[1] and as a Fife emigration to Shetland in the sixteenth century is a historical fact, the fanciful pistol-holes might denote distant connections.

More significant are the loops which penetrate the very angles of the building at the Earl's Palace and Noltland, and the spacious and imaginative handling of their stairways, those traditionally awkward necessities. The wheel stair at Noltland has unusual width and easy rise round a massive newel column. The renowned Fyvie stair (1598-1603) is of great size and elegance, and the large sculptured knop with which it is finished at the landing on the stairhead as a finial surmounts a Gothic buttress. There are few in this grand manner, and the Fyvie stair is unique. The parallel with Noltland reflects a contemporary improvement in communications evident elsewhere. Falkland, Elcho, Glamis and many others bear witness to a new interest in stairs as necessities worthy of creative ability and capable of an appeal to the imagination no less forceful than spirited indulgences at the wall-head. Their emergence from obscurity to distinction is a real gain.

With the general improvement in wheel stairs goes another improvement, a totally new conception introduced to the architecture of towers. This is the stair advancing decorously in straight flights and landings about a flat inner wall instead of revolving rapidly round a circular newel post or column. The old idea of this hub round which the steps revolved or radiated has a distant echo in Leslie (1661) (fig. 19) in Aberdeenshire, where straight flights and landings are worked about a square hollow newel. Hollow newels are not rare in Scotland but they are uncommon enough to be noteworthy. In a seventeenth-century description of Cassilis Castle, a fourteenth-century oblong tower to which a square tower was added in the seventeenth century, a round hollow newel is thus accounted for: " . . . a fine stone stair, turning about a hollow casement, in which are many opens from the bottom to the top, that by putting a lamp into it gives light to the whole turn of stairs".[2] Hollow newels are to be found in the Falkland, Glamis and Noltland stairs also, but the Fyvie newel is solid. The newel as a hollow square occurs in Early Renaissance houses in England. An example very similar to that in Leslie is included in the Thorpe

[1] W. D. Simpson (1952*c*), 148.

[2] R. Pitcairn (1830), 158.

drawings in the Soane Museum, which are illustrated by Gotch.[1]

The scale and platt stair is natural to square stair towers as the spiral stair is not, and the northern castles are conspicuously successful with their straight flights. While Noltland retains the orthodox spiral, albeit on the grand scale, the related works of the Earl's Palace at Kirkwall, Muness and Scalloway contain accomplished stairways in straight flights and landings, and they do not resort to the projecting stair tower, that hard-worked expedient capable of resolving many a difficulty in planning by the ease and the certainty of good effect with which it could be pushed outside a wall. They

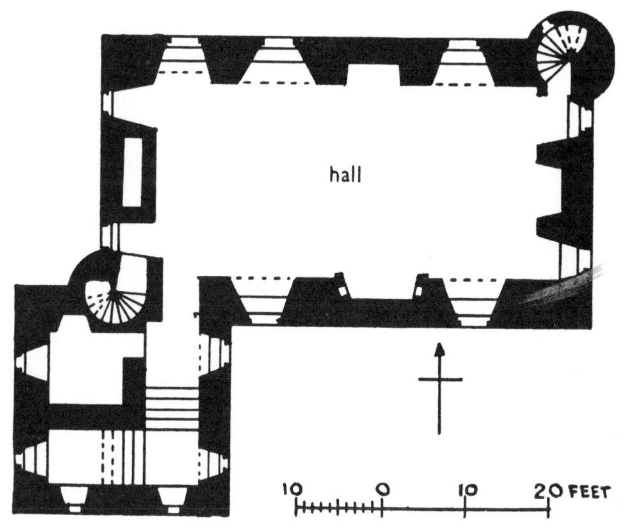

FIG. 23. Scalloway, first floor

become an integral part of the plan. They reveal a real awareness of spacial effects by changes in direction and varying ceiling heights and shapes produced by the semi-circular barrel-vaults which cover them as they ascend and turn. The Earl's Palace stair is particularly impressive in this respect. To stand at the foot of it, with the long vista of the barrel-vaulted corridor lit by courtyard windows on the one hand, and the return of the corridor and the ascent of the barrel-vaulted scale and platt stair on the other hand, is a most satisfying experience. It would doubtless be more so when the walls were plastered and the shapes and volumes were undisturbed by the distraction of exposed undressed masonry.

Scalloway follows the same scheme, while the Muness stair,

[1] J. A. Gotch (1901), pl. LXXIII, 5.

situated in the thickness of one of the long walls of the main block, is the earliest and less accomplished work. The 1580-90 Italianate block at Crichton affords direct evidence of foreign influence in one of the most sophisticated of Scottish stairways, enlivened by carefully considered detail more generously employed than is usual even in the more ambitious works. The stylistic mannerisms of construction and decoration in the northern castles indicate the same hand and mind at work. It has been suggested that "*ane gentilman Andrew Crafurd, sumtym servand and maister of vark to the Earl of Orkney, quha deperted the 1 Mai 160–*" was responsible, according to a broken tombstone in the old churchyard at Tingwall not far from Scalloway.

Master Lukup of Drumlanrig has already been referred to. In the old churchyard of Midmar, some half-mile from the castle, a plain and undecorated recumbent slab of granite has an equally interesting story to relate which likewise throws some light upon the building history and family relationship of the Midmar group of castles. It says: "*Heir lyis Georg Bel meason Deceisit in Balogy Ano 1575*". As Balogy is the old name for Midmar there is little doubt that the mason George Bell who was buried here played some important part in the construction of the castle, and references to other Bells in connection with the related works suggest that he was one of a family of some note to whose memory we may pay tribute.

Upon the giant frontispiece of Castle Fraser a small tablet commemorates "*I. Bell 1617*". At Pitfichie (1607) a David Bell was employed.[1] Upon a skew-putt at Tolquhon there are the initials TL for Thomas Leiper. Its gable belongs to a square chamber corbelled from a round stair tower projecting from the centre of the rear block in the courtyard. The corbel system carrying the square chamber has a curious upper member, flat and straight, resembling a frieze. The rounded corbel courses below it have a distinctive section which is paralleled at Esslemont nearby. We seem here to have stylistic connections, whose interest is enhanced by association with a known mason.

Such occurrences are unfortunately rare, if for no other reason that vernacular building was haphazard, and Scottish ambitions generally fell to the talented but uncommemorated artisan to realise, which he did in the conventional way or in some personal version of it without too drastic a change from the traditional. But there must have been a measure of enlightened patronage to encourage and

[1] RSS VIII. 635.

maintain the high standards achieved throughout the country, and for the outstanding accomplishments of the Aberdeenshire school an "Episcopalian culture" may be inferred, with roots in a mediaeval tradition of craftsmanship never so rudely severed as they were in the south.

FOREIGN INFLUENCES

French châteaux, particularly those of the Loire, make much of the round towers, turrets and dormer windows which invest the later tower-houses with their most engaging air. From this, and the recorded activity of French masons in Scotland in the sixteenth century, French inspiration is assumed. While convenient, pleasing and plausible, this assumption is not supported by the facts of the architecture, which refute it. Although French Court connections in the sixteenth century are undoubted, and French master masons were introduced and remained long enough to win distinction and permanent professional appointments and even citizenship,[1] Scottish work remains fundamentally unaffected. This is so not only in the detail (and in the significance of the detail which is conditional upon the use made of it), but also in the larger and more important aspects of planning, composition, rhythm and proportion. Where French masons have worked, or where French influence has operated, the effect is instantly imparted to the beholder who is familiar with contemporary Scottish work that here is something with a difference to account for, a departure, no matter how elusive, from normal practice and established tradition. A little research after such a reaction invariably yields a foreign connection to explain it—of Fyvie with the Earl of Dunfermline and continental scholarship, of Huntly with the Earl of Huntly and France, of Crichton with the Earl of Bothwell and Italy, and of Edzell with Lord Edzell and Germany.

Attention has been drawn to Fyvie (pl. 37) as a rare example of the extended frontage. It is the great show-façade of an intended but never completed quadrangular lay-out. The composition incorporates an earlier tower-house as a terminal feature. At the other end of the long elevation another was built to match it. The remodelling and enlargement of Holyroodhouse by the Duke of Lauderdale and Sir William Bruce for Charles II in 1671 repeated this process by adding to the old tower-house of about 1500 a long

[1] John Roytell, Frenchman, was appointed "principall maister masoun to all hir hienes workis" in March 1556-7, having been admitted a burgess of Edinburgh six years previously. He is associated with the fortification of the island of Inchkeith in the Forth by the French in 1564. (See AMW I.xxxiv.)

low frontage with classical orders flanking the main entrance in the centre. This is stopped at the other end on a replica of the old tower. Behind the Holyroodhouse frontage rises a quadrangle with elevations relieved by classical pilasters. The horizontal spread of the Fyvie frontage and the symmetry imposed upon it arrest the attention, not only because of the compelling interest of the composition which leads the eye from end to end, but because the experience is unique.

Yet although the result is French the means are not. The end towers are traditional. The mid-tower with its lofty arched recess recalls contemporary Craigston (1604). The squat corner roundels upon corbels, the stepped string-courses and the surface blankness of the main residential blocks which link the towers are typically Scottish of the Aberdeenshire school of the late sixteenth and early seventeenth century. Although for all their waywardness the incidental detail of the typical tower-house is rarely misapplied, the ambitious and on the whole extremely successful achievement of Fyvie is not altogether faultless. An early example of the pedimented window (properly a dormer with a pediment standing free above the wall-head in Scots work) is applied to the walling of the mid-tower, high up, and the pediment looks lost, as though it should not be there, which it should not, or built up by later work, which it is not. As MacGibbon and Ross say: "If a French architect designed this building, he must have changed his style very much to suit his Scottish patron". This is true of course; and if a native architect designed it he changed his style as much to suit his patron's taste.

Were there many castles as eloquent as Fyvie and Huntly there would be little justification in denying French sources. French quotations are even more clearly pronounced at Huntly than they are at Fyvie (pl. 28). A splendid series of oriel windows, oversailing the wall on richly moulded corbelling of unusual sophistication, is ranged along the wall-head of the main block and even upon the top of the great drum tower. They lack their pediments, but a false window and its pediment are worked upon the side of a chimney-stack to complete the series of dormers which it interrupts. A frieze with giant letters in relief commemorates

GEORGE GORDON FIRST MARQUIS OF HUNTLIE 16
HENRIETTE STEVART MARQUESSE OF HUNTLIE 02

Comparable statements enliven the wall-heads of the early

Plate 37

Fyvie, Aberdeenshire, *c.* 1600

left detail

below the show-façade

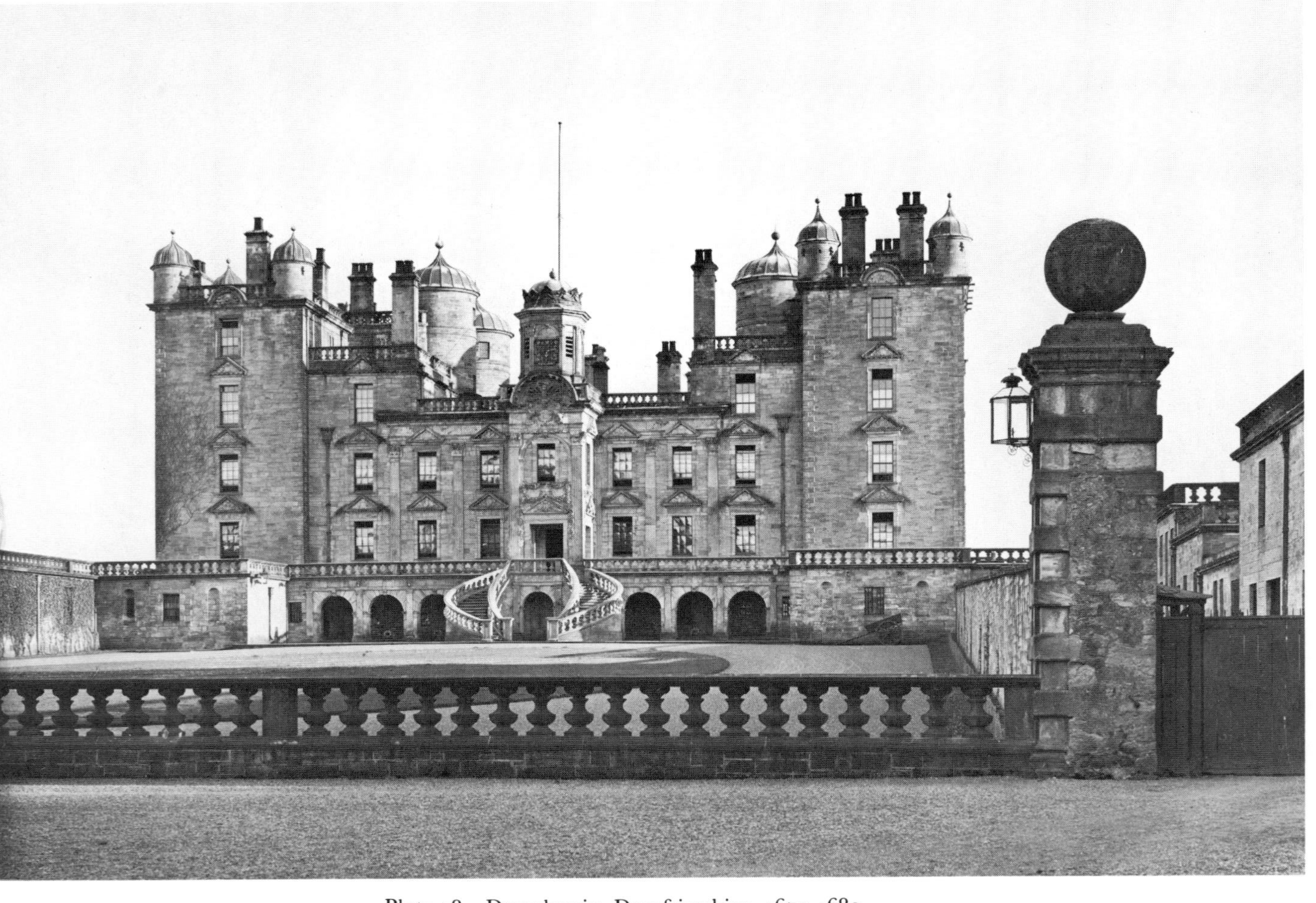

Plate 38 Drumlanrig, Dumfriesshire, 1675-1689

Plate 39 George Heriot's School, Edinburgh, 1627-1650

Plate 40

above, left Edzell, Angus: 'Mars', 1604

above, right 'Mars': engraving by the Meister I.B. of Nuremberg, 1528

below Crichton, Midlothian: the Italianate façade, 1581-91

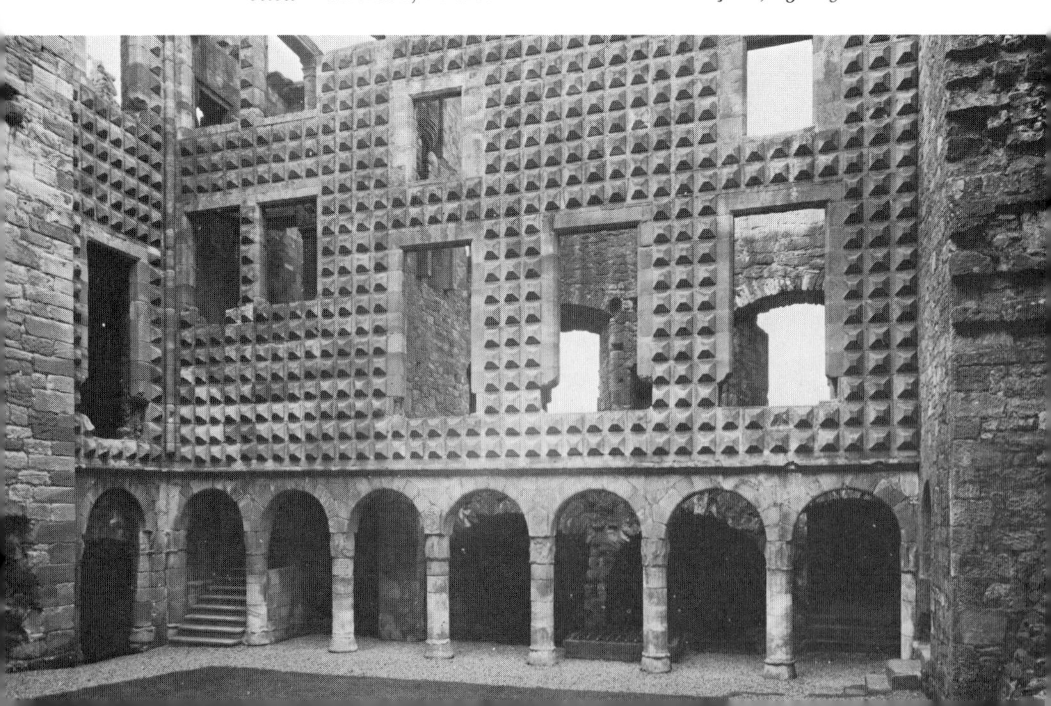

Jacobean ranges and octagonal turrets of Castle Ashby (Northamptonshire) which is attributed to Inigo Jones. But there the letters are cut in the round, as substitutes for the fashionable strap-work or traceried balustrade; and in like manner they appear in the crowned cyphers of Hardwick Hall (Derbyshire) in 1590-7. With the exception of Gordon Castle, Fochabers, now demolished, they do not occur elsewhere in Scotland: the wall-head emphasis was expressed in strictly architectural terms. During the course of the demolition of Gordon Castle an incomplete inscription was found behind friezes in adjacent rooms which had been added to the original castle.[1] This inscription was originally external and ran round at least two sides of an oblong block. It was cut in a fashion identical to that of Huntly, and in every way was a closely related declaration commemorating . . . GEORGE . GORD(ON) . . . HENRIETTE . ST(EWART) . . . .

The oriels are clearly derived from France, probably Blois. They were erected about 1600 by the Marquis of Huntly, who, when in exile in France, became a Knight of the French Order of St Michael. In all probability he brought French masons to Scotland for his ambitious remodelling of the upper part of the castle and the addition of the heraldic frontispiece over the entrance. A mason associated with the work is known, one Ralph Raleyn, which does not sound Scottish and could be French. The occurrence of oriels is itself a matter of interest. Although not unknown—they occur as widely spread as the Earl's Palace in Kirkwall, Linlithgow in West Lothian and Maybole in Ayrshire for instance—they were strangely ignored, despite the popularity of corbelling.

The startling and aggressive courtyard façade of Crichton, which was erected between 1580 and 1590 by the Earl Bothwell, is likewise the outcome of exile. Bothwell was exiled to Italy, whence he returned in 1581 to commence the rebuilding and enlargement of the castle, retaining the austere late fourteenth-century tower-house as a nucleus for a courtyard lay-out. There is even less doubt about direct foreign influence at work here. This elevation is one of the most unequivocal results of it to be found in Britain. The nail-head or diamond-facetted sculpturing of every stone is unparalleled in Scotland and occurs in England sparingly, as on the podiums of the

[1] Working drawings discovered in the muniment room (and now in the General Register House, Edinburgh, with related papers of considerable interest) show extensive additions of the late eighteenth and nineteenth centuries. The most important are signed by Baxter and Roumieux who seem to have established small drawing offices there while engaged on their projects.

columns which carry the porch at Cobham Hall (Kent) in 1594. It occurs more frequently in Italy and Spain—on the Palazzo dei Diamanti in Ferrara, for instance, in Florence, and on the Casa de los Picos in Segovia.

A still more striking case of foreign influence may be seen in the remarkable pleasance added in 1604 by Sir David Lindsay, Lord Edzell, to his notable castle in Angus (pl. 40). The wall of this pleasance is highly enriched with heraldic and symbolic decorations, including a unique series of panels portraying the cardinal virtues, the liberal arts and the planetary deities. These are of German origin, and all but one of the planetary series are actual copies of copperplate engravings by Meister I.B., usually identified as George Pencz, one of the most illustrious of the Nuremberg *Kleinmeister* and a pupil of Dürer.

Lord Edzell is known to have travelled in Germany and brought back with him a couple of mining engineers from Nuremberg to help prospecting for precious metals at the head of Glenesk, where the workings can still be traced. Probably he got the drawings which his mason copied from an *Album Amicorum* in the hands of one of these engineers. So scrupulously has he gone about his task that the master's initials I.B. have been included in the carving, upon the blade of the halberd of Mars, just as they appear in the engraving. Edzell is also one of the places where the characteristic German form of redented gunloops is found.[1] Upon the wall-head of the nearby castle of Balbegno, otherwise notable for its rib-vaulted hall with painted plaster severies, are figures sculptured by the same hand. They include figures looking out of a false window, as they do at the house of Jacques Coeur in Bourges (1443-51).

These instances of enlightened patronage introducing foreign notions are exceptional, and save for these works and those of the Court School in the first half of the sixteenth century there are no castles which prompt a search for foreign explanations. The gentry, however widely travelled, were evidently well satisfied with the customary style, the result of the slow and unconscious moulding of architectural form from generation to generation. For the innumerable tower-houses there is no hint of French masons or French influence, except in the alleged affinity of the architecture itself. This would indeed be sufficient if true, but upon analysis it will be seen that the resemblances are not at all convincing.

[1] W. D. Simpson (1931), 162.

The corner turrets, which so easily provoke French comparisons, are of early Scottish ancestry. They appear upon Scottish work long before the period of alleged French influence. They are present incipiently on the corners of Drum, the earliest tower-house, which dates from the end of the thirteenth century. They occur on the barbican covering the drawbridge pit of Dirleton (*c.* 1300), on the three vulnerable corners of the tower-house of Lochleven of the first half of the fourteenth century, on the mid-tower of Tantallon of the later fourteenth century, and on the internal re-entrant stair which oversails the basement upon continuous corbelling at Threave in 1390. At first they were open rounds, an outward swelling of the parapet. In this form they were commonplace throughout the fifteenth century. In the sixteenth century they were covered by conical roofs—just as the parapet was covered by the main roof advancing to the outer face of the wall-head. At first they were defensive, as was the parapet walk. Later they were ornamental, and provided additional accommodation when the desire for it grew greater and the need for defence grew less.

In the same way the parapet walk was absorbed into the interior, and the dormer window which had hitherto been obscured by the parapet wall also advanced to the wall face to become a conspicuous and ornamental feature. This is only to be expected. Architecture is a steady and consistent mover. From the wall-head the corbelled turret grew downwards to die away in corbelling at any level convenient to the interior arrangements, at any floor level, or even between floors, where a straight stair springs into a spiral and jumps out of the building. This happens in the kitchen tower of Doune before 1400. In this fashion it is employed as an expedient of planning and for outward effect, the unhampered freedom in which it could be used was fully exploited by well-instructed masons familiar with the features they were handling. In the same gable elevation one turret might be short, the other long; one rises high, the other is small; one corner has a turret, the other has not. And in most cases the crow-stepped gable between the turrets is asymmetrical, at times reduced to extreme narrowness in the battle of the turrets. The French roundel is never used in this eccentric fashion.

Arising from this free use of roundels and the ornamental importance of the dormer is another contrast. The Scottish profile is very different. The aspect changes as one walks round. The skyline is punctuated by a procession of turret roofs, gable chimneys and dormers, all contributing separate and emphatic notes of interest. On the other hand the French elevation is invariably dominated by the mass of the high steep-pitched roof. It overwhelms these features, so that they do not contribute to the variety of the skyline. As a consequence of this the French dormer asserts itself by standing high, the daylight opening of the window very frequently being wholly above the wall-head. Vertical emphasis and attraction is sought by high slender finials.

French dormers generally are rich in Gothic detail of this kind and the windows in the main walling are similarly treated. The Scottish distinction between the fanciful dormers of the wall-head and the plain windows of the main walling is not characteristic of French work, especially that of the Loire School, the alleged source and inspiration. The formal treatment of the French window expresses the interior: the windows express the rooms behind them. The Scottish façades are not like this: the masses seem to be solid, and the windows are irregular, small and unpretentious. French windows are underlined by a string-course; and the horizontal divisions of the interior are clearly indicated, sometimes by double strings joining cills and lintels, and continuing regularly across façades without fenestration. The Scots mason rejects the horizontal string, and uses the string arbitrarily, to link incidental features, not to define structure.

More general differences between French and Scottish work are equally significant. The relationship of plain to decorated surfaces is entirely different. The French elevation is sophisticated; an all-over treatment is carefully considered. This contrasts with Scottish simplicity and informality and the dominance of the plain wall over the designed wall. The attitude to the relationship of plain to decorated surfaces is fundamentally different, and in plan, the very basis of architecture, there is no affinity.

The introduction of foreign masons in number belongs to the exceptional first half of the sixteenth century when building in Scotland lapsed almost entirely, save for the royal works which are consciously and obviously un-Scottish. They were occasioned by the impending marriage of James V to a French princess and the efforts he made to refashion his palaces by architectural window-dressing in the style which would please her, and with which he had become familiar and envious during his residence at the court of his prospective father-in-law François I, who built the courtyard of

Blois. The Frenchmen worked side by side with Scots who greatly outnumbered them. In the Accounts of the Masters of Works for the years 1539-41 there appear regularly with Roytell, Roy, Martin and Peter Flemisman, all foreign, the names of John Brounhill, Thomas Gray, John Balquhanan, Thomas Lychtoun, Robert Liall, Andrew Harvey, Alexander Campbell and so on. Many of these native craftsmen are men of standing, accompanied by their "servitours" or apprentices. Nothing demonstrates more forcibly the native independence of foreign ideas than the failure of the Falkland façade to influence Scottish architecture. Let it be said that there is nothing commendable in this, for that work is of historic importance as the first Renaissance façade in Britain. But such is the fact. And when building activity was resumed after the return of Mary Queen of Scots from France in 1561 it was to the old tower-house that the new patrons turned for their model.

When Erik Rosencrantz rebuilt the great tower-house in Bergen in 1562-3 he engaged builders and masons from Scotland (*murmestere oc stenhuggere af Skotland*). Armorial panels (*c.* 1560) over the entrance of St Andrews Castle and on St Mary's College, St Andrews, have a striking resemblance to a large and conspicuous panel upon the Rosencrantz Tower. This is difficult to parallel in Norway, but earlier Norwegian records show immigrant Scots were at work. In 1548 Odn(?) Skotte (Odn the Scot) made a statue of St Hans for the rebuilt Greyfriars Church in Bergen; in 1558 a Scottish master-mason is included in a list of artisans.[1] Apart from the particular detail of its armorial panel the Rosencrantz Tower bears a strong general affinity with the traditional Scottish tower-house. There is no doubt of Scottish influence in Bergen and some probability that the masons who worked the frontispiece at St Andrews Castle—a remarkably fine thing incidentally—and the interesting elevation of St Mary's were shortly afterwards at work in Bergen, continuing a well-established connection in their own native style.

[1] R. Kloster (1930), 38.

8

Artillery and Fortification

ALTHOUGH tower-houses derive their most distinctive features from their residential and domestic functions, strong defensive qualities are obvious. This is particularly true of the earlier works of the fourteenth and fifteenth centuries. But if for curtain-wall castles evolving in response to the challenge of the elaborate apparatus of mediaeval siegecraft no wholly military explanation is admissible, and the strategic explanation of their distribution admits of doubt, even less would the humbler tower-house respond to military expediency. Several questions therefore arise. To what extent were defensive preparations seriously considered? What thought was devoted to defensive features generally, and how much to the aggressive part of them? How serious was the threat and what was its nature? What was current European military theory and practice in the long period of tower-house architecture and how did tower-houses submit to it? What were the weapons used in attack and defence? How faithfully do the ineloquent towers echo the changing circumstances of warfare? Such questions affecting the form of tower-houses have never been put. They are of importance for these late and peculiarly Scottish castles as well as for their predecessors of the earlier European and Byzantine tradition.[1]

The first recorded use of ordnance in Britain was against the Scots by Hainault mercenaries of Edward III when he invaded the country in 1327, the first year of his reign.[2] This is the date of the earliest known illustration of a cannon, which is in a manuscript treatise by Walter de Milemete in the library of Christ Church, Oxford. The text contains no allusions to the illustration. It is the only known picture of a gun which can be associated with a known

[1] For many references to the use of artillery see R. C. Clephan (1903 and 1911) and C. Oman (1924), vol. 2, bk. 10.

[2] J. H. Ramsay (1913), 1.194.

date until the official seal (1403) of Johan von Oppenheim, master of ordnance to the town of Hagenau.[1] This follows hard upon a document proving the existence of cannon in the early fourteenth century which authorises the priors, the gonfalonier, and twelve good men to appoint persons to superintend the manufacture of cannons of brass, and iron balls, for the defence of the commune, camps and territory of Florence in 1326.

The cannon of the Christ Church manuscript is vase-shaped, bulbous and long-necked. Lying upon its side on a table, bed, or stand, it is directed towards the crenellated gatehouse of a town or castle. Fired by a mail-clad soldier holding a bar of iron and fuse in his hand, with which he ignites the charge, the projectile emerges from the gun as a brass-feathered bolt or arrow. The garreau or garrot, as the projectile was called, was commonly used with early small ordnance and hand-guns as well as with the older mechanical throwing engine the espringal or springal, the forerunner of the cannon, an exceedingly large crossbow on wheels, spanned by windlasses and used as mobile field artillery to cast stones or bolts by tension not explosion. An inventory of stores in Berwick Castle handed over to the Constable, Sir Hugh de Audley, on 22 October 1290 includes "five corner pieces of iron for the springalds and three springalds on the walls with all their furniture excepting cords".[2] At the siege of Berwick by Edward II in 1319 springalds, engines and cranes were used by John Crabb, "a Fleming of great subtlety", a skilled artificer.[3] A "sow" or covered shed moving upon rollers was made "of greit joistis", with armed men within and "instrumentis for to mine".[4]

Barbour denies that Crabb had guns in this famous action—"gynnis for crakys had he nane"[5]—and he categorically asserts that the first guns ever heard of in Scotland were those employed by the English in the invasion of 1327, when two novelties were then experienced—plumes for helmets and "crakys of wer".[6] Clearly Barbour had cannon in mind when describing these events about 1375, but he may have antedated later occurrences, for he was young when these episodes took place and could only have written from hearsay and a familiarity with artillery. Edward is said to have used

[1] R. C. Clephan (1911), 57ff, 87.
[2] J. Stevenson (1870), II.322-5, quoted by W. C. Dickinson (1952), I.202.
[3] For Crabb see E. W. M. Balfour-Melville, SHR, XXXIX (1960), 31-4.
[4] John Barbour, quoted by Agnes Muir Mackenzie (1946), 219.
[5] John Barbour XVII, line 250. [6] John Barbour XIX, lines 394ff.

ordnance at yet another siege of Berwick in 1333.[1] For 1338 there is unquestionable proof of the use of ordnance in ships in letters referring to the delivery of "canons de ferr".[2] But from the unimpeachable evidence of the Christ Church illustration and the exceptional interest in the use and development of ordnance taken by Edward III, who in all probability used it at Crécy in 1346[3] and to whom the Christ Church manuscript was dedicated by its author, there can be little reasonable doubt that the "crakys of wer", the "novelty" alluded to by Barbour, were cannon. The statement, although not indisputable, is accepted by most writers.

The Scots were again at the receiving end of interesting early experiments in detonation in 1342, when, as Froissart records,[4] cannon were employed at the assault on Stirling Castle ("chatel de Sturmelin"): *Les Seigneurs d'Ecosse se hâterent tellement et contraignirent ceux de la dite garnison, par assauts d'engins et de canons, que par force les convint rendre aux Escots.* This formidable stronghold, the gateway to the Highlands, commanding a crossing and the upper reaches of the Forth, has in common with Edinburgh Castle a precipitous situation, a long and eventful history and the loss of most of its early work as the result of that history. It was the scene of one of the classic mediaeval sieges of the great period of siege warfare, by Edward I in 1304. On 20 July of that year Sir Walter de Bedewyne writes: "As for news Stirling Castle was absolutely surrendered to the King without conditions this Monday, St Margaret's Day, but the King wills it that none of his people enter the castle till it is struck with his war-wolf and that those within the castle defend themselves from the said war-wolf as best they can".[5] Evidently Edward was not a little displeased at the premature surrender of the garrison which threatened to spoil his demonstration of a great new war engine, to enjoy which event a number of ladies and gentlemen had assembled. This creation of his employed five supervisors and fifty carpenters much time and labour to construct, and caused the King's Treasurer and the Barons of the Exchequer to be firmly enjoined to send without fail, and that in haste, a horseload of cotton thread, a load of quick sulphur and another of saltpetre.[6]

This demand was addressed from St Andrews Castle, which had been improved by the construction of new houses by Robert de

[1] R. C. Clephan (1903), 5.
[2] H. Brackenbury (1865), 5.
[3] R. C. Clephan (1911), 72.
[4] Froissart I, 159.
[5] J. Bain (1884), II.405.
[6] Agnes Muir Mackenzie (1946), 157.

Bedeford, Master Carpenter, on the occasion of the royal visit of Edward and his Queen.[1] The record of the siege continues by mentioning expenses which John de la Mullier has incurred in throwing fire into the castle, and for sulphur bought by Gerard Doroms, and canvas for the stones (probably for the sling of a catapult) and other less important items such as the wages of a boy staying forty days at St Andrews by order of the letter-writer Sir Walter de Bedewyne.

Springalds and fire-and-stone-throwing engines such as were brought into play against Stirling were vastly superior in convenience (awkward though they were), rate of fire and destructive power to the new experimental ordnance which had appeared beside them in action. Up to the mid-fourteenth century cannon were breech-loading, shooting bolts no more effectively than large cross-bows and much less accurately. They were slow in action and required to be cleaned between salvos, when they were vulnerable and frequently captured. Materials were costly. The force of the charge was reduced below its maximum because of inherent structural weaknesses in the guns themselves. But with the advent of the heavy siege gun about the mid-century the whole situation changes, albeit slowly and difficult to assess because of imprecision of nomenclature. It was unpopular in its early stages and until long after its introduction in the early fourteenth century. Machiavelli consistently deprecated fire-arms and in 1513 was half-inclined to banish artillery from the battle-field altogether. To early fire-arms, arquebuses and the like he contemptuously assigned the role of overawing the peasantry as shot-guns are used to scare birds.[2] Claude Fauchet, writing as late as 1600, avers that cannon were used only by cowardly people and that valiant knights disdained them.[3]

In its early stages ordnance partakes of the traditional throwing engines. They are modified and given new names suggestive of changes more drastic than was usually the case. The word gun is a case in point. In the variations *gonne*, *gunne*, etc. it probably derives from an abbreviation of *mangonel* and descended to the new weapon destined to supersede it.[4] "Artillery" itself has an early history, long

[1] J. Harvey (1954), 27. [2] F. L. Taylor (1921), 170.
[3] C. Fauchet (1600), 57.
[4] And so "gunnar" might not mean artilleryman, but carpenter, wright, or artificer working with the old-style catapult. The word, like "gun", needs be received with caution, and the earlier the reference the greater the caution. Two different versions of Wyntoun's *Original Chronicle* give different renderings of the same passage and illustrate

preceding fire-arms. Thought to be derived from *aro bellaria*, meaning crossbows, it was used thus in 1180 by Alexander Neckham in *De Utensilibus*, and by Guiart in a poem of 1305 on the Battle of Courtrai (1302). An "artillator" was a maker of throwing engines in 1300.[1] Grose in his *History of the English Army* (1778) refers to a manuscript which gives the establishment of the English forces in Normandy and before Calais in the twentieth year of Edward III, and refers to engineers, gunners, and artillerymen ("ingyners, gonners and artillers").[2] In 1384 the Exchequer Rolls record payment for an instrument called a gun, bought for the Castle of Edinburgh (*Et pro uno instrumento dicto gun empto pro castro de Edynburgh, iiij li*), but when Robert Bruce's Parliament at Scone in 1318 passed a conscription act rendering all men between sixteen and sixty liable for compulsory service it stipulated that each should be clad in haqueton, bascinet and gloves, and bear a shield and sword or a spear and good bow with a sheaf of arrows, that is to say twenty-four arrows.[3] There is neither mention nor implication of fire-arms.

Throughout the fourteenth century tower-houses are reticent about weapons, whereas curtain-wall castles with projecting towers, arrow slits and long spreading bases proclaim the challenge they were designed to meet. No contrast in structures of similar kind is more striking than that between the two types of Scottish castle, the one inward-looking and passive the other turned and equipped to confront the danger without. Even the keep-gatehouse of the later curtained castle, the progenitor of the tower-house, advances boldly beyond the curtain.

No tower of the fourteenth century has any connection with the new weapon. Even the greatest achievements of the first half of the fifteenth century, Borthwick, Elphinstone and Comlongon, are wholly innocent of gun-loops and arrow slits.

the point. The earliest version (the Wemyss manuscript) in describing the assault of Dundarg Castle, Aberdeenshire, 1334, says:

> The wardane gert the gunnare syne
> Dress up stoutly the engyne.

The Cottonian manuscript gives it thus:

> The wardane gert his wrichtis syne
> Set up richt stoutly ane ingyne.

And the context suggests the stone-throwing engine, not ordnance. H. M. Paton (1957) xxxv-vi, is quite positive that "gunnar" is not necessarily an artilleryman even in the sixteenth century, but a carpenter. At this late date the connection must be with ordnance, presumably with gun-carriages and wheels.

[1] W. Porter (1889), I.13, 15. [2] F. Grose (1778),
[3] Agnes Muir Mackenzie (1946), 159.

Until the middle of the fourteenth century there was little advance in artillery. Heavy cavalry, the crossbow and the longbow were the popular and influential weapons, even though no force took the field without its complement of fashionable cannon and its attendant convoy of ammunition carts, ribaudequins or armed chariots, and pioneers to prepare its way. Little mention is made of the artillery arm in battle, and such passages as describe it in detail indicate its experimental character and uncertain efficacy. It is recorded with wonder that at the siege of Saaz a cannon fired seventy salvos in a single day[1], and when the Gantois besieged Ypres in 1383 two cannon discharged 450 rounds without injuring a single man.[2] The effect was largely fortuitous it seems, depending on the morale of the attacked. In some encounters the mere presence of ordnance won the day. When Henry IV besieged Berwick in 1405 the first shot from his large gun caused such an impact upon the walls that the garrison forthwith surrendered.[3]

Early cannon cast the same missiles as the older stone-throwing engines less accurately and with less effect, but with the advent of the heavy siege-gun projecting massive stone shot horizontally the balance of power between attack and defence was radically altered in favour of attack, hitherto at a disadvantage in the face of ditches, curtain-walls, spreading bases, and overhanging machicolated galleries. Modifications of walls and towers, constructed to resist high trajectory missiles not low trajectory horizontal "gunstones" of greater destructive power, were inevitable. Walls were made thicker to resist impact and to provide a wider platform for mounting guns for counter-attack. Tantallon Castle affords one of the best examples of such expediency to be found in the British Isles. The lofty curtains contain long flights of straight mural stairs ascending from the courtyard at ground level to the wall-head. Opening off them are sizeable chambers also in the thickness of the walls. After the surrender of the castle in 1529 the Crown blocked the mural chambers to strengthen the curtain against the forces of improved artillery.[4]

An account of the siege of Le Mans (1424) relates how "the Englishmen approached as nighe to the walles as they might without their losse and detriment, and shot against their walles great stones out of great goones which kinds of enginnes before that tyme was

[1] R. C. Clephan (1911), 103.
[2] R. C. Clephan (1911), 64.
[3] R. C. Clephan (1911), 88.
[4] J. S. Richardson (1937), 17-18.

very little seene or hearde of in Fraunce: the strokes whereof so shaked, crushed and rived the walles that within few days the citie was despoyled of all her toures and outward defences".[1]

In 1435 the Master of Ordnance at Nuremberg cast "a new kind of gun".[2] It was forged in two lengths for separate and easier transport, to be screwed together for use, and it is from about this date that artillery is frequently mentioned in Scottish royal records, usually with a foreign connection.

SCOTTISH RECORDS OF ARTILLERY

James I brought a great bombard of brass from Flanders in 1340 which was called "The Lion".[3] It, or others, are mentioned in the Exchequer Rolls for 1441-2, and 1449-50. There was a bombard at Hatton House (Midlothian) in 1452, as well as a "sow", and at the siege of Abercorn in 1455 where a French gunner "shot right well".[4] In the same year a great bombard and other ordnance were conveyed to the siege of Threave, and one of them was that famous piece of ordnance "Mons Meg". At first known simply as "Mons" she was first referred to by name in an entry of 1489 for "drinksilver" to the gunners when they "cartit" Mons on her way west to the siege of Dumbarton. Mons was in Edinburgh Castle in 1501, 1526, 1539 (when her wheels were greased with Orkney butter and she was overlaid with red lead) and in 1558 pioneers recovered her "bullet" after a salute carrying over two miles. She was still a force to be reckoned with in 1578, when she is referred to as "a great piece of forged iron called Mons", and in 1650 she is capable enough to be "the great iron murderer Muckle Meg". She burst in 1680 in firing a salute, was restored in 1829, and is now a much-loved, greatly admired showpiece before St Margaret's Chapel in Edinburgh Castle.

There is an identical cannon in Ghent which was forged between 1430 and 1452 for the Duke of Burgundy, probably in Malines, which could be Mollance in Scots, corruptible to "Mons".[5] It too was painted red and thus earned the soubriquet "De Roode Duyvel" (The Red Devil). It was also called "Dulle Griet" (Foolish, or Evil, Meg). The Duke of Burgundy was in Edinburgh in 1449 for the wedding of his niece, Marie of Gueldres, to James II; the cannon for his galleys were forged at Malines, and the state marriage established

[1] Richard Grafton (1569).
[2] R. C. Clephan (1911), 106.
[3] ALHT I.ccxxi.
[4] ALHT I.ccxxii.
[5] W. H. Finlayson (1948), 124-6.

a close intercourse between the Scottish and Burgundian courts. The payment of two bombards sent by the Duke of Burgundy to James in 1458[1] is an early instance of that monarch's fatal interest in artillery. It was an interest shared by succeeding Stewarts, particularly by James V, although without such fatal consequences as befell James II, whose death might indeed have been caused by one of these Burgundian products, if not by Mons herself, which exploded during his siege of Roxburgh in 1460 and killed him. Of this disaster Pitscottie relates: "The King, more curious than became him, did stand near the gunners when the artillery discharged; his thigh-bone was dung in two with the piece of a misformed gun that brake in shooting, by which he was stricken to the ground and died hastily."

Ordnance was indeed a royal liability as well as a royal monopoly, for although the feudal army was self-sufficient and decided the result of engagements until well into the sixteenth century—Churchill calls Flodden the last great victory of the long bow[2]—no army took the field without its complement of artillery. At Flodden the captured Scottish guns were varied and numerous and excited the admiration of English writers. The full term of feudal service was rarely demanded, but on 14 February 1496 Symon Spardour was paid for carrying the King's letters to the sheriffs of Stirling, Menteith Perth, Fife, Angus and Kincardine to warn them that all within these bounds remain in service the 6 April and forty days thereafter.[3] The instructions for conscripts to appear in arms of their own providing specify bows, spears and axes, but do not mention fire-arms among the requisite "abilyementis of were".

The expenses of artillery fell upon the Crown alone, and for the increasing independence of the feudal host which this specialised branch gave the government a heavy price was paid, so much so that as early as 1456 the security afforded by the royal monopoly in ordnance was compromised by an appeal to certain of the great barons of the land that were of any might to make carts of war with two guns and two chambers and to provide a cunning man to shoot them.[4]

Under a master of artillery, a court official, there were master gunners, Flemings, Germans and Frenchmen for the most part, assisted by artificers (some foreign) and pioneers or labourers. It

[1] ER vi.386.
[2] W. S. Churchill (1956), ii. 29.
[3] ALHT i.120.
[4] APS ii.45 c. 4.

was mainly Flanders which exported her superior products and the experts to operate them, but in 1474 messengers were sent to Haddington, Dunkeld and Perth to collect metal for the guns—probably old bells and the like—and Wil Turing obtained clay for gun-moulds.[1] This is the first evidence of guns being cast in Scotland whereas for England gun-casting is recorded as early as the 1380's.[2] Thenceforth the Scottish documentary evidence multiplies. Guns were taken to the siege of Dumbarton in 1489 and Burcar was paid for bringing them home; in 1496 he is paid for working irons for artillery; and John Lam of Leith makes gunchambers, sights, bolts for the bombards and a brass gun.[3] "Dymondis" (cubes of iron-shot) are made, serpentines and culverines are present, and two master gunners are on the staff, both Low Countries' men it seems—Hans, first mentioned in the Accounts for 1494-5, and Robert Herwort. In 1496 there is much activity in the royal workshops at Stirling and Edinburgh castles, in preparation for the Raid of Ellem in that year. Burcar is paid for working iron, wheels are iron shod, close-carts for ammunition are made and mustered, and gun-stones, gun-carts, wheels and limbers are made ready.

But artillery remained undecisive. The campaign petered out after two days across the Border, and thus justified the report to Henry VII of Sir John Ramsay, the forfeited Lord Bothwell, a traitor allowed to return to Scotland to be received intimately by James. He sent to Henry a full account of the aforesaid warlike preparations and concludes by assuring him he has little to fear from James's efforts to campaign on behalf of Perkin Warbek. He has inspected the provision of ordnance of the King of Scots and finds it wanting. It comprises 2 great curtaldis, 10 falcons, 30 cart-guns of iron with chambers, 16 close-carts for spears, powder, stones, and other stuff for the guns. The master-gunners as usual were foreign, Hans and Hendrik, and a Guienne Frenchman. The rest were artificers and labourers, to clear a route through narrow paths and mires. Although Perkin Warbek was scarcely helped by this adventure it sufficiently annoyed the English, and in February of the next year Henry VII issued a commission of array to Sir Thomas Dacre against the Scots, because they destroyed without remorse, castles, fortalices and towers, and intended further mischief.[4]

Without doubt the Scots intended further mischief and lost no

[1] ALHT I.
[2] R. C. Smail, *Antiquity*, vol. 36 (1962), 73.
[3] ALHT I.292.
[4] *Foedera* XII. 647.

time in preparing for it, but Ramsay's opinion was again justified, for once more a brave show of arms came to nought, despite the employment of foreign gunners. A greater raid—"the great raid of Norham"—was announced by general proclamation to sheriffs south of the Border. Preparations for warfare even more exacting than those of the previous year were undertaken with determination. The King coined "the great chain" of considerable weight and value (about £1500) and other personal ornaments, which in an age and society much given to expensive ostentation, would also raise considerable funds. With such assistance, a "spear tax" and other contributions considerable funds were raised. The number of men hired for artillery was even greater than before, for the great bombard "Mons" was to accompany the host. The guns, chiefly ox-drawn, were assisted by 187 horses and 110 drivers, 221 pioneers or labourers with spades and mattocks, 61 quarrymen and masons, and 12 carpenters for the smaller fire-arms (culverines and such). Sir Robert Ker, Master of Artillery, engaged no less than 100 workmen and 5 carpenters to accompany "Mons" alone. The specialist gunners included Robert Herwort, Hannis, John Kerrom younger and older, Burcar, Lam, Dande Achinsone and others.

The King rode ahead to Melrose with his pavilions and field kitchens. Next day "Mons" went to war, played out from Edinburgh Castle by minstrels, and then she broke down, and lay at St Leonards, a suburb, while trees were felled and a new carriage made. She arrived late, but the campaign had quickly proved ineffectual for reasons other than her absence.

The sixteenth century begins with royal preparations to subdue the ever-rebellious Islesmen. In 1503-4 the Earl of Huntly began operations, using artillery. Robert Herwort and Hans go to the siege of Carneburgh Castle, an island stronghold off the north end of the island of Mull, where a curtain-wall with rectangular loops in embrasures probably dates from this time. There are frequent payments for men and materials. Hans and Herwort continue to be conspicuous, but others assume importance also and like them were valued servants of the Crown. In 1504 the widow of the armourer Pasing received expenses to return to France when he was dead. His "furthbringing" was paid for, with wax, winding sheet and all expenses.[1]

But little progress was made. Shipments of guns continue. In

[1] ALHT II.432.

1506 Herwort returns to the Isles with wrights and gunners "needful to good compt". A bombard is taken to Leith from the Castle and shipped there with smaller ordnance, falcons, barrels of powder, "dis" or iron missiles (presumably "dymondis" referred to above), and furniture ("paraling") such as ram-rods ("chargeouris schafts").

Artillery was perhaps more successful as entertainment. In 1506 an iron gun performed before the King upon the sands of Leith. The next year Hans took guns and their chambers from Leith to the "barras" for the jousting. Royal interest in gunnery, fatally demonstrated by James II, was shared by all the Stewarts save James VI. James IV did much to encourage its development, and James V acquired a passion for shooting the hand culverine. Hans, Herwort and Pierson instructed him in his royal practising, first inside Holyroodhouse, then outside. He engaged in competitions and lost his wagers and paid his debts. He shot fowls with his new culverine, a weapon which seems to have taken his fancy and which may have been a foreign novelty, but not to the professional gunners, Hans and Herwort, who were his instructors with experience no doubt in continental service. Under George the Alemane he discharged big guns at Newhaven near Edinburgh. At first the king's efforts were directed at canvas targets, but after these preliminary experiments he shoots deer at Falkland with his culverine. In between times he shoots with bow and arrow.

In 1508 evidence for the casting of guns is specific and thereafter repeated. Alan Cochrane gets tin for gun-casting; a Dunfermline potter makes crucibles for smelting gun-metal; copper for gun-casting is purchased; and there is no doubt now that the Scottish arsenals were being equipped with home-made ordnance. Alexander Bow, an Edinburgh potter bought metal "to cast the first gun with",[1] and foundries were established at Stirling and Edinburgh Castles, especially at Stirling. Tallow is purchased to lay on the mould of a gun and wire to bind the mould. Two guns were made at this casting. Others being unsuccessful, George the Almane was sent to Stirling to cast guns. French gunners were prominent and Johne Veilnaif (?Villeneuf) who says he can make guns gets 20 crowns by the king's command.[2] In 1506 Bastion the Spaniard brings a gun.[3]

[1] This item doubtless refers to the first gun of a new series, not to the historical first gun which we have seen was made 1474. In 1498 Robert Borthwick cast guns for James IV which, according to Hollinshed v. 470, were inscribed *Machina sum Scoto Borthwic fabricata Roberto.*

[2] ALHT III.139.

[3] ALHT III.329.

Ravenscraig, Fife, 1460

Affleck, Angus, later fifteenth century (see pl. 15)

Tillycairn, Aberdeenshire, late sixteenth century

Leslie, Aberdeenshire, 1661

Muness, Unst, Shetland, 1598

Muness, Unst, Shetland, 1598

Plate 41 Gunports

Plate 42
above Noltland, Westray, Orkney, mid-sixteenth century
below Tolquhon, Aberdeenshire, 1594-8

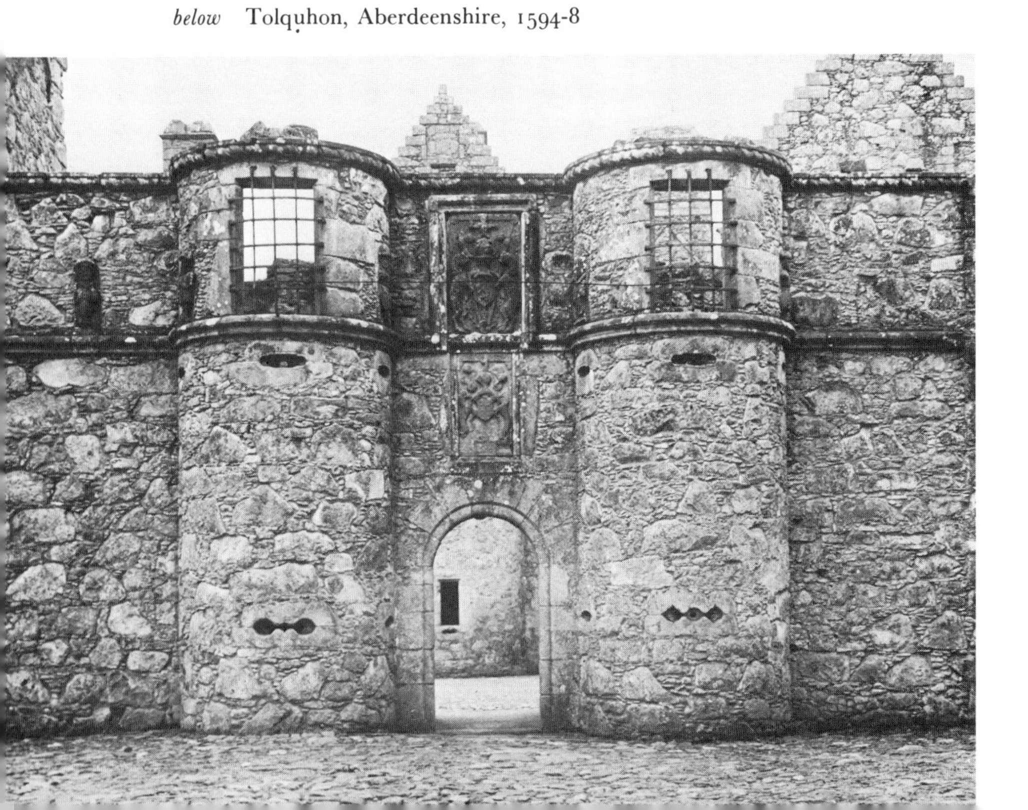

He or one of his kin is probably the Nicholls Bestiane who is on the staff in 1518. In 1511 more foreign experts come to join those already employed. Quantities of material arrive at the same time, and a great cast brass cannon called "Necar" is the result.

In this and the following year energetic efforts to collect and construct ordnance were being made in Edinburgh Castle. Ten carts went to Threave to bring back two great guns in June 1512, and the king more than once inspected the castle's workshops. Robert Borthwick is in charge of the foundry, with Dutch smiths, Scots smiths, and masons, wrights, gunners, powder-men, artificers and pioneers. Gervase, a Frenchman, joins the staff, and his fellow gunners receive drinksilver in June 1512. Wolf Urnbrig makes gun-powder. By August of that year three great guns were ready and taken to Leith docks to be shipped in the *Great Michael* which herself carried six guns each side, as well as three Flemish basilisks or large cannon and four hundred small pieces including crossbows and long-bows. Each of the three guns required six carts to bear it down from the castle. Work on ordnance continued busily until the eve of Flodden, at which there were, according to the Accounts of the Lord High Treasurer, seventeen guns altogether, five large cannon, two large culverines, four culverines pikmoyene (the smallest) and six culverines moyane (French *moyen*, "medium") all under the direction of Robert Borthwick, who is traditionally credited with the casting of the famous cannon "The Seven Sisters" which were mentioned in Venetian and other contemporary records as being guns of great power and beauty. These are probably the captured guns which the Earl of Surrey boasted were longer and larger than any in the arsenal of the King of England.[1] The attribution of these guns to Robert Borthwick may be wrong, but it could be correct. He was a skilled gunner and gunsmith, and in charge of ordnance at the battle, which might have had a different result had the king taken his advice. The tale is told of Borthwick falling upon his knees before the king, begging permission to fire, and of James refusing, declaring he would meet his adversary on equal terms and not with advantage.[2]

The advantage which James declined to accept was topographical. His artillery was equal to the occasion, according to all accounts. A contemporary English writer describes it thus: "Marvelous and great ordnance of guns, that is to wit, v great curtalles, ii great culveryns, iiii sacres, and vi great serpentyns, as goodly gonnes as have been

[1] P. F. Tytler (1845), v.82. [2] P. F. Tytler (1845), iv.76ff.

sene in any realme, and besides these wer other dyvers small ordnances."[1] And there is also Surrey's claim.

The Accounts of the Lord High Treasurer record that two cannon were drawn by thirty-six oxen each, and nine drivers. Four culverines pikmoyene were each drawn by sixteen oxen with four drivers and ten pioneers; six smaller pieces had each eight oxen and six pioneers; a crane was taken for slinging the guns onto their beds; gun-stones were borne in baskets by twenty-eight horses; and there were at least twelve carts of gunpowder. Borthwick had twenty-six men under his immediate supervision to work the guns, and Burcar or Barker had smiths and a travelling smithy, carrying its own coal, to make repairs. Owing to the arbitrariness of nomenclature about artillery, a source of confusion to the study of both home and continental works, it is difficult to obtain a true estimate of the position. But there is a correspondence between the Treasurer's Accounts and this contemporary description which leads one to suppose they refer to the same event.

Artillery henceforth is frequently mentioned, and with it smaller fire-arms such as arquebuses and hakbuts, which were discharged from or over a wooden stand. But when Robert Hectoure is paid by the Lord High Treasurer for making a piece of ordnance, so also is a crossbow maker for his craft, which indicates the continuance of older weapons in high quarters. Indeed James V was more partial to the bow than to fire-arms, it seems, shooting with bows discharging bullets in 1538, presumably the "pellok" bow or arquebus, which is the old-fashioned cross-bow modified to discharge the new missile. "Hans alias Cunynghame" now appears (1537) and is regularly paid £38 per annum. He seems to be a naturalised Scot, perhaps the son of "Hans gunner" of the early days of Scottish artillery in the later fifteenth century. With Robert Herwort he was very close to the king in gunnery affairs, both in major sieges with bombards in distant unruly parts and in competitions with the culverin in Holyroodhouse. The familiar names occur no more, but among their successors continental gunners continue to be prominent and highly valued, as for example Peris (?Piers, Paris) Rowane, who by the king's command received help to send his two sons to France for gunnery apprenticeship.[2] But gun-casting even by such an accredited expert as he was could still be unsuccessful in 1541. He failed twice at Stirling in that year, and was replaced by John de Lyones who with

[1] R. C. Clephan (1911), 135; D. Laing (1868), 146. [2] ALHT VI.402.

four men strove for three months to cast another, which they did successfully.[1]

About this time there is ample evidence to show that efforts were made to improve ordnance, which was still a royal taste. A Dutchman William Fandyk was employed casting guns—"makar of irne gunys".[2] The number or reserve of artillery is mounting: in November 1541 there are 413 hagbuts and 8 culverins, with gunpowder, bullets, moulds and accessories lodged in Edinburgh Castle. And there are frequent payments for the movements of guns and ammunition to various parts of the south country. These movements were slow, uncertain and on occasion hazardous both to material and personnel. In 1543 fourteen horses were hired, each to draw a cannon to Dalkeith, while twenty-three were used in the carts to pull smaller pieces and ammunition. A threat to Stirling in the same year caused Hans Cochrane with seven ordinary—including Hans Cunynghame—and thirty extraordinary gunners to be dispatched to Stirling, while their guns went in three boats from Leith, and fifty-four carthorses were sent to receive them. The fleet was dispersed by a storm and only one boat was required to return the guns; many seem therefore to have been lost, either in the action or upon the seas before it. A "moyane" or medium cannon, which cast a nine pound shot some 2,500 yards needed twelve horses to drag it from Leith Docks to the castle.

If this is uphill all the way, it is no more so than was frequently experienced in campaigns in the upland routes. These were varied as much as military expediency allowed, to minimise the hardship necessarily imposed upon those in the districts through which siege trains passed, whose duty it was to provide the oxen which usually pulled the guns. Accompanying the train were pioneers with picks and shovels to prepare the way. Smiths and other artificers were never far distant, ready to execute repairs *en route*. During the harrying of Hertford, for example, two culverins moyane were dispatched to the south from Edinburgh Castle. One train consisted of thirty-five horses and twelve labourers besides artificers. They took Caerlaverock without trouble, and were redeployed to Hamilton. One gun lay helpless for lack of oxen; gabions were made.

There are innumerable items of local interest in the records: much gathering of timber, carriage of it and parts of guns from place

[3] ALHT VIII.125-6. [4] ALHT VIII.118.

to place, frequently to ships. The Edinburgh Castle foundry is obviously busy making and repairing the metal and timber parts. New gunhouses are constructed here and at Leith at this time. There is almost no mention of large ordnance, and none significant. Robert Harp works six days upon the stocking of the great bombard after a Frenchman had worked one day before him. Stocks to slangs and double slangs are paid for. Double slangs and other pieces go aboard the *Mary Willobe*. Much of the movement of ordnance is to or from ships. The tops of the *Salamander* get nine hagbuts.

FORTIFICATION

Ravenscraig Castle, Kirkcaldy, is unique. It stands alone as an artillery fort among the many castellated structures of the troubled fifteenth century, when the knowledge of ordnance was steadily increasing. It is the first of its kind and, save for Cadzow, the only known example for some two hundred years thereafter. It is a suitable memorial to its royal builder James II, whose fatal interest in artillery caused his death while the castle was in course of erection. Begun in 1460, completed in 1463, its erection was due to as systematic a scheme of defence as contemporary notions and conditions demanded. With it went the erection of a fortified tower-house incorporated as a western tower in the church of St Serf at Dysart, less than a mile away upon the coast, and a plan to fortify the island of Inchkeith in the middle of the Forth, all of which combined with the Port of Leith opposite would constitute an effective barrier to sea-raiders. The island was not in fact fortified until 1547, and then by the English. In 1481 further steps were taken to defend the sea-coast of south and east Scotland by strengthening with victuals, men and artillery the castles near the Border and the sea: St Andrews, Aberdeen, Tantallon, Hume, Haddington, Hailes and Hermitage.[1] Ten years after, and in consequence of the enactments of 1481, the laird of Dundas received a licence to erect a stronghold on Inchgarvie, another Forth island, for the protection of ships; Sir Andrew Wood received retrospective licences to erect fortalices upon his land; and Sir John Towers of Inverleith was permitted to erect a house upon the sea-coast for the defence of his lands and goods from the English invasion.[2] None of these licences is commemorated by architecture especially designed to be defended by and against artillery.

[1] APS II.133.

[2] W. D. Simpson (1938*b*), 3.

The only fortification analogous in any way to Ravenscraig is the strange and little-known citadel of Cadzow Castle (Lanarkshire) hard by Châtelherault. Here, a natural eminence towering over the Avon Water has been enclosed by strong walls and a wide ditch. At each end of the vulnerable face, confronting the only approach, are two round towers projecting boldly into the ditch. One is much reduced; the other is apparently well-nigh complete. It has wide-mouthed gun-ports to enfilade the walls, and a backward sloping wall-head strongly reminiscent of the towers of Ravenscraig. But with this difference. The towers of Ravenscraig are high in the mediaeval tradition; at Cadzow the tower is low, does not rise above the ditch it commands, but is sunk into it, as a gun battery or casemate. The analogies for this singular defence, which has no known parallels in Scotland, are the rounded bastions of Henry VIII's coastal forts of Deal, Walmer etc., in 1538, and the writings of Dürer in 1527. The citadel of the early sixteenth-century fortifications of Schaffhausen on the Rhine has closed salient batteries strikingly like this.[1] Cadzow was probably constructed by the second earl of Arran, heir-presumptive and governor of the kingdom (1542-3), who was created Duke of Châtelherault by Henry II in 1548,[2] before and after which he spent much time on the continent.

Ravenscraig lies across the neck of a narrow pointed promontory whose sides fall precipitously to the sea. A wide ditch cuts it off on the landward side. It consists of a long frontal range with a barrel-vaulted entrance passage through the centre of the ground floor. Massive round towers flank this range at either end and project into the ditch (fig. 24). That at the west end, 38 feet in diameter, is entered only from the rear courtyard and has no communication with the central main block. It rises higher than this block, and higher also than the eastern tower. This is 43 feet in diameter and communicates with the central block. The western tower is the donjon, the residential building of James' queen, Mary of Gueldres, who spent her widowhood here. It contains a complete suite of chambers in four floors arranged in traditional tower-house style. The central building has vaulted basements, over which extends to their full length and breadth an artillery platform open to the sky and to the courtyard in the rear. It is protected at the front or landward side by a high parapet wall with wide-mouthed gun embrasures.

The towers and central building have walls of great thickness (as

[1] E. Viollet-de-Duc (1879*a*), fig. 101. [2] A. H. Dunbar (1899), 201.

much as 14 feet in the frontal parts of the towers), which are pierced by well-placed inverted key-hole gunports of large size. A formidable battery thus confronted the vulnerable landward approach from the higher ground and the exposed east and west sides of the towers. The seaward danger was less alarming because of the site (upon 80 feet of perpendicular cliff), and the narrow ranges of the courtyard buildings along the edge of the promontory, now reduced to ruin, reveal little of defensive preparations, which, although doubtless existing, could not and need not have been so formidable.

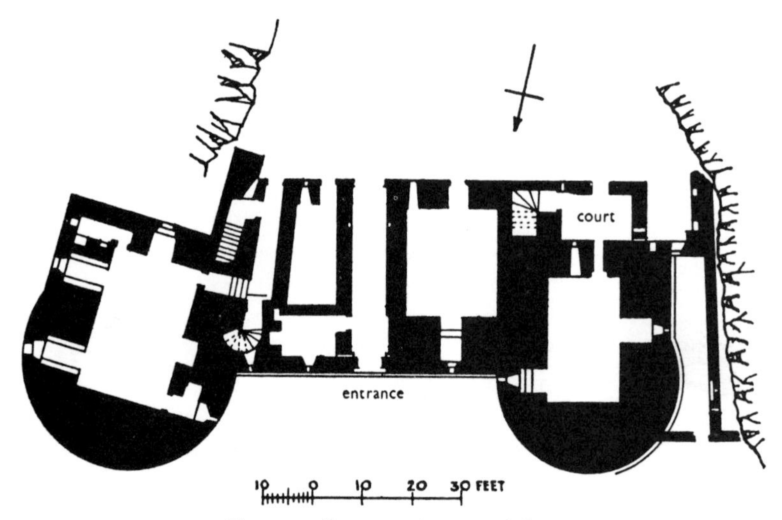

Fig. 24. Ravenscraig, ground floor

The plan of this bulky structure shows that the implications of defence by and against artillery were fully realised. The internal lay-out of the basements is no longer casual and traditional, intended merely for storage, but planned positively for gunnery and gun crews. Intercommunication is unorthodox, in the ground floor minimal, so that even the guardroom, the only chamber accessible from the entrance passage, and itself leading nowhere, was expendable, and could be surrendered without more loss than the one fire-point it contains. The rectangular embrasures are large and practical, unlike others to be described which serve similar gun-ports.

The gun-ports are of two types, wide-mouthed in the upper platform of the central mass, inverted key-holes below this and in the towers (pl. 41). There is a visible chronological difference in these two types. They occur in stratigraphical relationship. This is of importance, for gun-ports are datable features. The breastwork containing the wide-mouthed ports is a secondary construction. The wall was originally to have been considerably thicker, as tuskers in the east wall of the west tower prove. In this thicker wall there would have been cannon, firing through embrasures with rounded copes. The destruction of the battlements is greatly to be regretted, for the sloping wall-head of the great tower is uncommonly interesting. Itself unparalleled in Scottish military architecture, it suggests that the parapet of the frontal battery would be similar. The east tower was finished in the same fashion, but subsequently altered. Sloping and rounded parapets and a lowering of height were protective measures against artillery at the wall-head of a castle. Standard practice in Cromwellian and Hanoverian fortifications, these artillery features are almost non-existent in earlier works. Rounded parapets with wide-mouthed gun-ports are to be found only upon Carberry Tower (Midlothian) and Mains Castle (Dundee) of the pre-Cromwellian period. The significance of the change of type at Ravenscraig is that the wide-mouthed ports must be after 1463, when the original work containing key-holes had been completed.

It might seem that, with continuing royal interest in artillery and the free introduction of foreign guns and experienced master-gunners to work them, the early erection of a fortress like Ravenscraig would inaugurate a new type of fortification which the nobles and lairds would adopt. This was far from being the case. The well-tried tower-house continued. The Ravenscraig achievement was not repeated. New towers arose, not like it obeying strictly defensive requirements, but according to current demands of increasing comfort and convenience. Only by the presence of gun-ports do castles of the late fifteenth century and onwards reveal a familiarity with gunpowder. How close that familiarity was can only be discovered by critically reviewing their widespread occurrence, and by considering their shape in the light of contemporary armament and their tactical efficiency in the light of current theory and practice.

INVERTED KEY-HOLE GUN-PORTS

Inverted key-hole ports in Canterbury Westgate are original features of the building, which is dated 1380-1.[1] They are exactly like those at Ravenscraig. There are similar loops in Cooling Castle (Kent) which was licensed in 1381,[2] and others occur in the

[1] CPR 450. [2] CPR 596.

western part of Southampton Town Wall, possibly as early as 1360.[1] The Ravenscraig gun-ports of 1460-3 are the earliest in Scotland which are securely dated. Their appearance in an advanced royal work consciously designed as an artillery fortification by Henry Merlion, first of a notable family of master-masons to the Crown, suggests that this is their first appearance in a preconceived system of defence by cannon. Two appearances of doubtful priority are in less advanced fortifications; in the secondary curtain wall of Craigmillar (1427) they are associated with an open machicolated parapet, and at Threave they also occur in a secondary curtain surrounding a fourteenth-century tower entirely innocent of defensive loops. The great siege of 1455, in which Mons Meg took part, is the probable occasion for its erection. In both castles the conception is mediaeval, without adequate realisation of the qualities of the new weapon which rendered the old defences obsolete.

Key-hole ports occur throughout the precinct wall of St Andrews Cathedral in the lower courses which ante-date the reconstruction of the wall by Prior Patrick Hepburn after 1522.[2] In the Falkland gatehouse of about 1500 they are associated with the later wide-mouthed port which is commonplace throughout the entire sixteenth century and survives well into the seventeenth century in all classes of castle. After about 1500 the inverted key-hole of the early large size is no longer used, but smaller examples occur sporadically in later work at Affleck, Huntingtower, Tarbert, Cardoness and Dalquharran. At Affleck (pl. 41) there is one in the centre of each face. At Huntingtower they are more numerous but irregularly disposed. None occurs above the basement of either, nor is there any other defensive feature.

A curious loop of restricted distribution and retrospective tendencies is to be found in Aberdeenshire at Gight, Towie Barclay, Craig, Tillycairn (pl. 41), Inverugie and Ravenscraig.[3] The latter, near Peterhead, was licensed in 1491.[4] Regularly disposed round all its sides at ground level is a business-like array of loops in the form of long slits with a short crosslet slit near the top and a circular aperture at the bottom. This is a reminiscence of the mediaeval crosslet, with a round aperture for a gun-barrel added to the design. The internal embrasures are wide, with jambs deeply slotted at the outer end. In

[1] B. H. St J. O'Neil (1954*b*), 45. [2] S. H. Cruden (1950), 22.

[3] It also occurs, once in each basement wall, in the sixteenth-century tower-house at Kirkconnel House (Kirkcudbrightshire).

[4] RMS No. 2030.

these slots the wooden cills were housed which held the spiked gun-mounting. In the other castles named this agreeable aberration can hardly be earlier than about 1570—a hundred years out of date. As it makes a less purposeful appearance than that which impresses itself so forcefully upon the oncomer to the Aberdeenshire Ravenscraig it would appear to have been revived in the locality as ornament. At Gight, Towie and Craig, which share other peculiarities described elsewhere, and at Inverugie its appearance amounts to little more than a token of defence. At Tillycairn it is associated with wide-mouthed ports and between them they afford a tolerable field of fire all round the castle. The internal embrasures are spacious and practical, and despite the differences in the gun-ports they are identical.

Threave illustrates an interesting transitional phase of development. The curtain has long narrow slits with deep splayed embrasures. These converge to the outer wall-face above a waist-high cill extending from back to front. This would suit a rifleman or gunner better than an archer. Like these slits the round aperture of the inverted key-hole in the round corner tower has no external splay, nor has the slit above it. This continues the older arrow-slit form. But the circular aperture has a wide internal splay, which the slit above has not. This would facilitate the handling of fire-arms. Thus by omitting the traditional pre-gunpowder slit, we get the single wide-mouthed gun-port of long life and ubiquitous occurrence.

As well as key-holes the Threave curtain-towers have dumb-bell ports. These are surely designed with an eye to appearance, for function would be unaffected by this extra aperture. An explanation of sighting is hardly feasible. The guns of the period rested upon short crutches like rowlocks. These were stuck into wooden cills, which were housed in slots in the jambs and lay upon the cill of the embrasure.

The inverted key-hole port represents a typological stage in the development of firepower. It is the old arrow-slit modified to take the barrel of a gun by the addition, or insertion, or a circular aperture at its bottom end. Doubtless the long vertical slit above it would be of some use in sighting or observation from within, and useful in dispersing smoke from confined quarters. But these functional explanations tend to overlook its antecedents. It is not a new thing invented, but an old one adapted. Its short life is natural to its transitional nature. The succeeding type, the wide-mouthed port, had a long life.

WIDE-MOUTHED GUN-PORTS

The embrasures of key-hole ports converge steadily to the aperture which is flush with the exterior wall-face. The embrasures of wide-mouthed ports have double-splayed jambs. They converge inwards from both the inside and the outside faces of the wall to the throat or gorge, which is half-way in its thickness.[1] Two varieties of wide-mouthed port occur. The difference is seemingly of little significance, but worth recording. The more frequent is chamfered all round. The less frequent is straight and rectangular, rounded

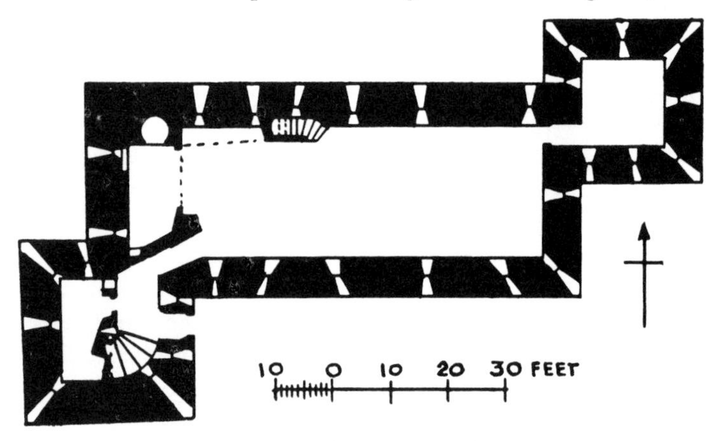

FIG. 25. Noltland, ground floor

only at the ends, and without a chamfer. They occur together in the frontal gatehouse towers of Caerlaverock. Save one all are rectangular and unchamfered, built into the later work at the top of the east tower and inserted into the earlier work below it. The single example of the more oval type with wide chamfer all round is inserted into the bottom of a blocked vertical slit. The two varieties occur together at Noltland in an astonishing parade of ranks of gun-ports (pl. 42). It has been suggested that the straight and narrower type is the earlier here, but a change in building material would account for the difference, the chamfers being necessarily worked in freestone.

[1] Some with single splays (i.e. long embrasures converging to the rear) occur in later sixteenth-century work: Blackness, Craignethan curtain, and the addition to David's Tower, Edinburgh. They always have extra-wide ports and suggest cannon.

The concurrence of the old and new forms—the key-hole and the wide-mouthed—at Falkland may be haphazard or due to a change of mind, an introduction into the scheme of a new and improved version. This is very probable, for the wide-mouthed form, used once in the basement of the eastern roundel of the gatehouse, continues eastwards exclusively in the basement of the adjacent chapel. Notwithstanding the advances in artillery and fire-arms, the wide-mouthed port introduced into use at the royal works by the royal engineers at Holyroodhouse and Falkland about 1500 were unchanged at the time of the building revival in the last quarter of the sixteenth century. As tower-houses were revived so were gun-ports. From 1569 at Claypotts, where wide-mouthed ports occur tactically all round the basement, to well into the seventeenth century when they are ornamental, they are commonplace. With the Aberdeenshire exceptions of the key-hole with crosslet, and small pistol-holes, frequently decorative, no other type of gun-port occurs.

A clue to the kind of gun used in the defence of tower-houses is to be found in the wooden cills referred to. Rarely do the cills survive, although the slots frequently do. In Elcho and Burleigh they exist, still with the central hole into which the tang or prong of the gun's support was inserted. This indicates the use of the *harquebus* or *hakbut*, a heavier weapon than the hand-gun, first mentioned in the Treasurer's Accounts under the year 1513 and frequently thereafter, usually as *hagbut* or *arquebus*. The weapon owes its name to the prefix *hak* or *harq*, which is the spur or rowlock-shaped support for the long barrel, which took the recoil and enabled the gun to be swivelled. The stem of the hak could be long like a crutch for use in the open, according to the height of the gunner, or of medium length when used on horseback. In a gun embrasure it raised the stock only the few inches necessary for manoeuvre.

These weapons were unsatisfactory. They were cumbersome and slow to load, fire and clean. They discharged a one-ounce ball whose effect was slight compared with that of a crossbow or longbow which had the added advantages of greater precision of delivery and rapidity of fire. It has been estimated that, while the longbow had a rate of fire of about six arrows a minute and the crossbow two to three bolts a minute, the hakbut discharged but six or seven balls per hour.

It seems clear that an uncertain reception was given to fire-arms by the nobles and lairds of the sixteenth and seventeenth centuries, when wide-mouthed ports are common but haphazard accessories. Many castles have none. Many castles are equipped without tactical assets. Some by well-placed gun-ports suggest a determination to resist. Others have them in some sides, but not in others equally vulnerable. A few castles are efficiently equipped, but only a few, and they have no history, position, or any circumstance to explain why they should be better fortified by guns than others which have none or too few. The matter seems to be of personal whim in which, doubtless, a contemporary partiality for bravado played its part. Even the same date and the same neighbourhood do not cause a like response to the possibility of attack and the necessity of defence.

Claypotts has a good provision of wide-mouthed ports all round its basement; so has Elcho of the same date. Drochil (also *c.* 1570-80) has them in the diagonally opposite towers covering the main block which has no ports at all. They are of two kinds, one with plain splays, outward and inward, the other with redented external splays. There is no practical significance in the difference, which it would appear is arbitrary, according to the notions of the builders. But the placing of the ports as a whole is significant, and indicates an attitude of mind. They cover only the walls of the central block, which itself has none at all. The field is not challenged; only close-range defence by enfilade is provided.

Fairburn has a business-like provision all round with three ports in each wall. Ardvreck has a gable passage which serves ports. Similarly Muness has a passage along an external wall which serves a series of small round shot-holes. They are numerous, decorative (set within quatre-foils), and they are in good supply in the towers also. Invermark is well-equipped with wide-mouthed ports in the basement. In its corner roundel is a vertical slit with two small pistol-holes beneath it. This also is decorative, and is paralleled at Schivas. Ballone has a very adequate display all round its ground floor. Burgie, like Fairburn, has a battery of three ports in each of its walls of L-plan. The associated group which includes Towie Barclay, Craig and Gight shares among other uncommon features a defensive peculiarity, a deflection of the ground-floor passage at the re-entrant angle, with a loop at the dog-leg bend. The front elevation of Leslie (1661), the last fortified house in Scotland, is well provided with redented ports, one of which covers the entrance (pl. 41), but the other three sides have no defences whatever.

The workmanlike provision of ports round the ground floor of

Tillycairn is symmetrical but inconsistent. Whereas the re-entrant door is covered by a crosslet key-hole and the gable walls have each another in the centre, the long back wall has two wide-mouthed ports only. Harthill (*c.* 1600) has a barmkin wall and gatehouse without ports. The tower has wide-mouthed ports ranging closely along the wall faces. The doorway is not protected by flanking side-long fire, but only by an adjacent port pointing directly out to the field. This defends it from frontal attack only. This is not uncommon. At Cumbrae, for example, there is some show of wide-mouthed ports in the front façade confronting the field.

This is the very opposite of the Drochil system. Without flanking towers the doorway is thus unprotected against advance along the walls. Some castles, e.g. Tilquhilly, are well provided with loops on all sides save one, or two, where strangely there are none. Leslie, for instance, is of the "stepped" plan and consequently has a front elevation in three planes. All are furnished with ground-floor ports and there is even one in the very junction of the re-entrant, but the other three sides have no ports at all. Timpendean has a wide-mouthed port but not in the entrance façade. Likewise Little Cumbrae has wide-mouthed ports low down but none cover the entrance. Lachlan has one without tactical significance, and its doorway is unprotected.

Many castles have no gun-ports at all. Drum, Hallforest, Craigmillar tower, Threave tower, Crichton tower and the other fourteenth-century castles have none. Borthwick, Comlongon and Elphinstone of the fifteenth century have none. Kellie, Glamis, Craigievar, Crathes and Midmar of the later sixteenth and early seventeenth century have none.

At least the doorway should be protected. The large arched entrance to the outer court of Tolquhon is flanked on either side by a triplet of decorative pistol-holes. They point to the field. There is no flanking fire. The entrance to the inner court is between two projecting round towers (pl. 42). Each has a triplet of pistol-holes similar to those at the outer gate. They, likewise, point straight out and there is no cover for the curtain but what is provided by a massive drum tower projecting from the corner of the inner enceinte. Here are more severe wide-mouthed ports, for use not display, one covering the curtain low down, another high up. In their workmanlike qualities they differ from the triplets as the corner tower differs from the entrance towers. At the diagonally opposite corner of the enclosure a square projecting tower matches the drum tower—an ingenious adaptation of the L-plan to an enclosure. It, too, has wide-mouthed ports covering its curtains. Otherwise the Tolquhon defensive arrangements were apparently not taken very seriously.

The twin towers flanking the main entrance are embellished with sculptured figures. The reduced scale and thinness of wall and the inadequacy and decorativeness of the shot-holes proclaim a feudal display of pride rather than stern or even reluctant military intention. Toy towers, designed not to impress the warlike but the peaceful visitor, these playthings could have been of little use in the face of a determined threat. The triplet in the mid-tower of the main block within the inner court opens from the wheel-stair it contains. It is plunged and directed downwards to the entrance, superficially conveying an impression of thoroughness which is illusory. Only the bottom of the doorway could be protected by a marksman stationed here, and not very well at that. A little more care, a little more sense of necessity and function in a patron or mason with knowledge sharpened by experience, and this expedient could without difficulty have been efficiently contrived.

Ornamental shot-holes are not uncommon; they occur at Edzell, the Earl's Palace in Kirkwall, Muness (pl. 41), Schivas, Castle Fraser and Collairnie. Noltland has a quatre-foiled port in the stairway. Double shot-holes occur at the Bishop's Palace in Kirkwall, Finhaven and Fordyce. Terpersie (1561), the earliest authentic example of the Z-plan (after the doubtful original of Huntly *c.* 1543), has plain round pistol-holes. Leslie, Tillycairn, Glenbuchat and many others have plunged pistol-holes in the continuous corbelling of their overhanging roundels. Castle Stewart has a good series of wide-mouthed apertures with redented outer splays, all round its lower parts. The arbitrariness of all this is so pervasive that one tends to accept it, noting existence or absence of these features without reflection on purpose and practicability.

Craignethan causes a more critical examination however. All round its unusually large outer court—a feature to be compared with Tolquhon—there is a systematic and regular series of wide-mouthed ports and projecting towers. So regular and extensive is the lay-out that one recalls to mind the curtains of earlier times. A difference in attitude to defensive measures is emphasised hereby. Thirteenth- and fourteenth-century curtains and towers were conscientiously equipped for defence, and had to be. Later work in the artillery and hand-gun era was slow to come to grips with current technique of attack and was rarely systematic.

At some point an impressive show of strength might be made, as at the frontal battery of Dunottar. But the wide-mouthed ports overlooking the entrance from the basement and first floor of Benholm's Lodging there could have been of little use in defending the castle's entrance, and the single port in the centre of the second floor could only have discharged its shot into the bay. The battery of four gun-ports with a square aperture in the centre of the pattern, which pierces the screen wall of the chamber confronting the entrance from the inside is equally of doubtful efficiency. Although placed across the inner end of the entrance passage it does not line up with it but inclines to one side. Also, the gun-ports are checked for glass! The long barrel-vaulted chamber, which is cut into the rock, would assuredly be disagreeable and unsafe with no openings other than the gun-ports and the doorway beside them cut through the screen wall at its outer end.

Even the Craignethan arrangements, methodical though they seem to be, leave room for honest doubt, for the impressive display of curtain walls with gun-ports and towers is placed at the bottom of a steep slope. Artillery or any concentration of throwing weapons could dominate the outer court and be above the fire-power of the curtain below. The gunners manning their posts round the other three sides of this large promontory castle would on the other hand largely discharge into space, for from the base of these walls the ground falls steeply away. Yet defensive measures were not entirely ill-considered. Upon the wall-head of the corner tower, a building of reasonable size, wide-mouthed ports are present, which is unusual, and plunged downwards moreover, the better to cover the approach up the slopes. Failure to hold the enemy at a safe distance was a probability evidently admitted.

The tower-house of this castle was separated from the court by a wide deep ditch, an immensely thick wall and a strong gatehouse.[1]

[1] See I. MacIvor, "Craignethan Castle" (p. ix above). Prolonged excavations have revealed the ditch uncommonly deep, with, across the bottom, a complete caponier—a stone vaulted loop-holed passage which could rake the ditch with shot, and being low was itself invisible until close-quarters. In the late fifteenth century advanced Italian engineers were writing of these defence-works, and in 1527 Dürer drew experimental versions. We can find only one other early example in Britain, at Hurst Castle (Hampshire). A caponier at Craignethan, probably *c.* 1540, is remarkable, and so is its preservation, beneath the débris of the curtain from which it was entered, which was demolished after a siege in 1579. Evidently Arran meant business when he built this and Cadzow (see above, p. 213).

In critically examining the arrangements which result wholly from ordnance the conclusion seems inescapable. Gun-ports were fashionable rather than essential items of defensive equipment. They were included as much to reduce the enemy's morale as to inflict real damage. Certainly one would be impressed by the double tier of wide gun-ports in Benholm's Lodging and more than a little afraid of the battery within the gate, but not for long. The inference to be drawn from the standard plans agrees with this conclusion. And in architecture the plan is the heart of the matter, more revealing than the elevation or appurtenances such as gun-ports.

In the foregoing pages attention has been drawn to the placing of projecting jambs, and some conjectures have been advanced in explanation of their long-lived and widespread popularity. As with the use of gun-ports, motives seem to have been mixed. The early promise of Claypotts, with its gun-ports and Z-plan systematically organised, was not sustained. The multitude of tower-houses which were erected throughout the later sixteenth century and beyond, with never another type of building to rival them, include many important castles whose plans defy military explanation. The lords and lairds at large about the continent were not ignorant of the great Italian artillery fortifications of a hundred years before, or of the achievements of contemporary military science. They doubtless numbered among them a few like Captain Ogle who became a hostage at the siege of Breda in 1625.[1] And then they returned to tower-houses and the tactics of Lord Dacre in 1513: "thei layed corne and straw to the dore and burnt it [the tower] both rofe and flore and so smoked theym owt."[2]

Such was the challenge the tower-house was designed to meet in the late waning of the Middle Ages in Scotland. "Please God", William Forbes is said to have vowed when he built Corse Castle in Aberdeenshire about 1581 after its predecessor had been plundered, "I will build me such a house as thieves will need to knock at ere they enter".[3]

CROMWELLIAN FORTIFICATIONS

Throughout the Middle Ages, and in Scotland until the mid-seventeenth century, warfare was characterised by the triumph of the defensive, and blockade was the only sure means of reducing a

[1] H. Hugo (1627), 129. [2] W. M. Mackenzie (1927), 200.
[3] NSA XII.1123.

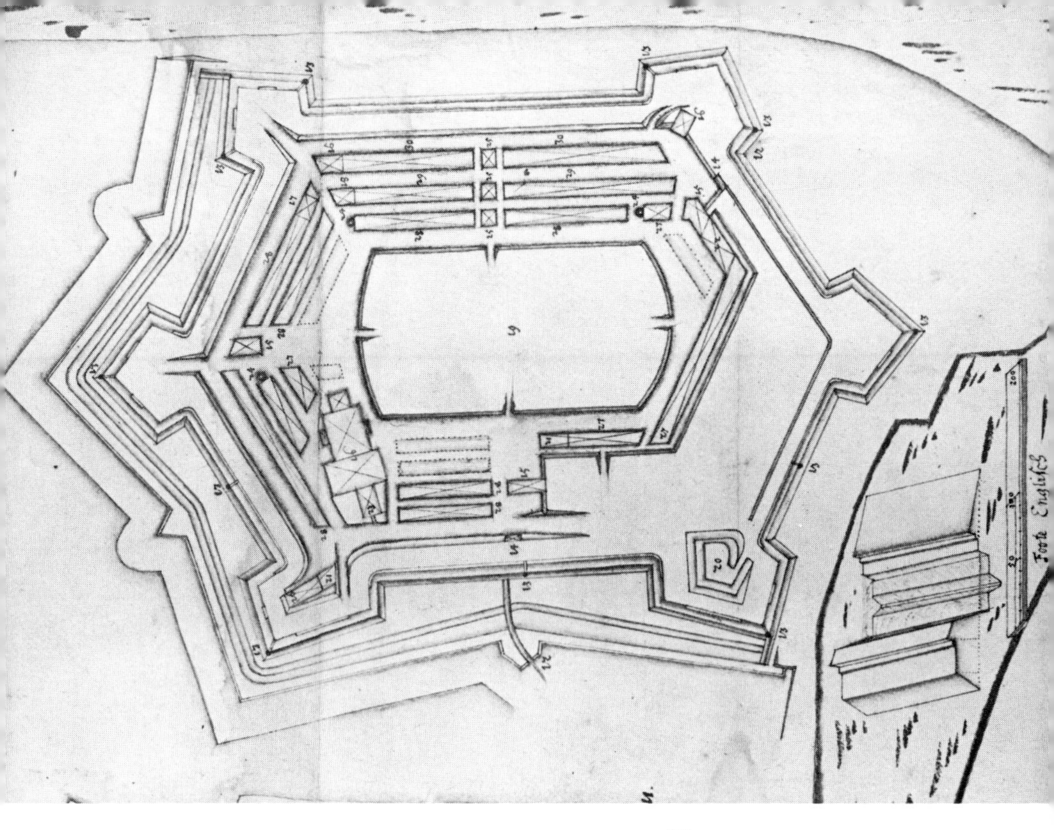

Plate 43

above

Part of 'The Citadell and Town of Ayre, 1654'

left

'Oliver's Fort', Inverness. Project drawing, 1746 ('on the Vestige of an old FORT demolished')

Plate 44

above Corgarff, Aberdeenshire: tower-house, sixteenth century; curtain, 1749

below Fort Charlotte, Lerwick, Shetland: plan of 1783

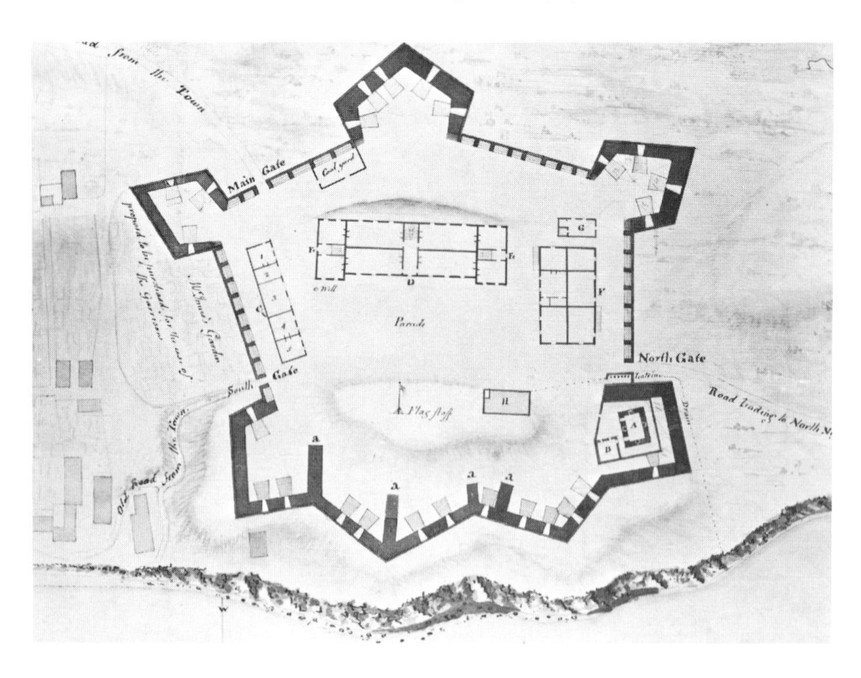

Plate 45 'Ruthven of Badenoch' barracks, Inverness-shire, 1719

above view from the west, 1959

below Board of Ordnance plan, 1719

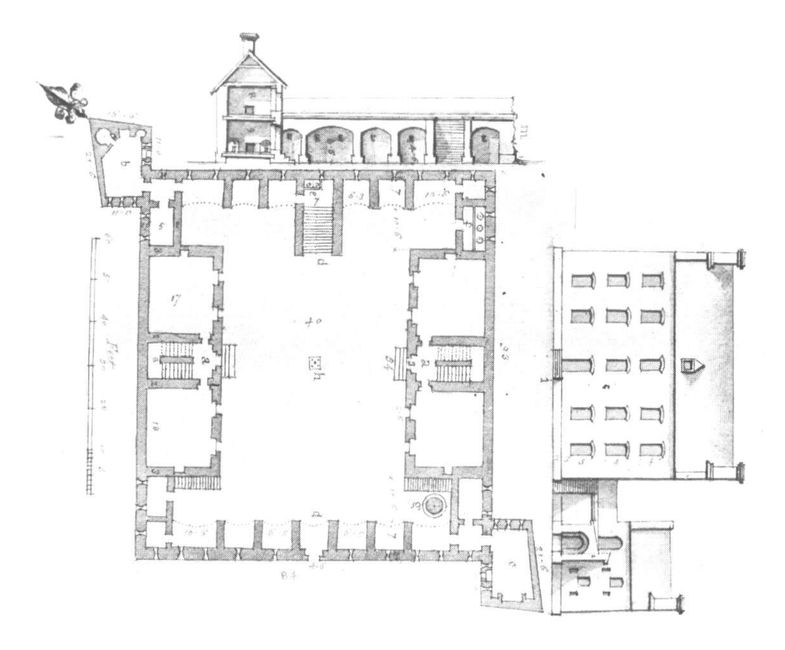

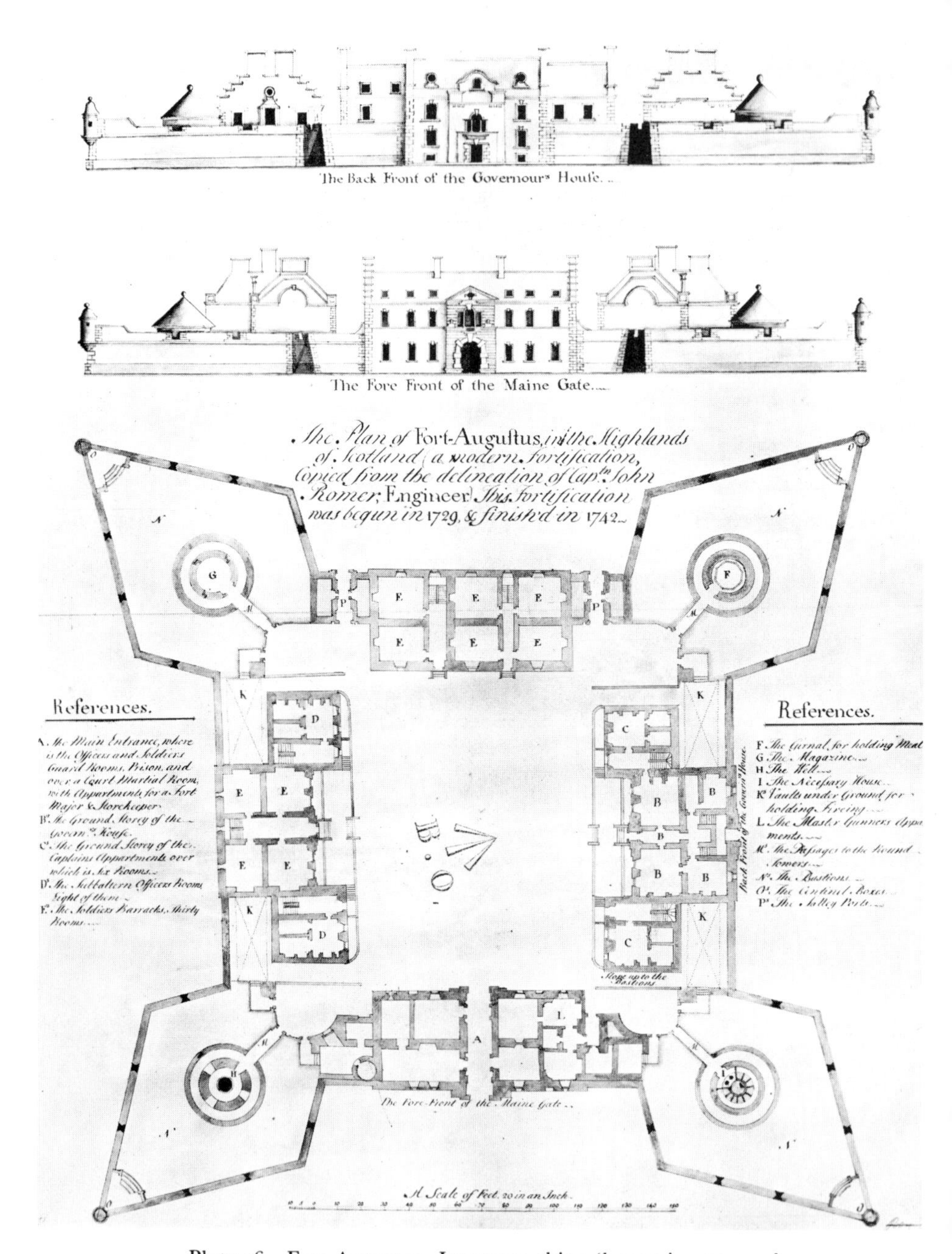
The Back Front of the Governour's House.
The Fore Front of the Maine Gate.
The Plan of Fort-Augustus, in the Highlands of Scotland, a modern Fortification, Copied from the delineation of Capt.n John Romer; Engineer. This fortification was begun in 1729, & finish'd in 1742.
References.
References.
The Fore Front of the Maine Gate
A Scale of Feet. 20 in an Inch.

Plate 46 Fort Augustus, Inverness-shire: 'begun in 1729 and finished in 1742'

well-manned stronghold. The new battering cannon was singularly ineffective in Scotland on several notable occasions in the first half of the sixteenth century. In 1528 James V failed to take the castles of Douglas, Coldstream and Tantallon.[1] At the latter "two great cannon, throwen-mouthed mow and her marrow" supported by cannon borrowed from Dunbar, and "bombards, moyens, double-falcons and quarter falcons, with powder, bullets and gunners for to use them", failed to take the castle in a twenty-day siege. The rebellious Earl of Angus, whose stronghold it was, in describing the event in a letter to the Earl of Northumberland, remarks upon the presence of Scots and French gunners ("ingenious men"), and says "there was never so much pain, travail, expense and diligence done and made for the winning of a house and the same escape in Scotland since it was first inhabited". The circumstances, result and derisive comment are paralleled in the case of the great siege of St Andrews Castle in 1546-7. There, two great cannon, "thrawn mow" ("crooked mouth") and "Deaf Meg", probably the same distinguished pieces that featured in a leading role at Tantallon, were brought to batter the walls and with the assistance of sundry lesser pieces did so, but "it was never ane hair the war". A dearth of ammunition may partly account for this, for the great roof of Holyroodhouse was stripped of its lead for the siege,[2] but the failure of the big guns is undoubted, and when they failed in royal engagements it is not surprising that they failed to influence castle design and construction also. The only defensive measures directly attributable to the threat of cannon are expedients such as the filling solid with stones and mortar of the mural passages and chambers of the Tantallon curtain.

On the continent political conditions accelerated the progressive developments of warfare in organisation, equipment and tactics. These in turn radically influenced the design of fortifications. The hindrances to the development of strategy and tactics, and consequently of castle-building, by the restrictive character and duration of feudal military service, the disputes and ambitions of the nobles and their want of discipline and knowledge, particularly evident in Scotland, were sooner dismissed on the continent. In 1494 the big guns of Charles VIII opened the way to Naples and by spectacular demonstration proved the old defences obsolete.[3] An immediate consequence of this war was an astonishing output of able treatises

[1] ALHT v.lxiv. [2] ALHT ix.xv. [3] F. L. Taylor (1921), 129.

on warfare as an art with particular reference to artillery technique.

Francesco di Giorgio Martini, architect and engineer, employed on fortifications by the Duke Federigo of Urbine, published about 1494 his *Trattato di architetture civile e militaire* and therein stressed a new and influential theory, i.e. that bombardment was resisted less by strength than by the plan of walls. Among others following, Michele Sanmichele (1484-1559), Architect and Military Engineer, author of a masterly report on the fortifications of Udine in 1513,[1] and Sangallo the Younger (d. 1546) translated the provisional earthwork into stone with the essence of the defensive system residing in the bastion projecting as the successor of the mediaeval tower from the angles of the curtain to give lateral and diagonal fire. Within a few years Dürer (1471-1528) embodied the theory in fortresses of the Low Countries. The theories and type of fortress originating at this time brought fame to Vauban, and influenced the art of fortification as late as the nineteenth century.

It is against this background that Cadzow and other Scottish castles of the sixteenth and seventeenth centuries should be assessed. Tower-houses continuing the traditional style do not reveal the slightest influence of contemporary European ideas, but sixteenth-century fortifications demonstrating theories expressed in Continental treatises have been identified in earthworks at Eyemouth and Dunglass and in a battery at Dunbar Castle, all on the coast between Edinburgh and Berwick, and the defences of Craignethan mentioned above are of singular interest.

Built to consolidate the Government's military success against the rebellious clansmen and "to suppress disorders and obviate dangers", the Cromwellian forts were strategically placed and well constructed. As General Monck said in a despatch to the Protector's Council in September 1655, they so effectively curbed the people that their garrisons had more command of the hills and Highlands than ever Scots or English had before.[3] By means of five important forts at Ayr, Leith, Perth, Inverlochy and Inverness, and twenty

[1] E. Langenskiöld (1938).

[2] The War of the Rough Wooing caused islands in the Forth to be fortified and garrisoned. In 1548 the strategically important town of Haddington (East Lothian) was fortified by the erection of a square earthen fort with corner bastions and a ditch, the work of Sir Thomas Palmer, an experienced English engineer. This fort was "the most scientific military work of its class hitherto constructed in Scotland". Cf. RCAMS VIII (1924), xxix. In the following year Scotland's French allies built a similar fort at Aberlady nearby, to intercept supplies. In both allied and English armies were many mercenaries from Switzerland, Spain, Italy, and Germany.

[3] C. H. Firth (1899), 304.

smaller forts elsewhere, and by spies and a strict police force any attempts at insurrection could quickly be suppressed.[1] In form and function these fortifications were entirely alien, highly specialised professional garrisons, separate from ordinary civilian life. Thus they did not immediately influence architecture generally, but the simplified version of the classic idiom in which their principal buildings and gate-ways were expressed must have accelerated the reception of the style throughout Scotland. The elevations of the administrative and domestic buildings of the later Government forts invariably express an austere classicism, most impressive in the fortresses of the Hanoverian occupation of the second quarter of the eighteenth century (pl. 46).

Such works have been somewhat overlooked in Scottish studies, but field-work in search of Cromwellian forts shows that indeed more is visible than might be expected from the silence on the subject. None is complete, most are mixed up in modern building sites, but good stretches of a rampart, a corner of a bastion, an entrance gate-way, and so forth taken together give the plan of a structure whose plan it is more than usually valuable to have, for this purely military architecture of occupation soldiers, professional and exclusive, was set in a defensive scheme of ramparts specifically designed according to theory in a manner unprecedented in Scottish military architecture. The value and significance of those parts which have fortuitously survived is enhanced by the existence of Cromwellian correspondence and contemporary plans in the Clarke Papers in the Library of Worcester College, Oxford, which feature them and to which they form an essential complement. For example, Cromwell's Citadel at Ayr whose plan that collection contains (pl. 43) can be traced in substantial remains through the harbour, a modern barracks, a gas works, a school, a public thoroughfare and a warehouse. Such documentary evidence, exact, accurate and official is of unusual importance.

Nor is it all. There has in recent years come to light an extensive and important collection of drawings of fortifications, batteries, barracks and other undertakings mostly of the Hanoverian Government after the Risings of 1715 and the '45, but including earlier work also in surveys of their remains made in connection with these undertakings. Beautifully drawn to explain progress reports and projected schemes they indicate in colour and marginal legend works completed and

[1] P. Hume Brown (1902), II.373.

intended. Many are signed and dated. Deposited in the National Library of Scotland by the War Office in 1934 they afford for research an invaluable source of authentic information. The King's Collection in the Map Room of the British Museum includes a long series of comparable drawings relating to Scottish fortifications of only slightly less interest, and the Public Record Office holds more. As documents illustrative of the last phase of military architecture in Scotland they are of the utmost value and interest, and, related to the surviving parts of the fortifications they depict, do much to compensate for what has been destroyed.[1]

It is greatly to be regretted that of these military works only fragments remain. Because of their situation at seaports and towns they have been vulnerable to the destructive forces of urban expansion and building development. With the exception of Fort Charlotte (pl. 44) at Lerwick, a work of the later seventeenth century, and the incredible survival of Fort George undamaged and complete from the mid-eighteenth century, not one complete fort remains to be studied on the ground.

The first fort at Fort William, known as Inverlochy, considered essential for the destruction of the "stubbornest enemy in the hills—the Clans Cameron and Glengarry and the Earl of Seaforth's people"—was of turf and wattles thrown up by Monck. Salmond says that this was in 1650 but gives neither authority nor evidence for this date.[2] A plan in the Clarke Papers probably represents the same fort consolidated. It lies on the promontory at the confluence of the River Nevis and Loch Linnhe. A zigzag trench cuts across the landward side of the fort which was thus surrounded by water on all sides. The drawing is crude but effective. It shows in awkward simple elevation the barracks of companies named after their respective captains and the disposition of store-houses, guardrooms and the like. The fort has one full three-pointed bastion at the south-east corner covering the trench and the bog on the landward side of the fort, and demi-bastions or "half-bulwarks" at the other four angles of the irregular enceinte. The demi-bastions enfilade one wall only.

Stretches of undistinguished but authentic walling have survived the comprehensive destruction of the entrance and outworks on the landward side of the fort which to-day is wholly occupied by railway

[1] Copies of all of the most important drawings in these collections are in the Scottish National Buildings Record (Ministry of Works) Edinburgh.

[2] J. B. Salmond (1934), 48.

yards, tracks and sheds. But about half the rampart perimeter survives in two long stretches along the shore of the loch and the river with the demi-bastion at the angle between them, to an average height of about 20 feet. The masonry indicates two building periods: the first of river boulders along the loch side, the second of superior masonwork in roughly squared stones laid in courses and supported by small pinnings. In this is a well-wrought sea-gate in dressed ashlar, round arched with long and short voussoirs as shown in a plan of 1656.

General Mackay followed Monck's strategy in 1690 by consolidating his position and the advantage he had won against the western Highlands whence future trouble was most likely. He erected on the site a fort of stone, which he called Fort William. This, he considered a "perfect defence" against such an enemy as the Highlanders.[1] A specific mention of stone and a short period of building construction suggest that Mackay strengthened the earlier earthworks by facing them with stone. The probable first building period characterised by unhewn boulders could represent this work. The second period could be of the eighteenth century. Mackay's opinion was justified by later events. In 1746 the Jacobite army, upon its retreat to Scotland from its unsuccessful venture in England, actually reduced Fort George, Fort Augustus and the barracks at Bernera, Inversnaid and Ruthven. Fort William alone held out, although in hostile territory.[2]

In accordance with Monck's strategy a fort had been erected at the other end of the Great Glen, the citadel or fort of Inverness known as "Oliver's Fort", founded by Major General Deane in 1652.[3] Little could have been done until twelve months later when Colonel Fitch was requested to submit an estimate and Cromwell was asked to send Joachim Hane, Engineer, to supervise the laying of foundations.[4] Local labour was employed for digging and most of the skilled artificers came from England, but not Hane who was otherwise engaged in England and France.[5] It was probably completed in the summer of 1657.

There are two contemporary descriptions of "Oliver's Fort", one by Richard Franck in his *Northern Memoirs* and a better by the minister of Kirkhill who gives a very lively account in his *Highland*

[1] P. Hume Brown, III (1909), 17, quoting the Melville and Leven papers, 609ff.
[2] R. C. Jarvis (1954), 391n; P. Hume Brown, III (1909), 318.
[3] C. H. Firth (1899), xliii.
[4] CSPDom (1652-53), 335.
[5] C. H. Firth (1899), xliv.

Notebook.[1] The fort was all but completed in 1655 for a garrison of about one thousand men. In plan a large regular pentagon with a three-pointed bastion at each corner,[2] it lay upon the east bank of the River Ness which washed its west side and bastions. From the river water was led to surround the whole in a wide flat-bottomed ditch capable of taking boats in a deep-water channel and of providing protected harbours. Considered of impregnable strength, the fort promised additional security by reason of its being on an isthmus surrounded by boggy morasses. The establishment was self-sufficient and of considerable size, with broad and spacious streets, avenues and parade-grounds.[3] The entrances were served by timber bridges across the ditch. That to the main entrance was long and provided with a drawbridge at its inner end leading to a stately entrance, vaulted, about seventy feet long and with seats on each side. Among the various buildings necessary for a garrison, such as magazines, stables and barracks were the "English" building, erected by English masons, and the "Scotch" building, erected by Scottish masons. The minister describes with wonder and admiration this achievement of the English and the English goods they introduced and observes that "they not only civilised but enriched the place".

Here surely is the origin of the claim of Inverness to speak the best English, which Mackay enhances with the following words: "They speak as good English here as at London and with an English accent; and ever since Oliver Cromwell was here they are in their manner and dress entirely English."[4] Defoe, in his turn, asserts that English cookery was introduced to Inverness during the English occupation.[5]

However, despite the influence of the fort and its garrison, it did not last ten years. In 1661 by Act of Parliament it was slighted and never rebuilt. The Government seriously considered its reconstruction soon after the demolition of its successor—Wade's Fort upon the Castle Hill—by Prince Charles Edward in 1746. In that year a comprehensive survey of the ruins was made by Major Lewis Marcell and detailed drawings were prepared for a new star-shaped fort "on

[1] Both accounts are quoted by C. H. Firth (1899), xliv-xlvi.

[2] *Let them be pentagons, for this figure is fittest, for the square is weaker and not so capacious. The rest of the figures above a pentagon are larger than needs and are too costly.* Cf. A. Tacquett (1672), 41.

[3] The street in the town of Fort William which crosses the estimated position of the hornwork shown on the plan of 1656, alongside the railway, is called the Parade to this day, and the locality is known as "The Fort".

[4] J. Mackay (1729), 123.

[5] Daniel Defoe (1769), III.196.

the vestiges of an old Fort demolished". But nothing was done, and all that remains of Oliver's Fort to-day are crumbling parts of a rampart and a bastion, and a small isolated tower in the interior.

Besides the Highland forts strategically placed at either end of the Great Glen were three in the south of comparable size, the citadels of Ayr, Perth and Leith. The forts of Ayr and Perth were also founded by General Deane in the spring of 1652 and by the autumn of the next year the hexagonal outworks ("six main bulwarks") of Ayr were complete. Lilburne informed the Protector in 1653 that it was a most stately thing and very strong but a great deal too large and costly to maintain. The work was designed "against England's foe for England's friend, whom ever God protect" by one Hans Ewald Tessin who signs himself thus as "military architect" on a plan of the town and citadel of Ayr which is dated 1654 (pl. 43). It was evidently a most accomplished work, a symmetrical elongated hexagon with a bastion at all six corners, an outer ditch with a deep-water channel, a terraced counterscarp bank and a long glacis. The outer bank had *places d'armes* and extended round the three landward sides of the fort, but the three which faced the river nearby had no such outerworks in support. The fort was large enough to have a spacious "market-place" in the centre with three ranges or streets of buildings around it. The ditch has long since been filled and lost, the buildings are gone and the ramparts which contained them are for the most part destroyed. But not entirely; here and there they remain, involved in modern works as has been said above.

On the main thoroughfare serving the harbour on the south side of the river a corner of a bastion is occupied by a warehouse which has encroached into its solid earthen core to leave its sloping revetting wall standing high and unsupported with an alarming inward inclination and a rough inner face. Upon a salient angle there overhangs a remarkable "sentry-box", one of an original number of eleven according to the plan which shows them irregularly disposed throughout the outer rampart, mostly at the bastion angles. The turret is carried by eight orders of continuous corbelling. This is not unusual for a Scottish corner turret, but the design is quite without parallel even in the extensive repertory of the Scottish mason. Two unexpected and unmilitary windows, closely set side by side, light the small interior of the turret which admits to the parapet walks on either side of it. Each window has a prominent frame, curving and pulled out from the curve of the turret as it were, and the whole is surmounted by a bold cable moulding. A singular feature is a break in the curve of the turret's main walling so as to make it of two planes. The break grows upwards from the parapet to the cable moulding on either side of the window heads with a fascinating profile resembling a section through a corbel table. Although corbelling is used freely and decoratively in castellated architecture it remains functional and its effectiveness is in its mass and sculptural qualities. It is never used in this sophisticated manner as linear decoration.

In a country which has perhaps more corbelled angle turrets than any other this turret projects as a unique phenomenon. German originals suggest themselves to explain this curiosity[1] and introduce a further point of interest concerning the employment at this time in Scotland of foreign exponents of military theory and practice. Although provincial as compared with the major continental fortifications of Verona, Antwerp, Lille, Breda, Constantinople and Rhodes (the place of origin of the bastion in 1480-96) and smaller than the English Civil War fortifications of Oxford, Liverpool, Newark etc., the late artillery works in Scotland are surprisingly ambitious having regard to their purpose, danger, and environment. As they are sponsored by the authorities who created the English forts their conception is the work of the same minds.

As no national school of design in military architecture existed in England in the seventeenth century the sources of these artillery fortifications must be sought on the continent. Of these the so-called Dutch school (it includes the German by mistranslation of "Deutsch") was undoubtedly the most influential.[2] Now Hans Ewald Tessin's plan of the citadel at Ayr (pl. 43) shows an isolated free-standing battery behind the rampart and the legend in the margin of the sheet calls this a "Katte". The town walls of Breda at the siege of 1625 were of turf and upon them gun-platforms were raised. These are also called "Katte". The German signature, and the use of this distinctive word for the same thing in the plans of both Ayr and Breda—and the Netherlands fort of St Sebastian at Choma ("Katte plaats")—indicate Dutch or German influence in Cromwellian times.

It is clear at "Oliver's Fort" also. As we have observed Joachim Hane was requested to attend its commencement. In his absence,

[1] This singular turret must be regarded with caution. Local tradition attributes it to a "Baron" Miller, a notable character who refashioned the old St John's Tower nearby about 1850. Old photographs, though not conclusive, support this tradition.

[2] W. G. Ross (1887), 8.

Firth surmises, John Rosworm was probably engaged.[1] Rosworm was a German engineer of note, employed by Parliament on major undertakings despite generous inducements by the Royalists. He fortified Manchester, Liverpool, Preston and Blackstone Edge. In 1659 he was nominated to Parliament as Engineer-General of the Army,[2] ten years after he had dropped a hint with a tract entitled "Good service hitherto ill-rewarded".[3] In the Army lists of the Civil War period Scottish names are among the most distingiushed, including John Mansfield, engineer with Prince Rupert at Bristol in 1645; Sir Alexander Hamilton, Surveyor-General of Fortifications; Sir John Meldrum, who designed and executed praiseworthy hornworks at Portsmouth; and Colonel Wemyss, who served with Gustavus Adolphus like many another and was "Master Gunner of England" in 1638.[4] The blowing-up of Wade's Fort George, so dramatically portrayed in a plan among the subsequent survey drawings, was the work of a French artillery sergeant named L'Épine who was hoist with his own petard.

The Cromwellian fort at Perth was, according to a letter of March 1652,[5] contemporary with the others, planned and begun by Richard Deane. It was a simple square with a bastion at each corner. This fort was greatly ruined at the time of the '45 when the Government military engineers surveyed its ruins when contemplating the erection of another up-to-date fort in the near vicinity. The contemplated fort, as a matter of fact, was very like that of Oliver's Fort at Inverness, being a pentagon but with ambitious circumvallations and two ravelins.

Leith was the last of these five great forts to be erected. It superseded an earlier and unsatisfactory fortification upon an important strategical site. Begun in 1656 and finished in two years, it was considered by Monck in a letter to the Protector, dated at Dalkeith 11 July 1657,[6] to be exceedingly strong and easy to defend and be relieved by sea if necessary. He assures the Protector, in his recommendation to support a request for money to complete the work, that there can always be six feet of water in the moat "so that it cannot be undermined and, if the enemy should make a gallery over it, he may let in the water and destroy it at pleasure".

[1] C. H. Firth (1889), 163 (Letter of General Monck to the Protector, probably 25 August 1654).
[2] CSPDom cciii.
[3] G. Ormerod (1844), 215-47.
[4] W. G. Ross (1887), 27ff.
[5] C. H. Firth (1899), xlviii.
[6] C. H. Firth (1899), 360-1.

Leith was perhaps the greatest of these Cromwellian forts, and all were imposing and effective. Approved by Monck they were praised and admired by others. John Ray, who saw Leith citadel in 1661, thought it "one of the best fortifications that ever we beheld, passing fair and sumptuous". Richard Franck said it would be fabulous to enumerate the advantages and conveniences of the citadel of Inverness. The minister of Kirkhill admired that fortress at length, albeit it was a "sacrilegious structure and could not stand" because it was constructed with stones robbed from Kinloss Abbey, Beauly Priory, St Mary's Church, Inverness, and other ecclesiastical quarries. It is clear from the surviving contemporary plans that the approbation was fully justified.

HANOVERIAN FORTIFICATIONS

The strategic importance of the Great Glen, recognised in the thirteenth century by the planting of curtain-wall castles at Duart, Dunstaffnage, Inverlochy, Urquhart and Inverness was not overlooked by Cromwell in the middle of the seventeenth century. His method of controlling the disaffected clansmen by forts at either end of this great natural division between the Highland and Lowland zones was followed by General Wade in the eighteenth century in circumstances and purposes not greatly different from those of Cromwell's day.

In 1724 George I instructed Wade to proceed to the North and there narrowly to inspect the situation of the Highlands, their manners, customs and the state of the country in regard to alleged depredations. He did so immediately and from his report stems the erection of Fort George, Inverness, at the head of the Great Glen, and Fort Augustus in the middle. These were first-rate undertakings, in architectural effect if not in efficiency greatly superior to the Cromwellian fortifications and the works which immediately followed the Rising of 1715, after which emergency lesser forts and garrison posts were erected. The ramparts of Edinburgh and Dumbarton castles contain component parts of such defences (pl. 48). These were also erected in accordance with Wade's comprehensive review, but they were added as expedients to older castles, and the tactical principles they demonstrate are adjusted, as they are at Stirling, to the irregularities of their precipitous sites.

A group of lesser forts and garrison posts which were erected in a period of vigorous Government activity after the Risings of 1715 and

1719 fall to be considered before the final achievements of the Hanoverian occupation. They are well represented in surviving ruins and are classic examples of a standard Government type of smaller fort or barracks of European ancestry. These are Ruthven-in-Badenoch, Bernera, Kiliwhimin (Inverness-shire) and Inversnaid (Stirlingshire). Of this early eighteenth-century group only Ruthven at Kingussie survives complete in all essentials.

Close parallels to this type are to be found at two fortifications in Malta,[1] the Palace at Verdala at Rabat and the Selmun Palace at Mellieha. Each combines with unusual distinction a systematic scheme of defence and the elements of an Italian villa such as the Villa Farnese at Caprarola. The Verdala Palace, designed by Gerolamo Cassar in 1586, is square, three storeys high, with acute-angled bastions projecting diagonally from all four corners and rising one storey higher than the main block. On plan this is divided into three main divisions: a large vaulted hall running down the centre from the central doorway, two smaller rooms in the divisions on either side of it, and three rooms across the end opposite the entrance front. The Selmun Palace, nearly two hundred years later, by Cachia (1700-?90) who designed the auberge de Castile at Valletta, is almost identical. The lines are more exaggerated, the bastions thrust forward more acutely, but it was undoubtedly influenced by Verdala whose antecedents are to be found in the military treatises which circulated among commanders and engineers in the sixteenth century. Zanchi[2] gives a perspective drawing of just such a plan which differs only in that the walls and corner bastions enclose an open court and are not components of a building block, as the Maltese examples are.

At each of two diagonally opposite corners of Ruthven are projecting towers (pl. 45). The Board of Ordnance plans show that two more towers were to have been built on the remaining angles "in case money answers". This work was not carried out. The fort occupies the summit of a mound of early mediaeval aspect, probably a motte-hill. The entrance is on the east side. On the west side a postern leads to the parade-ground beyond which is an isolated stable-block erected by Wade in 1734. These two sides of the edifice are constructed with a series of embrasures with elliptic arches. Each has a gun-loop. Above is a banquette with a parapet. The men's quarters consisting of two large plain blocks of three storeys and a garret

[1] J. Q. Hughes (1956), 38-40. [2] Giovanni Battista Zanchi (1556), 34.

flank the other two sides of the courtyard. The angle towers were each of two storeys and a garret. The elevations are as plain as could be. Round the whole area ran a low breastwork about 2 feet thick.

The plans of the barracks at Kiliwhimin show that they were designed on precisely the same principles as those expressed at Ruthven, but that each barrack formed a double tenement containing on each floor six rooms with two staircases. Here also it was proposed to add towers at two free corners if funds permitted and to insert a frontal building containing a guardroom and a bakehouse. The same plan was adopted at Inversnaid and at Bernera, and for each of these a regular star-shaped covered-way was designed as an outer defence. About the old tower-houses of Braemar and Corgarff an elongated star-shaped curtain with loops ('créneaux') was built, and may still be seen.[1]

Much information is available as to the reasons that led the Hanoverian Government to build the barracks of Ruthven-in-Badenoch. In 1699 a *Report of the Committee anent this peace off the Highlands*, dated 6 December in that year, begins as follows[2]

> It is the opinion of the Committee that a garrison be established at Ruthven of Badenoch consisting at least of thirty Sentinels with a Captain and Subalterns, two Sergeants, two Corporals and a Drum.

Other posts were to be established at Ardclach in Nairn and at Invermoriston; and

> it is the opinion of the Committee that all the parties posted for guarding of the country shall consist of detached men, and not of entire companies and that they be highlanders where they can be had as fittest for that highland service.

The building of Ruthven Barracks, however, was not carried out until 1719 when the recent experience of the first Jacobite rising had driven home the wisdom of the Committee's report of twenty years before. In General Wade's first report on the state of the Highlands, submitted to the king in 1724, it is recommended that the garrison of Ruthven Barracks be supplied from Fort William, and also that quarter sessions be held there.[3] His second report, made three years later, contains the recommendations that a military way should be constructed between Loch Ness and Ruthven-in-Badenoch, and also

[1] See below, p. 237.
[2] W. J. Allardyce (1896), 1.1.
[3] W. J. Allardyce (1896), 142, 147.

> That a stable for 30 horses be erected at Barrack of Ruthven which, being over the middle of the Highlands and on the road proposed in the preceding article, I conceive to be a proper station for a party of dragoons to serve as a convoy for money or provisions for the use of the Forces as well as to retain that part of the country in obedience.[1]

Evidently it was as a result of this recommendation that the existing stables, not shown on the original plans, were in due course built and the postern gate in the west wall of the barracks made to provide access to them. In the King's Warrant Books it is stated that General Wade in 1734

> Erected and built in a workmanlike and substantial manner a stable for thirty dragoons with all conveniences thereunto belonging together with a Guard House for the security thereof upon a piece of ground within the compris of the Barracks of Ruthven where three of the roads lately made through the said Highlands do meet.

Kiliwhimin (1718) was of the Ruthven type, but somewhat larger, with barrack-blocks of double-tenement size, having a double-gable, strong central wall on the long axis and two internal stairs in place of the single Ruthven stairway. In all essentials they were alike, even in respect of the two missing diagonally opposite towers. Inversnaid has precisely the same plan as Ruthven, also with two of its bastions provisional. Both were surrounded by a regular star-shaped curtain, probably erected about 1749, at which date the native tower-houses of Corgarff at the head of the Don valley and Braemar on Deeside were commandeered as garrison posts and instantly brought to a state of readiness by the addition of similar ramparts.

The nucleus of Corgarff (pl. 44) is a plain oblong tower of late sixteenth- or early seventeenth-century date, complete and roofed but derelict. This was remodelled as a Hanoverian garrison after the suppression of the last Jacobite rising. Low wings were added to each end and all was encompassed by a regular zigzag curtain wall with long narrow loops for musketry defence. By Cock Bridge at the foot of the formidable Lecht Road it commands the passes of the Dee, the Avon and the Don, and was of considerable strategic importance. The castle has a dolorous situation and a long and eventful history. In 1571 it was the scene of the outrage commemorated in the well-known ballad "Edom o'Gordon" which relates how Margaret Campbell, wife of the laird, was burnt to death with her family and

[1] W. J. Allardyce (1896), I.165.

servants, to the number of twenty-seven, by a party of Gordon raiders from Auchindoun Castle. In 1645 Corgarff was the headquarters of Montrose and was at that time much dilapidated. In the rebellion of 1689 it was fired. In 1746 it was occupied by a detachment of Dragoons. In 1748 it was taken over by the Government, with Braemar, and thereafter reconstructed as a Hanoverian garrison with the above mentioned additions. From 1748 to 1802 it was a Government post. In 1802 the Government contemplated its desertion and a lease was drawn up which contained this preamble:

> The Barrack and Military Post of Corgarff situated in the parish of Strathdon and county of Aberdeen and appurtenance thereof belonging to His Majesty for a number of past years used as a Military Station for the use of Troops has been judged proper for the present to be discontinued.

The lease seems not to have been executed and the castle was re-garrisoned between 1827 and 1831 by a captain, a subaltern and fifty-six troops against a revival of smuggling in Strathdon. At the same time a detachment of the 74th Foot was stationed at similarly fortified Braemar castle for the same purpose.

The Hanoverian fortifications give a distinctive character to these buildings and because of their rarity and significance in Highland history greatly enhance their interest. They also afford unusual demonstrations of late mediaeval tower-houses having a prolonged military history down to the nineteenth century, with structural alterations illustrating that history.

In summing up the consequences of the '45 and its suppression Trevelyan says that "Lowland law was applied to Highland tenures and customs with harsh uniformity and with all the customary ignorance of civilised man in his dealing with a primitive society of which he despises the appearance too much to study the reality".[1] He goes on: "Devoted Presbyterian missionaries converted the Highlanders to the common stock of the nation's religious and educational ideas." These words recall the apprehensions of travellers to Scotland from south of the Border in the late seventeenth and early eighteenth century, of whom it has been observed that before their departure the luckless adventurers made their wills, took solemn leave of their friends, and asked to be prayed for in the churches.

A comparison of the plans of those forts with strikingly similar

[1] G. M. Trevelyan (1945), 538.

plans of contemporary fortified trading stations on the Gold Coast and elsewhere—James Fort, Accra (1717); William's Fort, Whidah; the forts of Dixcove and Commenda, etc.[1]—adds to the impression of conditions not far removed from barbarism which these words convey. And indeed conditions must have been hard and disagreeable, even for professional soldiers accustomed to privation. Active service at Inverlochy, for example, was regarded as so severe and unpleasant that the Cromwellian garrison stationed there was perforce composed of one company drawn by lot from each regiment of foot in Scotland, so that there should be no suspicion of favouritism or prejudice; and these companies were changed annually.[2]

Wade refers to His Majesty's Highland Barracks then in existence at Fort William, Kiliwhimin, Bernera and Ruthven, all of which he has visited. He suggests improvements to prevent the insurrections of the Highlanders, to bring criminals to justice, and to hinder rebels and attainted persons from inhabiting that part of the kingdom. The fort at Kiliwhimin,[3] situated at the southern end of Loch Ness, being considered too far from the water, was superseded in 1727 by a new fortress on the loch side named Fort Augustus after the Duke of Cumberland. Because it was in the centre of the Highlands and midway between Fort William at the south end of the Great Glen and Fort George at the north end, it was designed as a fortified residence suitable for a Governor with the Chief Command not only of these forts but of all the Barracks and Independent Companies in the Highlands. Conceived in the light of Wade's recommendations that it should constitute a G.H.Q. the impressive elevations of the domestic buildings (pl. 46) proclaim an administrative centre and a seat of civil power more than a garrison barracks. Attack seems an incongruous possibility, its success improbable. Yet Fort Augustus fell after a two-day siege, even after massive outer works were erected round the central complex.

An undated plan copied from an original of Captain John Romer, Engineer, bears the legend "this fortification was begun in 1729 and finished in 1742". It gives excellent elevations of the "Fore Front of the Main Gate" advancing beyond the flanking curtains which link it to the corner bastions. These elevations and that of "The Back Front of the Governor's House" reveal competent early Georg-

[1] Copies in the library of the Society of Antiquaries of London (O'Neil Bequest).
[2] C. H. Firth (1899), xl.
[3] The south wall of Kiliwhimin stands in the back-yard of the Lovat Arms Hotel, Fort Augustus.

ian treatment of the façade in simple orthodox style. The first floor has a venetian window over a rusticated main doorway lintel. There are lintelled windows with keystones, raised quoins and jambs, stepped gables and oillettes for dormers.

This conception is quite different from that of the Ruthven-type forts. The scale of the residential quarters and the complexity of the defences are vastly superior. The acutely pointed bastions projecting from each corner of a square enclosure are basically the same as Ruthven, but the bastions are real bastions, solid, and not towers; and, instead of plain windowed external walls of two barrack blocks overlooking the field, the two sides of the courtyard or parade consist of these two great administrative and domestic buildings. Neither had aggressive function or military appearance save for a monumental and formal severity and neither had gun-ports or any kind of military equipment. The curtains, or ramparts as they should now be called, have no gun-ports either, but the long pointed bastions have two in each face and one in the flank. Tactical and economical siting of ordnance such as this is vastly different from the earlier artillery and musketry forts with their long series of "vaulted ramparts" or firing embrasures along two sides of the enclosure and with windowed and loopholed external walls of the barrack blocks which form the other two sides. The bastions project far beyond the square enceinte. The parapet rises to overhanging round corner turrets capped with an ogee roof with a ball upon it. The turret is carried on continuous corbelling and it has small narrow windows.

Fort Augustus is now absorbed into the Benedictine abbey of that name. The original fort was captured and slighted by the Jacobites in 1745. A water-colour by Paul Sandby in Windsor Castle shows the salient angles of the bastions lying each in a heap of ruins and the buildings with their roofs destroyed. Otherwise the fort seems to be in fair shape. It surrendered to the Jacobites after a direct hit upon a powder magazine from the old fort of Kiliwhimin about half-a-mile away. After Culloden it was re-taken and repairs immediately effected. The Sandby picture must therefore be close to the action, and, being by him, as accurate as one could hope for. The interest lies in its illustration of slighting as a technical operation, the explanation it affords of the absence of the distinctive sentry-boxes shown in the pre-'45 drawings, and the evidence of rebuilding at the salient angle of the bastions which is visible still to-day.

The situation of Inverness at the head of the Great Glen has made

Plate 47 Fort George, Inverness-shire

above the great ditch, fort on left, ravelin on right (to be read with plan below)

below plan of 1752

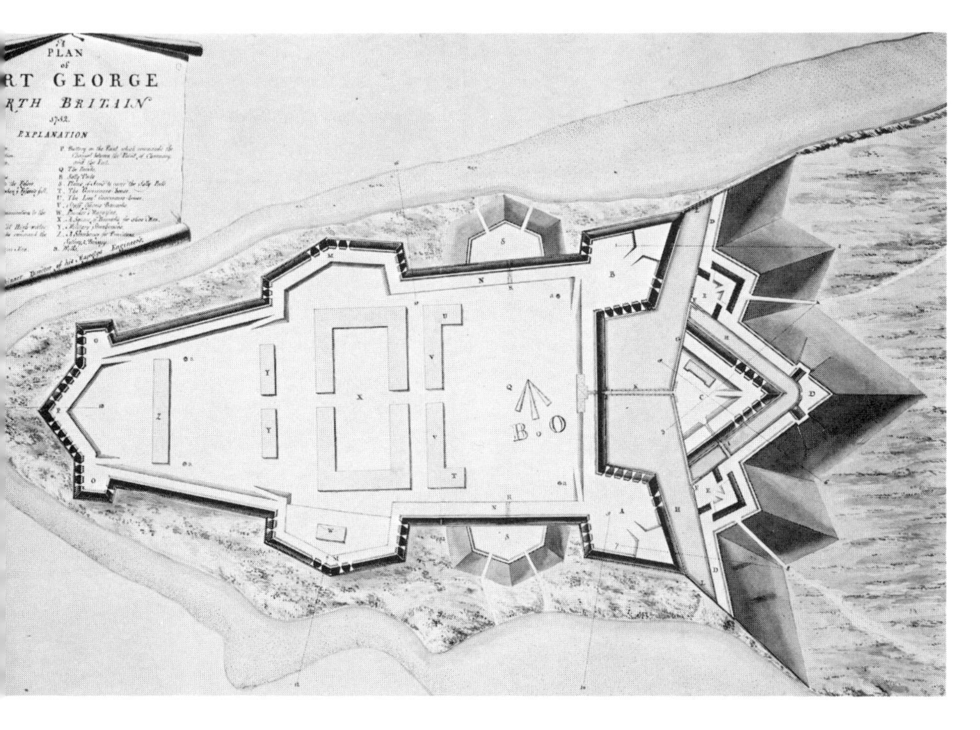

Stirling, 1708

Fort George, *c.* 1750

Edinburgh, *c.* 1735

Dumbarton, *c.* 1735

Plate 48 Sentinel turrets

it one of the most fortified positions in the British Isles. From earliest times until the present day powerful strongholds have been erected there. Nothing remains of the mediaeval castles. Three important late artillery forts were erected: "Oliver's Fort" on the east bank of the River Ness, Wade's Fort George upon the Castle Hill in the town, and its successor, also called Fort George, at Ardersier, on the south shore of the Moray Firth some ten miles distant, which is still in use by the Seaforth Highlanders and has been since the day of their formation.

The first successor to Oliver's Fort at Inverness, which was demolished in 1661 and never rebuilt, was erected, probably by Mackay, about 1690 upon the Castle Hill. It is a site of long and eventful history as a stronghold and it commands the town closely. Mackay's fort had ramparts and demi-bastions and embodied an older towerhouse and an irregular system of curtain walls doubtless mediaeval. This adaptation was out of commission by 1719 when the site was surveyed by the Government. Then the buildings were no longer weatherproof, the mansion-house was ruinous, and the well was choked with rubbish. In 1726 Wade erected a second fort—the original Fort George. In 1732 Romer prepared a further project for the site which envisaged an outer rampart, but this was not completed when a further survey was made in 1750.

Romer's survey and project drawings show the old tower-house surviving still, five storeys high, dominating a gate-house and barrack blocks of typical 1727 Fort Augustus style with round corner turrets overhanging the salient angles of the bastions. The survey of 1750 shows great damage to all buildings. Some are severely fractured and, although on the whole they are complete to their wallheads, all are roofless. The great tower has suffered and is riven and roofless, but its late fifteenth-century corbelled parapet is clearly illustrated in the survey drawings with gun-ports which must be late seventeenth- or early eighteenth-century insertions. Small corbelled roundels overhang its corners in characteristic tower-house fashion. The building is referred to as "the Old Castle formerly used as officers' barracks part blown up".

This fort of Wade, that of 1726, was totally destroyed in 1746 when it was reduced by the Highlanders only two days after Prince Charles Edward had entered the town. As has been said above, the Government promptly considered a reconstruction of Oliver's Fort. But nothing came of this save a series of most interesting plans of the scheme by Major Lewis Marcell for another pentagonal fort "on the vestiges of an old fort demolished".

If Hanoverian authority in the rebellious Highlands was strengthened by these forts, it was assured by the construction of a second Fort George.

The new Fort George, like the Edwardian Caerphilly of the late thirteenth century, was so powerful that it has no history. By great good fortune it has enjoyed a remarkable survival and affords to-day a unique example of a mid-eighteenth-century military architecture erected as a purely professional's work, in every respect a complete text-book example of a self-sufficient garrison fortress. Without doubt it is outstanding, and there is reason to believe from what is known of English works that it is unrivalled in the combined merits of size, completeness and scenic and academic interest. Its plan and details are determined by theoretical considerations of fire-power and are adjusted with typical eighteenth-century attention to symmetry along the long axis of the flat promontory projecting far out into the Moray Firth. The design is quite simple—simpler than it seems to be on the plan (pl. 47)—and the essence of the defence is typically the bastion.

Conforming to the site, the lines of the fort converge to a point. The fort thus projects spearlike towards the sea with an extended base laid across the neck of the peninsula. The apex is flanked by demi-bastions; flat bastions project from the centre of each long side and full bastions at each of the basal angles. Across the base, to confront and halt the landward approach, there is a wide water ditch. Before it is a ravelin, a triangular work connected to the main fort by a long timber bridge on fourteen pairs of uprights with a drawbridge at each end. The ravelin is itself no mean construction. It could for instance contain Caerlaverock Castle quite easily. Ditches and further outworks, traverses and lunettes, covered ways with fire steps and so forth go round the ravelin and carry the defensive effort as far beyond the main batteries in the bastions as the barrack blocks are withdrawn behind them. It will be noted that no guns were mounted upon the curtains but on the bastions and ravelin only, and that the essential was flanking fire along the curtains, not out to the field except from the ravelin which covered the field by diagonal fire from its two outward flanks. Beyond these defences was the ultimate glacis, zigzagging and darkly shaded at the extreme right-hand of the plan. This is a long sloping surface of no great height extending from the covered way to the field to expose an onrush to muskets in the foreworks and to the artillery behind them. The so-called "covered way" was not in fact covered but was an open communication way with a narrow trench containing a palisade over which the incomer had to leap, with every chance of impaling himself.

The curtains or ramparts, bastions and ravelin are in point of fact immense earthworks retained by the massive stone walls which fill the view from all aspects (pl. 47). They are exceedingly wide even along the top, and at suitable places at ground level vaulted chambers, magazines and the like are built into the earthen core. This earthwork construction, apparently primitive, is strictly according to the book. Andrew Tacquett of the Society of Jesus expounding the "*Orthographical Dimensions of the Profiles of Fortifications*" in 1672 states that the rampart must not be made of wood nor stone but earth, which is easy to come by and to use and besides, by its yielding, breaks the force of shot.[1] It did more than that, as he subsequently thought proper to confess, and as Sir Josies Bodley found to his cost at St Augustine's Fort near Galway, when its earthen ramparts had collapsed. (When he repaired it in 1609 he erected another fort of stone around the original earthen rampart some five feet away from it.[2]) A British Museum plan of St Augustine's shows a simple quadrangular fort with an acute-angled bastion at each corner, a gateway in the middle of one side and a single street or row of houses extending from end to end of the enclosure. However, Tacquett goes on to prefer a stone-faced rampart after all, because, among other enumerated advantages, "it is a stable and everlasting work; whereas a bare Rampar, unless it be continually repaired, falls to the ground".

Fort George is the creation of William Skinner, Director of Engineers. His signature, associated with that of a draughtsman or architect, Tarrant by name, occurs with gratifying frequency on the drawings covering the long period in which the undertaking was proceeding. Their collaboration begins with an undated plan—very probably of 1747—of "the designed fort". The work is well under way by 1749, and further yearly progress is indicated on a plan of that date accompanying a progress report.

In 1750 a palisade was erected round the base of the ramparts "for the security of the works". It followed the profile closely save

[1] A. Tacquett (1672), 14-18. [2] M. D. O'Sullivan (1934), 31.

at two *places d'armes* intended to cover sally-ports in the middle of the long sides of the fort. Here there was uncertainty, or at least a change in plan. In Skinner's early schemes the *places d'armes* are merely palisaded enclosures projecting outwards from the centre of each long side. In 1751 they are shown as improved, and had become obtusely pointed bastions with a covered way. But the timber palisade of 1750 which surrounded the fort cuts through these flank bastions, on the drawing, which suggests that they were not erected but only contemplated in the year after the palisade "to secure the works" was built.[1]

In 1753 we have a sheet of drawings by Tarrant of barracks for 1600 officers and men, in 1754 the barrack blocks are complete to their first floor. They are in two facing U-shaped lay-outs about a parade. Each range comprises double tenements with a central corridor. They were completed and dated by pediments of 1757 and 1763. In 1756 the sally-ports and ravelin are completed and the frontal *places d'armes* are doubled. The entrances through the ramparts and barracks are in good bold Georgian style. The parapets were served by ramps for the transport of wheeled guns. According to the drawings Skinner was still responsible for the work in 1762, by which time it must have been all but complete. The garrison church, still in use like the rest of the fort, appears for the first time on a plan of 1769.

The documentation of Fort George and the surviving completeness of the finished work, by which the whole scheme can be studied in the closest and most authentic detail, is unparalleled in the castellated architecture of Scotland and probably of England also. The only part of the defence works which has been vitiated is the glacis. Modern barrack blocks encroach into the foot of its slope but the fort is otherwise almost wholly unaffected.

Fort George affords a striking example of military architecture determined by established principles of artillery warfare and executed with due regard to local conditions and a sensible avoidance of extravagance. Having nothing of the seemingly *ad hoc* improvisation and excessive enlargement of continental fortifications, it shows Skinner if not as a genius at least as competent and far-sighted. In

[1] *Despite the strength of the defences there was a fault discovered during an attack, which was a lack of palisades in front of the redoubts and trenches, which fell, which had not been built through forgetfulness or lack of material.* Also, *palisades with sharp nails on the top of them* were placed along the bottom of the town walls and bastions, and around the bastions of hornworks. Cf. H. Hugo (1627), 116, and plan p. 28.

the advancement of the work from project to completion there is little alteration and no fundamental change at all. And it admirably fulfils its function as a garrison H.Q. even in the mid-twentieth century. What he conceived was well suited to the purpose and of sufficient strength. One might expect a hornwork in advance of the ravelin, but such an expedient seems at no time to have been considered or to have been found wanting.

LIST OF REFERENCES AND ABBREVIATIONS

ActaArch — *Acta Archaeologica*, Copenhagen.

Agricola — *P. Corneli Taciti Agricola*, ed. R. F. Davis, London 1892.

ALHT — *Accounts of the Lord High Treasurer of Scotland* (*Compota Thesaurariorum Regum Scotorum*), 11 vols., Edinburgh 1877-1916.

Allardyce, W. J. (1896). *Historical Papers relating to the Jacobite Period 1699-1750*, 2 vols., Aberdeen 1895-1896.

Amours, F. J. — See Wyntoun.

AMW — *The Accounts of the Masters of Works*, ed. H. M. Paton, vol. I 1529-1615, Edinburgh 1957.

Anderson, A. O. (1922). *Early Sources of Scottish History*, 2 vols., Edinburgh 1922.

Anderson, J. (1890). "Notice of the excavation of the brochs of Yarhouse . . . and an Appendix . . .", ArchScot v (1890), 131-198.

AntJ — *The Antiquaries Journal*, London.

APS — *The Acts of the Parliament of Scotland 1124-1707*, 11 vols., Edinburgh.

Apted, M. R. (1957). *Claypotts*, Ministry of Works Official Guide, Edinburgh 1957.

Arch — *Archaeologia or Miscellaneous Tracts relating to Antiquity*, London.

ArchAel — *Archaeologia Aeliana*, Newcastle-upon-Tyne.

ArchCamb — *Archaeologia Cambrensis*, Cardiff.

ArchJ — *The Archaeological Journal*. London.

ArchScot — *Archaeologia Scotica*, Edinburgh.

Armitage, Ella S. (1912). *The Early Norman Castles of the British Isles*, London 1912.

Bain, J. (1884). CalDoc II (1884).

Barbour, John — *The Bruce*, ed. W. W. Skeat, 2 vols., Edinburgh 1894 (STS 31, 32, 33).

Barnes, H. D. (1952*a*). See Simpson, W. D. (1952*a*).

Barrow, G. W. S. (1956*a*). "The beginnings of feudalism in Scotland", BIHR XXIX (1956), 1-31.

(1956*b*). *Feudal Britain*, London 1956.

(1973). *The Kingdom of the Scots*, London 1973.

BIHR *The Bulletin of the Institute of Historical Research*, London.

Billings, R. W. (1852). *The Baronial and Ecclesiastical Antiquities of Scotland*, Edinburgh 1852.

Boece, Hector (1526). *Scotorum Historiae Prima Gentis Origine*, first published 1526. Edinburgh 1938-1941.

Brackenbury, H. (1865). *Ancient Cannon in Europe*, Woolwich 1865.

Brand, J. (1703). *A brief description of Orkney, Zetland, Pightland Firth and Caithness*, 2 vols., Edinburgh 1701-1703.

Brieger, P. (1957). *English Art 1216-1307*, Oxford 1957.

Brown, R. Allen (1976). *English Castles*, London 1976.

(1902-9). *History of Scotland*, 3 vols., Cambridge 1902-9.

Bruce-Mitford, R. L. S. (1956). *Recent Archaeological Excavations in Britain*, ed. R. L. S. Bruce-Mitford, London 1956.

Bryant, A. (1954). *The Story of England: Makers of the Realm*, 2nd imp., London 1954.

Buchan, John (1928). *Montrose*, Edinburgh 1928.

BullMon *Bulletin Monumental*, Paris.

CalDoc *Calendar of documents relating to Scotland and preserved in H.M. Public Record Office, London*, 4 vols., Edinburgh 1881-1888.

ChetSoc Publications of the Chetham Society.

Child, F. J. (1898). *The English and Scottish popular ballads*, 5 vols., Boston 1898; another edn. New York 1956.

Christison, D. (1883). "On the grated iron doors of Scottish Castles", PSAS XVII (1882-83), 98-135.

(1888). "Additional notices of yetts or grated iron doors", PSAS XXII (1887-88), 286-320.

Churchill, W. S. (1956). *A History of the English-Speaking Peoples*, 4 vols., London 1956-1958.

Clephan, R. C. (1904). "Early Ordnance in Europe", ArchAel XXV (1904), 1-61.

(1911). "The ordnance of the fourteenth and fifteenth centuries", ArchJ LXVIII (1911), 49-138.

Clouston, J. S. (1931). *Early Norse Castles*, Kirkwall 1931.

Clusa, Walter de *Historia Ardensium Dominorum*, quoted from Ella S. Armitage (1912).

Collemedio, Johannes de. *Vita S. Joannes Morinorum*, quoted from Ella S. Armitage (1912).

Collingwood, R. G. (1923). See Graham, A. (1923).

CPR *Calendar of Patent Rolls*, London.

Cruden, S. H. (1951*a*). *The Brochs of Mousa and Clickhimin, Shetland*, Ministry of Works Official Guide, Edinburgh 1951.

(1951*b*). "Glenluce Abbey: finds recovered during excavations", TDGAS XXIX (1950-51), 177-194.

(1952). "Scottish mediaeval pottery: the Bothwell Castle collection", PSAS LXXXVI (1951-52), 140-170.

(1953). *Castle Campbell*, Ministry of Works Official Guide, Edinburgh 1953 (2nd imp. 1958).

(1954*a*). *St Andrews Castle*, Ministry of Works Official Guide, Edinburgh 1954 (2nd edn. 1958).

(1954*b*). *St Andrews Cathedral*, Ministry of Works Official Guide, Edinburgh 1954 (4th imp. 1957).

(1956). "Seton Collegiate Church", PSAS LXXXIX (1955-56), 417-437.

CSPDom — *Calendar of State Papers, Domestic.*

Defoe, Daniel (1769). *Tour through the whole island of Great Britain, divided into circuits or journeys*, London 1769 (7th edn.).

Dickinson, W. C. (1952-54). *Source Book of Scottish History*, 3 vols., ed. W. C. Dickinson, with G. Donaldson and I. A. Milne, Edinburgh 1952-1954.

Donaldson, G. (1953). "Scottish Bishops' Sees before the Reign of David I", PSAS LXXXVIII (1952-53), 106-117.

Dowden, J. — See Lindores Charters.

Dryburgh — *Liber S. Marie de Dryburgh*, ed. W. Fraser, Edinburgh 1847.

Dunbar, A. H. (1899). *Scottish Kings*, Edinburgh 1899.

Dunlop, Annie I. (1950). *Life and times of James Kennedy, Bishop of St Andrews*, Edinburgh 1950.

Edwards, J. G. (1946). "Edward I's castle-building in Wales", PBA XXXII (1946), 15-81.

EHR — *English Historical Review*, London.

ER — *The Exchequer Rolls of Scotland (Rotuli Scaccarium Regum Scotorum)*, 23 vols., Edinburgh 1878-1908.

Evans, Joan. — *Art in Mediaeval France 987-1498*, Oxford 1948.

Fauchet, Claude (1600). *Origine des chevaliers, armories*, etc., Paris 1600.

Fedden, R. and Thomson, J. (1957). *Crusader Castles*, London 1957 (2nd edn.).

Finlayson, W. H. (1948). "Mons Meg", SHR XXVII (1948), 124-126.

Firth, C. H. (1899). *Scotland and the Protectorate. Letters and Papers relating to the military government of Scotland from January 1654 to June 1659*, Edinburgh 1899 (SHS).

Fischer, G. (1951). *Norske Kongeborger*, Oslo 1951.

Floud, P. (1954). *Castell Coch*, Ministry of Works Official Guide, London 1954 (2nd imp. 1959).

Foedera — See T. Rymer.

Forbes, A. P. (1872). *Kalendars of Scottish Saints*, Edinburgh 1872.

Fordun, John of — *Johannis de Fordun Chronica Gentis Scotorum*, ed. W. F. Skene, Edinburgh 1871.

Fraser, W. — See Dryburgh.

Froissart, Jean — *Chronicles*. trans. Thomas Johnes, 2 vols., London 1839.

Gotch, J. A. (1901). *Early Renaissance Architecture in England*, London 1901.

Grafton, Richard (1569). *A Chronicle at large and meere history of the Affayers of England*, London 1569; another edn. London 1809.

Graham, A. and Collingwood, R. G. (1923). "Skipness Castle", PSAS LVII (1922-23), 266-287.

Graham, A. (1947). "Some Observations on the Brochs", PSAS LXXXI (1946-47), 48-99.

Graham, R. C. (1895). *The Carved Stones of Islay*, Glasgow 1895.

Grose, F. (1788). *Military Antiquities respecting a History of the English Army*, London 1786-1788.

Hamilton, J. R. C. (1956). *Excavations at Jarlshof, Shetland*, Edinburgh 1956.

Harvey, J. (1954). *English Mediaeval Architects*, London 1954.

Hemp, W. J. (1926). *Denbigh Castle*, Ministry of Works Official Guide, London 1926.

(1929). *Flint Castle*, Ministry of Works Official Guide, London 1929.

HMSO — Her Majesty's Stationery Office.

Hollinshed — R. Hollinshed, *The Scottish Chronicle or complete history and description of Scotland*, 2 vols., Arbroath 1805 (1st edn. London 1570).

Hope-Taylor, B. (1956). "The Norman Motte at Abinger, Surrey, and its wooden castle", R. L. S. Bruce-Mitford (1956), 223-249.

Hughes, J. Q. (1956). *The Buildings of Malta, 1530-1795*, London 1956.

Hugo, Herman — *The Siege of Breda* (*Obsidionis Bredana*), Brussels 1627.

Innes, C. — See OPS, RegEpMor.

Jarvis, R. C. (1954). *The Jacobite Risings of 1715 and 1745*, Carlisle 1954.

JGAS *Journal of the Galway Archaeological and Historical Society*, Galway.

JWI *Journal of the Warburg Institute*, London.

Kendall, M. (1923). "The siege of Berkhampstead Castle in 1216", AntJ III (1923), 37-48.

Kloster, R. (1930). *Skulpturen på Rosenkrantztarnet*, Bergen 1930.

Laing, D. (1868). "A contemporary account of the Battle of Flodden 9th September 1513", PSAS VII (1866-68), 141-152.

Langenskiöld, E. (1938). *Michele Sanmicheli, the architect of Verona*, Uppsala 1938.

Leask, H. G. (1941). *Irish castles and castellated houses*, Dundalk 1941.

Lethaby, W. R. (1955). *Architecture*, 1911; 3rd edn. Oxford 1955.

Lindores Charters. *Chartulary of the Abbey of Lindores*, 1195-1479, ed. J. Dowden, Edinburgh 1903 (SHS XLII).

Lindsay, R. (Lindsay of Pitscottie). *The Historie and Cronicles of Scotland*, ed. A. J. G. Mackay, 3 vols., Edinburgh 1899-1911 (STS 42, 43, 60).

Low, G. (1774). *Tour through the islands of Orkney and Shetland 1774*, Kirkwall 1829.

McCombie, C. (1845). See Robertson, J. (1845).

McFarlane, K. B. (1944). "Parliament and 'bastard feudalism' ", TRHS 4th Ser. XXVI (1944), 53-79.

MacGibbon, D. and Ross, T. (1887-92). *The Castellated and Domestic Architecture of Scotland*, 5 vols., Edinburgh 1887-1892.

Mackay, A. J. G. (1911). See Lindsay, R.

Mackay, J. (1729). *Journey through Scotland*, London 1729.

Mackenzie, Agnes Muir (1946). *Scottish Pageant*, Edinburgh 1946.

Mackenzie, W. M. (1927). *The Mediaeval Castle in Scotland*, Edinburgh 1927.

(1934). "Clay Castle-building in Scotland", PSAS LXVIII (1933-34), 117-127.

Martin, E. (1872). *Roman von Guillaume le Clerc*, ed. E. Martin, Halle 1872.

Marwick, H. (1951). *Orkney*, London 1951.

Melville and Leven Papers. Quoted from P. Hume Brown (1902-09).

Mersier, A. (1923). "Hourds et machicoulis", BullMon LXXXII (1923), 117-129.

Mooney, J. (1952). *Charters and other records of the city and royal burgh of Kirkwall*, Aberdeen 1952.

Mylne, R. S. (1896). "The Masters of Work to the Crown of Scotland, with the writs of appointment, from 1529-1768", PSAS xxx (1895-96), 49-68.

Nicolas, N. H. (1828). *The Siege of Caerlaverock*, London 1828.

Nisbet, A. (1816). *A System of Heraldry*, 2 vols., Edinburgh 1816.

NSA *The New Statistical Account of Scotland*, Edinburgh 1845.

Oman, C. (1924). *The Art of War in the Middle Ages*, 2 vols., London 1924.

O'Neil, B. H. St J. (1944). "Criccieth Castle", ArchCamb XCVIII (1944), 1-51.

(1946). "The Castles of Wales", *A hundred years of Welsh archaeology*, Gloucester 1946 (Cambrian Archaeological Society Centenary Volume).

(1949), with Randall, H. J. *Newcastle, Bridgend*, Ministry of Works Official Guide, London 1949.

(1951). "Castle Rushen, Isle of Man", Arch XCIV (1951), 1-26.

(1952). *Caerlaverock Castle*, Ministry of Works Official Guide, Edinburgh 1952.

(1954). "Rhodes and the origin of the bastion", AntJ XXXIV (1954), 44-54.

(1960). *Castles and Cannon*, London 1960.

OPS *Origines Parochiales Scotiae*, ed. C. Innes, 3 vols., Edinburgh 1851-1855.

Orkneyinga Saga *The Orkneyinga Saga*, transl. A. B. Taylor, Edinburgh 1938.

Ormerod G. (1844). *Civil War Tracts of Lancashire*. ChetSoc II. 1844.

O'Sullivan, M. D. (1934). "The fortifications of Galway in the sixteenth and early seventeenth centuries", JGAS XVI (1934), 1-47.

Painter, S. (1949) *The Reign of King John*, London 1949.

Paton, H. M. (1957). See AMW.

PBA *Proceedings of the British Academy*, London.

Peers, C. (1947). *Berkhamstead Castle*, Ministry of Works Official Guide, London 1947.

(1952). *Pevensey Castle*, Ministry of Works Official Guide, London 1952.

Piper, Otto (1905). *Burgenkunde; Bauwesen und geschichte der burgen zunächst innerhalb des deutschen sprachgebietes*, Munich and Leipzig 1905.

Pitcairn, R. (1830). *Historical and genealogical account of the principal families of Kennedy*, Edinburgh 1830.

Pitscottie, Lindsay of. See Lindsay, R.

POAS *Proceedings of the Orkney Antiquarian Society*, Kirkwall.

Porter, W. (1889). *History of the Corps of Royal Engineers*, London 1889.

Powicke, F. M. (1953). *The Thirteenth Century*, Oxford 1953.

PPCRE *Professional Papers of the Corps of Royal Engineers*, Chatham.

PPS *Proceedings of the Prehistoric Society*, Cambridge.

PRAI *Proceedings Royal Artillery Institution*, Woolwich.

Prestwich, J. O. (1954). "War and finance in the Anglo-Norman state", TRHS 5th Ser. iv (1954), 19-43.

PSAS *Proceedings of the Society of Antiquaries of Scotland*, Edinburgh.

Radford, C. A. R. (1946*a*). *Dolwyddelan Castle*, Ministry of Works Official Guide, London 1946.

(1946*b*). *White Castle*, Ministry of Works Official Guide, London 1946.

(1947). *Restormel Castle*, Ministry of Works Official Guide, London 1947.

(1954). *Skenfrith Castle*, Ministry of Works Official Guide, London 1954.

(1956). *Acton Burnell*, Ministry of Works Official Guide, London 1956.

(1957). "Balliol's manor-house on Hestan Island", TDGAS xxxv (1956-57), 33-37.

(1959). *The Early Christian and Viking Settlements of Birsay; Orkney*, Ministry of Works Official Guide, Edinburgh 1959.

Ramsay, J. H. (1913). *The Genesis of Lancaster*, 2 vols., London 1913.

Randall, H. J. (1949). See O'Neil, B. H. St. J. (1949).

RCAMS *Reports and Inventories of the Royal Commission on the Ancient and Historical Monuments of Scotland*, Edinburgh (HMSO).

RegEpMor *Registrum Episcopatus Moraviensis*, ed. Cosmo Innes, Edinburgh 1837.

Reid, R. C. (1926). "The excavations at Auchencass", TDGAS XIII (1925-26), 104-123.

(1953). "Edward I's peel at Lochmaben", TDGAS XXXI (1952-53), 58-77.

(1957). "Edward de Balliol", TDGAS XXXV (1956-57) 38-63.

Richardson, J. S. (1937). *Tantallon Castle*, Ministry of Works Official Guide, Edinburgh 1937.

Riformagioni — The *Riformagioni* of Florence, quoted by H. Brackenbury (1865), 3.

Ritchie, R. L. G. (1954). *The Normans in Scotland*, Edinburgh 1954.

RMS — *Register of the Great Seal of Scotland* (*Registrum Magni Sigilli Regum Scotorum*), 11 vols., Edinburgh 1912-1914.

Robertson, J. and McCombie, C. (1845). "The parish of Lumphanan", NSA XII (1845), 1079-1095.

Ross, T. — See MacGibbon, D.

Ross, W. G. (1887). *Military engineering during the great Civil War: 1642-9*, PPCRE XIII (1887), paper IV.

RS — *Rotuli Scotiae in turri Londinensi et in domo capitulari Westmonasteriensi asservati*, London 1814-1819.

RSS — *The Register of the Privy Seal of Scotland* (*Registrum Secreti Sigilli Regum Scotorum*), Edinburgh 1908-1957.

Rymer, T. (1717-35). *Foedera, conventiones, literae*, etc., 20 vols., London 1717-1735.

Salmond, J. B. (1934). *Wade in Scotland*, Edinburgh 1934.

Saxl, F. (1938). "A heathenish fountain in St Wolfgang", JWI I, (1937-8) 182-3.

Scott, W. L. (1947). "The Problem of the Brochs", PPS XIII (1947), 1-36.

SGTS — Publications of the Scottish Gaelic Texts Society, Edinburgh.

Shetelig, H. (1945). "The Viking Graves in Great Britain and Ireland", ActaArch XVI (1945), 1-58.

SHR — *Scottish Historical Review*, Edinburgh.

SHS — Publications of the Scottish History Society, Edinburgh.

Simpson, W. D. (1926). "The development of Balvenie Castle", PSAS LX (1925-26), 132-148.

(1928*a*). "James de Sancto Georgio Master of Works to King Edward I in Wales and Scotland", TAAS (1928), 31-41.

(1928*b*). "A new survey of Kildrummy Castle", PSAS LXII (1927-28), 36-80.

(1930). "Craig Castle and the Kirk of Auchindoir", PSAS LXIV (1929-30), 48-96.

(1931). "Edzell Castle", PSAS LXV (1930-31), 115-173.

(1935). "The Castles of Dunnideer and Wardhouse", PSAS LXIX (1934-35), 460-471.

(1936). "Excavations at the Doune of Invernochty", PSAS LXX (1935-36), 170-181.

(1937). "Rait Castle and Baraven Church", PSAS LXXI (1936-37), 98-115.

(1938*a*). "The two castles of Caerlaverock, a reconsideration of their problems", TDGAS XXI (1936-38), 180-204.

(1938*b*). *Ravenscraig Castle*, Aberdeen 1938.

(1941). "The development of Dunnottar Castle", ArchJ XCVIII (1941), 87-98.

(1944). *The Province of Mar*, Aberdeen 1944.

(1946). "Bastard feudalism and the later castles", AntJ XXVI (1946), 145-171.

(1948). *Threave Castle*, Ministry of Works Official Guide, Edinburgh 1948.

(1949). *The Earldom of Mar*, Aberdeen 1949.

(1952*a*), with Barnes, H. D., "Caister Castle", AntJ XXXI (1952), 35-51.

(1952*b*). "Drochil Castle and the plan *toute une masse*", PSAS LXXXVI (1951-52), 70-80.

(1952*c*). "Noltland Castle", J. Mooney (1952), 131-157.

(1953*a*). "Caerlaverock Castle", SHR XXXII (1953), 123-127.

(1953*b*). "Crookston Castle", TGAS XII (1953), 1-14.

(1954*a*). "The broch of Clickhimin", W. D. Simpson (1954*b*), 19-45.

(1954*b*). *The Viking Congress*, ed. W. D. Simpson, Edinburgh 1954.

(1954*c*). *Huntly Castle*, Ministry of Works Official Guide, Edinburgh 1954.

(1955). "The Valliscaulian priory of Beauly", AntJ XXXV (1955), 1-19.

(1957). *Hermitage Castle*, Ministry of Works Official Guide, Edinburgh 1957.

(1958). *Bothwell Castle*, Ministry of Works Official Guide, Edinburgh 1958.

Skeat, W. W. (1894). See Barbour, John.

Skene, W. F. (1867). *Chronicles of the Picts, Chronicles of the Scots and other Early Memorials of Scottish History*, ed. W. F. Skene, Edinburgh 1867.

SRO Scottish Record Office.

Stevenson, J. (1870). *Documents illustrative of the history of Scotland from the death of Alexander III to the accession of Robert the Bruce, 1286-1306*, 2 vols., Edinburgh 1870.

STS Publications of the Scottish Text Society, Edinburgh.

Summerson, J. (1953). *Architecture in Britain* 1530-1830, London 1953.

TAAS Transactions of the Anglesey Antiquarian Society.

Tacquett, A. (1672). *Military Architecture or the Art of Fortifying Towns together with the wayes of Defending and Besieging the Same*, i.e. Book II of *Military and Maritime Discipline in three Books*, London 1672.

Taylor, A. B. (1938). See Orkneyinga Saga.

Taylor, A. J. (1949). *Rhuddlan Castle*, Ministry of Works Official Guide, London 1949.

(1950). "Master James of St George", EHR LXV (1950), 433-457.

(1953). "The castle of St George D'Espéranche", AntJ XXXIII (1953), 33-47.

(1954). "The date of Clifford's Tower, York", ArchJ CXI (1954), 153-159.

(1955). "English builders in Scotland", SHR XXXIV (1955), 44-45.

Taylor, F. L. (1921). *The Art of War in Italy, 1494-1529*, Cambridge 1921.

TDGAS *Transactions of the Dumfriesshire and Galloway Natural History and Antiquarian Society*, Dumfries.

TELAS *Transactions of the East Lothian Antiquarian Society*, Edinburgh.

TGAS *Transactions of the Glasgow Archaeological Society*, Glasgow.

Thompson, M. W. (1959). *Conisburgh Castle*, Ministry of Works Official Guide, London 1959.

Thomson, J. (1957). See Fedden, R. (1957).

Thomson, T. (1825). *The Historie and Life of King James the Sext*, ed. T. Thomson, Edinburgh 1825.

Toy, S. (1953). *The Castles of Great Britain*, London 1953.

Trevelyan, G. M. (1945). *History of England*, 3rd edn., London 1945.

TRHS *Transactions of the Royal Historical Society*, London.

Tytler, P. F. (1845). *History of Scotland*, 7 vols., 3rd edn., Edinburgh 1845.

Viollet-le-Duc, E. (1879*a*). *Military Architecture*, 2nd edn., Oxford and London 1879.

(1879*b*). *Dictionnaire d'Architecture*, Paris 1879.

Vita S Joannis Morinorum Episcopi. by Johannes de Collemedio (Jean de Colmein), *Acta Sanctorum*, Bolland, ii, 799.

Watson, G. P. H. (1949). *Crookston Castle*, National Trust Official Guide, Edinburgh 1949.

(1923). "The development of Caerlaverock Castle", PSAS LVII (1922-23), 29-40.

Watson, W. J. (1937). *Scottish Verse from the Book of the Dean of Lismore*, ed. W. J. Watson, Edinburgh 1937 (SGTS I).

Weaver, L. (1913). "Drumlanrig", *Country Life* xxxiii (15 March 1913), 382-390.

Webb, G. (1956). *Architecture in Britain, The Middle Ages*, London 1956.

Wyntoun, Andrew of. *The Original Chronicle of Andrew of Wyntoun*, 6 vols., ed. F. J. Amours, Edinburgh 1902-1914 (STS).

Young, D. C. C. (1955). *Romanisation in Scotland: an Essay in Perspective*, Tayport 1955.

Zanchi, Giovanni Battista (1556). *Del Modo di Fortificar le citta*, Venice 1556.

INDEX